HOW GOD
BECAME
KING

HOW GOD BECAME KING

The Forgotten Story
of the Gospels

N. T. WRIGHT

HarperOne
An Imprint of HarperCollinsPublishers

HarperOne

All Old Testament quotations are taken from the New Revised Standard Version, copyright © 1989, National Council of Churches of Christ in the U.S.A. All New Testament quotations are taken from *The Kingdom New Testament: A Contemporary Translation,* by N.T. Wright, copyright © 2011 by Nicholas Thomas Wright.

HarperCollins books may be purchased for educational, business, or sales promotional use. For information please e-mail the Special Markets Department at SPsales@harpercollins.com.

HarperCollins website: http://www.harpercollins.com

FIRST HARPERCOLLINS PAPERBACK EDITION PUBLISHED IN 2016

Library of Congress Cataloging-in-Publication Data is available upon request.

ISBN 978–0–06–173060–3

20 LSC(H)   10 9 8 7 6 5

To the faculty and students of

St. Mary's College,

St. Andrews

CONTENTS

PREFACE

IT HAS BEEN slowly dawning on me over many years that there is a fundamental problem deep at the heart of Christian faith and practice as I have known them. This problem can be summarized quite easily: *we have all forgotten what the four gospels are about.* Yes, they're about Jesus, but what exactly are they saying about Jesus? Yes, they're about God, but what precisely are they saying about God? Yes, they're about the beginnings of what later became known as Christianity, but what are they saying about that strange new movement, and how do they resource it for its life and work?

As I have both studied and written about Jesus and the gospels, and as I have tried to lead and teach Christian communities that were doing their best to follow Jesus and order their lives by the gospels, I have had the increasing impression, over many years now, that most of the Western Christian tradition has simply forgotten what the gospels are really all about. Despite centuries of intense and heavy industry expended on the study of all sorts of features of the gospels, we have often managed to miss the main thing that they, all four of them, are most eager to tell us. I have therefore come to the conclusion that what we need is not just a bit of fine-tuning, an adjustment here and there. We need a fundamental rethink about what the gospels are trying to say, and hence about how best we should read them, together and individually. And—not least—about how we then might order our life and work in accordance with them.

The problem of forgetting what the gospels are about is not confined to one segment of the church. Different branches— Catholic, Protestant, Reformed, charismatic, evangelical, liberal, social-gospel, and the many segments of church life that bear two or more of these rather misleading labels at the same time— come at things from different angles. Naturally. But it is my belief that all of them, over many centuries now, have backed off from facing the full challenge of Matthew, Mark, Luke, and John. It would be fascinating to chart the ways in which different parts of the church have read (and, in my view, misread) the gospels. But that would require a different sort of book and is in any case way beyond my competence.

Instead, I want to come at the question from the angle of the parts of the church I know best. After nearly twenty years in senior ministerial roles in the Church of England, seven of them as Bishop of Durham, and with fairly wide experience of traditions very different from my own, I think what I have to say reflects not a narrow or idiosyncratic viewpoint, but one at which many Christians from many traditions will nod with recognition. The question, then, is not only: Can we learn to read the gospels better, more in tune with what their original writers intended? It is also: Can we discover, by doing this, a new vision for God's mission in the world, in and through Jesus, and then—now!—in and through his followers? And, in doing so, can we grow closer together in mission and life, in faith and hope, and even in love? Might a fresh reading of the gospels, in other words, clear the way for renewed efforts in mission and unity? Is that what it would look like if we really believed that the living God was king on earth as in heaven?

That, after all, is the story all four gospels tell. I am aware, of course, that there are other documents that have been called "gospels," and I shall say something about them in passing. But I am here dealing with the four that were recognized, from very early on, as part of the church's "rule of life," that is, part of the "canon": Matthew, Mark, Luke, and John. And the story that the four evangelists tell is the story, as in my title, of "how God became king."

This, I discover, comes as a surprise to most people, and an unwelcome shock to some. It appears, as we say today, counterintuitive; that is, the claim that God has become king doesn't seem to square with the world as we know it. "If God is really king, why is there still cancer? Why are there still tsunamis? Why are there still tyranny, genocide, child abuse, and massive economic corruption?" What's more, as we shall see, some people, not least some Christians, appear allergic to the very idea of God becoming, or being, "king." "Isn't God as king triumphalist? Doesn't that lead us toward that dreaded word 'theocracy'? And isn't that one of the problems of our day, not one of the solutions?"

Questions like that are important. But even if the gospel writers had heard us asking them, they would not have backed off from the claim they were making. To discover why not and to see what they might have said in reply to such comments, we have to take a deep breath and go back to the beginning.

The book proceeds in four parts, or stages. Part I introduces the problem as I see it and attempts to sharpen it up, so that readers come to see that there really is a problem that demands some fresh work and, if possible, some fresh attempts at a solution. The second part explores four dimensions of the canonical gospels that, again, have normally been screened out in modern Western readings and that we need to recover if we are to allow the gospels to tell us the story they intend to tell. Then, in Part III, we reach what is really the heart of the picture. Using the four dimensions set out in the second part, I try to show how the two vital themes so often separated, the kingdom and the cross, come together in the gospels, knock sparks off one another, and reinforce each other in setting out a claim that today's church has all but forgotten, a claim as much in what we call the political as in what we call the religious or spiritual sphere. That central combination of kingdom and cross then leads to further considerations about the meaning of these themes in the light of the gospels' story of Jesus's resurrection and ascension.

Then, in the final part, I come back to the great creeds and suggest that, though we have indeed allowed them to lull us into a frame of mind in which it's all too easy to screen out the central message of the gospels, it is just as possible, once we realize that mistake, to say or sing them as rich affirmations of that full message. This will generate some suggestions about how we should rethink our basic traditions of teaching and practice, so as to be more faithful to the documents that are, after all, at the heart of the Christian faith.

It may be worth pointing out at this introductory stage that this book is not primarily about Jesus himself. I have written plenty on Jesus within his historical context, including a recent short book, *Simply Jesus*.* I intend to go on working at that subject, but that isn't what this present book is about. The two questions that are interlinked at every point are: Who was Jesus (including, What did he do and say and think? Why did he die? and What happened next?). And why did the four gospels tell his story the way they did? But these two questions are in principle also separable. Indeed (and I hope this doesn't sound too Irish), unless we hold them apart, we shall never be able to put them together. Having, then, addressed the Jesus question elsewhere, I turn now to address the gospel question once more, following, for instance, the treatment I offered in *The New Testament and the People of God*.† The gospel question is all the more interesting because there were, as I just mentioned, other documents in circulation by at least the second half of the second century that told the story very differently. (I think, of course, of the so-called *Gospel of Thomas*

***Simply Jesus: A New Vision of Who He Was, What He Did, and Why He Matters* (San Francisco: HarperOne, 2011).

†*The New Testament and the People of God* (London: SPCK; Minneapolis: Fortress, 1992), chap. 13.

and similar books.) Why did Matthew, Mark, Luke, and John do it in the ways they did?

In case anyone should think at this point that I am simply lumping the four canonical gospels together without paying proper attention to their very considerable differences, let me say right away that, though these four share a great deal with one another that is not shared with the noncanonical gospels, in other ways they are just as different from one another as they are from those other traditions.* Within the quartet itself, of course, a similar point is to be made. Matthew, Mark, and Luke are much more like one another than any of them is like John, but they are still very different works. But my question is: What story is it they are trying to tell?

We could still ask this question, in fact, even if it could be proved that Jesus of Nazareth never existed, or never did most of the things ascribed to him, or was never crucified or raised from the dead. In such a case, of course, we would conclude that their story is fiction in the full sense. (All writing, all history, is "fiction" in the sense that someone has constructed it, put it together, decided what to put in and leave out, and determined how to structure the whole. But the word "fiction" is normally used, of course, to denote stories that do not correspond to anything that ever actually happened in real life.) But, even if the gospels were "fiction" in that full sense, it would still be perfectly possible, and worthwhile, to ask: What story or stories do these writers think they are telling? That is the question, bracketing out issues of historical referent, that I shall be addressing in this book.

In the same way, I shall not be raising or addressing questions about the prehistory of the gospels or indeed about their date, authorship, or possible place of composition. This may be a disappointment to some. I have nothing but admiration for those who have devoted their lives to the study of gospel sources and origins.

---

*See, again, my discussion in *New Testament and the People of God,* chap. 13.

This study remains a hugely important subject within the larger enterprise. But again, for the purposes of this book, I am going to assume that it is possible, from the documents we actually have, as opposed to the hypothetical documents that may lie behind them, to ask the central question: What story did the gospels think they were telling? Even if the traditional picture proposed by most twentieth-century scholarship is correct, that Matthew and Luke both used, as basic sources, Mark, on the one hand, and a second source, generally known as Q, on the other; or even if one of the alternative proposals now on the table is preferred, perhaps the one in which Luke used Matthew as well as Mark and no Q is postulated; or even if matters are yet more complicated, with multiple oral and written sources now almost impossible to reconstruct—even if any of these proposals is correct, we are still left with the documents we actually have in front of us, and it still makes sense to ask what story they think they are telling.

The same goes for what is called form criticism. Again, the question form critics ask (What were the original forms in which the traditions were told and transmitted, and what can we learn about the early church from the study of these forms?) is a perfectly sensible and good question, but it isn't my question in this project. I think, for quite other reasons, that the way form criticism has normally been done needs a great deal of rethinking, but that is another story.*

In the same way—just to complete the holy trio—I am not doing what is often called redaction criticism. I am not lining up the gospels to see how, granted some theory about sources, they have altered one another's material and thereby tipped their hand, revealing their theological or ecclesial leanings. That too is a worthy discipline, though with the fragmentation of synoptic studies in recent years the quest for such "redactive" hints is far more problematic than used to be thought. Rather, what I am doing

---

*On all this, see *New Testament and the People of God*, chap. 14.

here is more like that second cousin of redaction criticism sometimes called composition criticism. We actually have Matthew, Mark, Luke, and John. It makes good sense to ask of them, as it does of a Jane Austen novel or a Shakespeare play: What story was the author telling, and how did he or she go about it? That is the question I shall be trying to address. If we get the answer right, it might well have spin-off effects for those other disciplines, but that lies beyond the remit of this book.

This book has grown, in part, out of the Durham-based program we named "The Big Read," the brainchild of my dear friend and former colleague Bishop Mark Bryant of Jarrow. One of my tasks during that program of large-scale Lenten Bible reading, launched in Durham in 2010, was to go around the northeast of England giving a series of open lectures about how to read the gospels (in that year, it was Luke in particular, though I have done similar talks, recorded and distributed, on Matthew in 2011 and on Mark in 2012). Doing those talks and discussing the material with local people made me realize then and there just how many misconceptions people have about Christianity in general and the gospels in particular. And if that is true for the faithful few who are prepared to turn out on a February evening, how much more true is it for those who stayed at home watching that most inappropriately named thing reality TV. It was the spring of 2010 that led me to believe that this book was necessary.

But the project reached its present shape in a memorable week in Salisbury Cathedral in May 2011, when I gave the four Sarum Lectures. I am very grateful to Sarum College for the invitation to give this series and to the principal and his colleagues for the warm hospitality I enjoyed in that delightful place. The book follows the line of the lectures, with the first three parts corresponding to the first three lectures. I wanted to make the fourth lecture particularly relevant for the many in my audience who were engaged in parish and pastoral work; for the present book I have widened the scope quite a bit to include proposals I hope will be taken seriously by theologians as well as biblical scholars. The question of "canon and creed," which underlies quite a bit of this book, has become quite urgent and controversial and needs to be addressed from the point of view of those of us who are actually working with the biblical canon itself rather than using the word "canon" as shorthand for the systematic theology they already possess. The practical outworkings are then framed within that larger agenda.

In preparation for the Sarum Lectures, I gave preliminary statements at a conference at Duke Divinity School in Durham, North Carolina, in October 2010. I then tried out the material at more leisure, later in the same month, with the clergy of the Diocese of Down and Dromore, Ireland. I am grateful to the Dean of the Divinity School, Professor Richard B. Hays, and the Bishop of Down and Dromore, the Right Reverend Harold Miller, for their invitations and hospitality. I also had the chance to sharpen the ideas up into an individual lecture that I gave, in various forms, at the Institute of Biblical Research in Atlanta, Georgia in November 2010 and at the Bristol School of Christian Studies in January 2011. Finally, I translated the Sarum Lectures into American the week after they were given and delivered them to church groups in Greenwich, Connecticut, and Nashville, Tennessee, in May 2011 and (in English again) to a gathering of Naval Chaplains in Hampshire in June 2011.

Wonderful memories surround each element of this rambling itinerary, and my gratitude goes out to the clergy and laity involved in its various stages (not least to Dr. Michael Bird for his response to the Atlanta paper). In particular, I express my gratitude to Chuck and Deborah Royce for the use of their apartment in New York, providing some quiet space in which I was able to translate the material once more, this time from the lecture format into the complete book. That a book on the gospels should be surrounded by so much gratitude and the memory of so much hospitality is only right. This too is part of their meaning.

I am also grateful to my editor at Harper, Mickey Maudlin, for his enthusiasm for this project and his guidance in holding back my earlier attempts to say too much too quickly. I hope that this finished product will encourage Christians from all backgrounds, as well as those looking over the fence and wondering just what the central Christian documents are actually all about, to read these explosive first-century books again with fresh eyes and to face once more the questions and challenges they actually offer, rather than the questions and challenges, important though they are in themselves, that we have regularly imagined they do.

The book is dedicated to my colleagues in St. Mary's College, the Divinity Faculty of the University of St. Andrews. It is no light thing to welcome into a faculty one who has been out of the academic mainstream for the best part of two decades, and it speaks volumes for their charity and faith that they have done so with open arms. Just as my lectures on the gospels, in the settings described above, were an attempt to relate the academic study of the gospels to the street-level life of the church, so I hope my new friends and colleagues here at St. Mary's will see the book into which these lectures have grown as a kind of contribution in the other direction, bringing reflections that were occasioned by my work in the wider world into the bright light and searching scrutiny of the academy. There is, of course, much more to do, and I hope to return to the four gospels in a much fuller academic context before long. But this book may perhaps provide a start, and a signpost.

N. T. Wright
St. Mary's College
St. Andrews
September 2011

PART ONE

The Empty Cloak

I

The Missing Middle

THE PROBLEM I WISH TO ADDRESS in this book can be introduced with a personal story from nearly fifty years ago. I was in high school, trying with some friends to run a small Christian Studies group. We decided one term that we would do a series of studies about Jesus, each beginning with "Why?" The topics included such questions as: Why was Jesus born? Why did Jesus live? Why did Jesus die? Why did Jesus rise again? And why will he return? (I don't think we had one on why Jesus ascended, though we should have.) Anyway, for some reason I was assigned the task of preparing and leading the second of these: Why did Jesus live?

I soon realized, even as a raw teenager, that I had drawn the short straw. After all, if you were given Jesus's birth, you could talk about the incarnation, about God becoming man. We all had memories of Christmas sermons, and we knew how important it was that Jesus wasn't just an ordinary human being: he was God in person. There was even the whole question of the virgin birth. No shortage of material there.

The same was true too for the person who was to speak about Jesus's death. Even at that tender age we knew not only that it was important to say "he died for our sins," but to push a little bit farther and ask how that happened, how it made sense. For myself, that is, so to speak, where I came in: my earliest memory of personal faith was when, as a very small boy, I was overwhelmed, reduced to tears, by the thought that Jesus died for me. What the cross says about the love of God has always been central and vital for me. I don't think we schoolboys quite grasped the range of what is called "atonement theology." But we knew there were some important questions to look at and some important and central beliefs to grasp hold of.

So too with the resurrection. And, indeed, the second coming. Again, I'm not sure we went very deep or even necessarily explored the most helpful biblical passages. But these were thrilling topics. There was plenty to talk about, plenty to chew over, plenty to make us not only think hard, but also celebrate the excitement of believing in Jesus and of trying to live as a Christian.

But what about that question in the middle—my question? Why did Jesus *live*? What, in other words, about the bit between the stable and the cross? There were, after all, Christmas carols and other hymns that took Jesus straight "from his poor manger to his bitter cross." Did it matter that, according to the four gospels, he had a short period of intense and exciting public activity at the latter end of his life? What truth could we learn from it? Why did it have to be like that? Does it matter that he did all those things, that he said all those things, that he *was* all those things? Would it have made any difference if, as the virgin-born son of God, he had been plucked from total obscurity and crucified, dying for our sins, without any of that happening? If not, why not?

I realized then, and have realized increasingly in recent years, that many Christians read the gospels without ever asking those questions. Adapting a phrase from a well-known book on management, *The Empty Raincoat,** such readers experience the four

---

*Charles Handy, *The Empty Raincoat* (London: Hutchinson, 1994).

gospels as an empty cloak. The outer wrapping is there—Jesus's birth, death, and resurrection. But who is inside the cloak? What did Jesus do in between? Is there anybody there? Does it matter?

Now comes the frustration. I have absolutely no idea what I said in that teenage talk. I don't know what sense I tried to make of why Jesus lived. It's possible that somewhere, deep in a dusty box, I have some scribbled notes from that early attempt to answer the question that has haunted me all my life. But at least I remember the fact of being puzzled. And that is part of the point of this book. It wasn't an accident that I was puzzled. It wasn't that most Christians knew the answer and I just hadn't grasped it yet. I had stumbled, without realizing it, on a weak spot in the general structure of Christian faith as it has come to be expressed in today's world—and, I suspect, for a lot longer than we might imagine. Here is all this material in Matthew, Mark, Luke, and John. Why? What are we supposed to make of it all?

The Puzzle of a Lifetime

Come forward about fifteen years from that early experience. In my late twenties, out of the blue, I was asked to give a Bible exposition to the student Christian Union at Cambridge. I don't know who inspired the question or what they expected me to say, but the title I was given was "The Gospel in the Gospels."

Preachers and indeed theologians may well recognize the problem posed by that subject (quite apart from the challenge of addressing such a vast topic in fifty minutes, not to mention the fact that my research was in those days on Paul, not on the gospels). I now realize, though I don't think I did at the time, that this problem is quite close to the puzzle I had faced as a teenager. Let me unpack it like this.

When C. S Lewis wrote his famous *History of English Literature in the Sixteenth Century,* he naturally included a section on the writers of the English Reformation, not least the great translator William Tyndale. Writing for a nontheological audience, Lewis had to explain one point that had obviously puzzled other readers. When William Tyndale, one of England's earliest Protestants, a disciple of Martin Luther, wrote about "the gospel," he didn't mean "the gospels"—Matthew, Mark, Luke, and John. He meant "the gospel" in the sense of the *message:* the good news that, because of Jesus's death alone, your sins can be forgiven, and all you have to do is believe it, rather than trying to impress God with doing "good works." "The gospel" in this sense is what the early Reformers believed they had found in Paul's letters, particularly Romans and Galatians—and particularly Romans 3 and Galatians 2–3.

Now, you can explain that "gospel" in Paul's terms. You can make it more precise, fine-tuning the interpretation of this or that verse or technical term. But the point is that you can do all of that without any reference whatever to "the gospels," to the four books that, along with Acts, precede Paul in the New Testament as we have it. Thus in many classic Christian circles, including the plethora of movements that go broadly under the label "evangelical" (and we should remember that in German the word *evangelisch* means, more or less, "Lutheran"), there has been the assumption, going back at least as far as the Reformation, that "the gospel" is what you find in Paul's letters, particularly in Romans and Galatians. This "gospel" consists, normally, of a precise statement of what Jesus achieved in his saving death ("atonement") and a precise statement of how that achievement could be appropriated by the individual ("justification by faith"). Atonement and justification were assumed to be at the heart of "the gospel." But "the gospels"—Matthew, Mark, Luke, and John—appear to have almost nothing to say about those subjects.

Now of course at one level "the gospels" contain this "gospel," simply because they tell the story of the death of Jesus. Without that—if someone were to suggest, for instance, that this "Christ" of whom Paul speaks never lived at all or never died on a cross—Paul's whole "gospel" makes no sense. That, indeed, is what some people in the second century tried to say, offering instead a "Jesus" who was simply a teacher of spirituality. But is that all? Is "the gospel in the gospels" simply a matter of the bare fact of Jesus's death, which Paul and others would then interpret as "good news" even though nobody saw it like that at the time?

That, I think, is the problem to which I, in my invited address at Cambridge, was supposed to offer an answer. Sadly, once more, I can't remember anything about what I said. Perhaps it's still in a file somewhere, but to be honest I haven't looked. There may even, for all I know, be a tape recording—though cassette tapes (remember them?) were still in their infancy in 1978, the year I gave the address.

I might, though, hazard a guess at some of what I said. There are of course the famous passages, such as Mark 10:45: "The son of man . . . came to be the servant, to give his life 'as a ransom for many.'" Ah, think readers, there we have it: a reference to Daniel 7, coupled with a reference to Isaiah 53:5, the famous passage in which the "servant of the LORD" is wounded, bruised, and killed "for our transgressions" and "for our iniquities." That sounds—to some!—as though Mark had after all been taking lessons from Paul. That's enough—there is our "atonement theology" in a nutshell, right there in Mark.

There is a problem, though. Matthew has the same line (20:28), but when Luke has an opportunity to reproduce it, he appears to leave out the crucial element (22:27, where Jesus simply says, "I am with you here like a servant"). Some have even claimed, because of this and other features, that Luke has no "theology of the cross," no doctrine of "atonement," at all. I regard that as a grievous misunderstanding; I will explain why later. But, even if Luke had reproduced Mark's phrase exactly, it doesn't look as though the gospels really make "atonement," *in the sense the church has come to use that word,* their main theme.

When it comes to "justification," there is one passage in Luke, in the parable of the Pharisee and the tax collector (18:9–14), in which the sinner is said to be "justified" in something like a Pauline sense. After all, he confessed his sins and trusted solely in God's mercy, unlike the self-righteous Pharisee.

And there are several sayings in John's gospel, not usually discussed when people talk about "justification," that might be regarded as relevant to the topic. There is, above all, the well-known John 3:16: "This, you see, is how much God loved the world: enough to give his only, special son, so that everyone who believes in him should not be lost but should share in the life of God's new age." But how does that saying fit into the story John is telling? How does it prepare for the final cry of Jesus on the cross, *tetelestai,* "It's all done!" (19:30)? Many preachers have turned to that verse for a statement of "atonement" theology, making the point that *tetelestai* was what ancient Greeks wrote on a bill when it had been paid: "Finished!" "Done with!" "The price has been paid!" There are many ways in which you can extract a "Pauline" resonance from all that.

But is *that* enough? Is what we mean by "atonement" something John was really interested in, and if so how does he express it? Or, to put it another way, what were the main themes John was exploring, and how does his understanding of the cross and its meaning fit into those, rather than into the scheme of thought that we have devised and inherited?

In any case, these passages and a few others like them have to be, as it were, prized out of their context. It is assumed that that context—the actual story that Matthew, Mark, Luke, and John all tell, in their different ways, of what happened to Jesus after his birth and before his death—is not actually "the gospel" in the same way as the saving death of Jesus and the Pauline doctrine of justification are "the gospel." That, I think, is the problem to which I, in my Cambridge address, was supposed to offer an answer. And it is the puzzle, I now realize, that has been a major theme of my lifetime. The puzzle of Jesus's lifetime—what was his *life* all about?—has crept up on me and become the puzzle of mine.

Come fast forward again, another twenty-five years. In 2003 I attended a conference where a well-known Christian leader from another continent requested some time with me. He had been reading my book *Jesus and the Victory of God** in the weeks before the conference and was intrigued by it. He wanted to know how it all made sense in terms of "the gospel" that he believed and taught. We had a cup of tea (some British and Anglican stereotypes don't change) and talked for an hour or so. I tried to explain what I thought I was seeing: that the four gospels had, as it were, fallen off the front of the canon of the New Testament as far as many Christians were concerned. Matthew, Mark, Luke, and John were used to support points you might get out of Paul, but their actual message had not been glimpsed, let alone integrated into the larger biblical theology in which they claimed to belong. This, I remember saying, was heavily ironic in a tradition (to which he and I both belonged) that prided itself on being "biblical." As far as I could see, that word was being used, in an entire Christian tradition, to mean "Pauline." And even there I had questioned whether Paul was really being allowed to speak. That's another story.

We got to the end of our hour. It was time to stop.

"Well, Tom," he said, summing it all up. "I think what you're saying is that I'm insufficiently biblical."

I gasped inside. That was quite an admission.

"Yes," I replied. "That's exactly what I'm saying."

And if that was true of him, it is true of a great deal of the Western Christian tradition (I can't speak about Eastern Orthodoxy): Catholic and Protestant, liberal and evangelical, charismatic and contemplative. We use the gospels. We read them aloud

---

Jesus and the Victory of God (Minneapolis: Fortress, 1996).

in worship. We often preach from them. But have we even begun to hear what they are saying, the whole message, which is so much greater than the sum of the small parts with which we are, on one level, so familiar? I don't think so. This is the lifetime puzzle. It isn't just that we've all *mis*read the gospels, though I think that's broadly true. It is more that we haven't really *read* them at all. We have fitted them into the framework of ideas and beliefs that we have acquired from other sources. I want in this book to allow them, as far as I can, to speak for themselves. Not everyone will like the result.

Canon and Creed

This problem about the puzzling relationship between "the gospel" and "the gospels" is reflected in the equally puzzling relationship between the gospels and the great Christian creeds. A good friend of mine, in a sparkling presentation, once let slip the remarkable line, "The canonical Jesus is, of course, the Christ of the church's creeds." In other words, the Jesus we find in the four canonical gospels is the Jesus Christ we confess when we say the Apostles' Creed, the Nicene Creed (properly, the Niceno-Constantinopolitan Creed), or even the so-called Athanasian Creed (a much longer formula that the old Anglican prayer book instructs worshippers to include on special occasions). My friend was distinguishing this supposedly both creedal and canonical Jesus from the reconstructed "Jesus" figures of so much would-be historical scholarship. Over here to one side, he implied, we have that mountain of historical scholarship, with characters such as Schweitzer and Sanders and even N. T. Wright peeping out from under the great pile, offering their various historical reconstructions. Over here to the other side, a very different thing, we have the Jesus whom the canonical gospels actually present, who is the same as the Jesus of the great creeds.

My problem with this is that the canonical gospels and the creeds are not in fact presenting the same picture. This, actually, is a question that goes much wider and deeper than we have time to explore in this book, but at the heart of it we could sum up the problem like this. The great creeds, when they refer to Jesus, pass directly from his virgin birth to his suffering and death. The four gospels don't. Or, to put it the other way around, Matthew, Mark, Luke, and John all seem to think it's hugely important that they tell us a great deal about what Jesus did between the time of his birth and the time of his death. In particular, they tell us about what we might call his kingdom-inaugurating work: the deeds and words that declared that God's kingdom was coming then and there, in some sense or other, on earth as in heaven. They tell us a great deal about that; but the great creeds don't.

Before we examine the great creeds in more detail, let's remind ourselves of the reason why they came to be formulated in the first place. The early church faced many problems and battles. This is hardly surprising. Jesus himself told his followers it would work out like that. Sometimes it was direct persecution; there were many martyrs in the first three centuries. Sometimes it was internal division, as devout followers of Jesus discovered that other devout followers of Jesus saw things very differently, but held their position equally strongly. There were ongoing debates with Jewish groups and individuals who did not believe that Jesus was the promised Messiah and found themselves in an awkward position vis-à-vis the expanding Christian church, which claimed so much from its Jewish heritage (not least the ancient scriptures) and yet saw so many other things in a very different light and ordered its life accordingly. In particular, there were the great battles with Gnosticism in the second and third centuries, in which Christian teachers like Irenaeus and Tertullian stood firm for belief in God as the good and wise creator, and with Arianism in the fourth and fifth centuries, in which teachers like Athanasius stood firm for belief in Jesus as "being of one substance with the Father." All these serious and long-lasting controversies, many of them against a background of fierce persecution from the imperial authorities, were enormously important in shaping the way the early Christians understood and articulated what was significant to them.

These controversies, then, and many others like them, left their mark on the church and its common life. As Christian teachers gradually came to realize that some things were absolutely essential to the faith and others of lesser importance, the things that were essential, but that had been controversial, were listed and agreed upon for the avoidance of doubt. These lists turned into a rule of faith, an agreed-upon shared statement of what Christians believed; and the rule of faith was codified into the great creeds. These creeds, though they too have been controversial from time to time, have functioned for over a millennium and a half as a sign and symbol of Christian faith and life. Where you find this belief, Christians have said, you find the church, the body of Christ, the company of "true believers." The creeds were dramatic developments within the early church. They stand to this day as a remarkable achievement of brevity, dense clarity, and evocative spiritual power. In the tradition to which I belong, we say the Apostles' Creed twice a day and the Nicene Creed at every Eucharist or at least on Sundays.

And yet. The one thing the creeds do not do—to return to the point I made a minute ago—is to mention anything that Jesus did or said between his birth and his death. Early Christians read and studied the gospels and tried to live by them. Their allegiance to them is not in doubt. But they saw no need to mention the central substance of the gospels in the creeds as well. This has had a massive, and I believe completely unintended, consequence. It is, in fact, one major part of the reason why Christians to this day find it so hard to grasp what the gospels are really trying to say.

Take the second article of the short fourth-century statement of faith we know as the Apostles' Creed:

I believe . . . in Jesus Christ, God's only son, our Lord;
Who was conceived by the Holy Spirit;
born of the Virgin Mary;
Suffered under Pontius Pilate;
Was crucified, dead and buried;
He descended into hell;
On the third day he rose again from the dead;
He ascended into heaven, and is seated at the right hand of God,
the Father almighty;
From thence he will come to judge the living and the dead.

So much detail, and yet nothing at all about what Jesus did in between being conceived and born, on the one hand, and being crucified under Pontius Pilate, on the other. Why not? If the aim were to summarize the key focal points of Christian faith, did that imply that that faith didn't really need, shall we say, Matthew 3–26? Would chapters 1–2 (Jesus's birth) and 27–28 (his death and resurrection) have done just as well? Was Matthew, and were Mark, Luke, and John for that matter, wasting time telling us all that stuff in the middle? Were they just giving us the "backstory" to satisfy any lingering curiosity the church might have about the earlier life of the one Christians now worshipped as Lord?

This problem, as we began to notice in the previous section, resurfaced in twentieth-century scholarship in the form of the question scholars associate with Rudolf Bultmann in particular (though with many antecedents and many followers): Why should the church, worshipping the living Lord, be bothered by the history of what he had done in the past? The answers given by conservative scholarship seem thin and flat. They amount to what we now refer to as arm-waving: they maintain that early converts, eager to worship the risen Lord in the present, wanted to know about the earthly life of this same Jesus. But although that was undoubtedly the case, responding to a request for information doesn't seem to come anywhere close to describing what the gospels seem to be doing. They do not seem merely to be providing background biographical details. They are not merely "filling in gaps" to help the present faith and life of their readers. They are telling a story, a story that is almost entirely missing in the great creeds of the early church.

The same point comes out even more strongly in the Nicene Creed, which developed to its present form by the middle of the fifth century. I quote the second article in its traditional English form:

> *I believe . . . in one Lord Jesus Christ*
> *the only-begotten Son of God;*
> *begotten of his Father before all worlds;*
> *God of God; light of light; very God of very God; begotten,*
> * not made;*
> *Being of one substance with the Father; by whom all things*
> * were made;*
> *Who for us men, and our salvation came down from heaven;*
> *And was incarnate of the Holy Spirit from the Virgin Mary,*
> * and was made man.*

Then we can imagine a deep breath, a dramatic pause, as we wait to see if anything further will be said about Jesus. But no, the creed leaps right over the whole "middle story" and lands once more at the end:

> *And was crucified also for us under Pontius Pilate; he suffered*
> * and was buried;*
> *And the third day he rose again according to the Scriptures;*
> *And ascended into heaven; and sitteth on the right hand*
> * of the Father;*
> *And he shall come again in glory to judge both the living*
> * and the dead,*
> *And his kingdom shall have no end.*

Again, lots of detail, filled in in new ways to answer new problems and challenges. But again no detail at all, no *mention* at all, of anything between the second person of the Trinity becoming human and this human/divine man being "crucified for us under Pontius Pilate." There is nothing there about what Jesus *did,* or why he did it, or how anything he did relates to either his birth or his death. There is, in short, an enormous gap. At precisely the point where Matthew, Mark, Luke, and John think something very important needs to be said, the creeds say nothing at all.

What they do say makes this problem still more acute. The gospels speak a good deal, as we shall see, about the "kingdom of God" as, in some sense or other, a present reality in the ministry of Jesus. This, indeed, is at the heart of what we need to explore in this book. But not only do the creeds fail to mention this in connection with Jesus's life (or indeed with his birth or his death). The Nicene Creed implies, to the contrary, that Jesus's "kingdom" will be established only when he "comes again in glory": "He will come again in glory to judge the living and the dead, and his kingdom shall have no end." It doesn't actually say that his kingdom will only be set up at that point, but the sequence of clauses gives that clear impression.

True, in both these ancient creeds it also says that Jesus, through his ascension, was "seated at the right hand of the Father." In ancient Jewish thought, with echoes of Daniel 7, this could only mean that, from that moment, Jesus was the Father's right-hand man, in charge of the whole world. But in our own day the "ascension" is just a way of saying that Jesus "went to heaven when he died." To speak of him "sitting at the Father's right hand" has become simply a fancy, perhaps even a fanciful, way of saying "he entered into a very splendid and glorious position." We have been lured, perhaps by our embarrassment at the literalistic sense of Jesus flying up like a spaceman to a "heaven" located a few miles up within our universe, into ignoring the real meaning both of "heaven" (which is not a place within our universe at all, but God's place, intersecting with our world in all sorts of ways) and of the ascension itself, which is about the sovereignty of Jesus as the Father's accredited and appointed agent. We have, as a result, understood the ascension in vague terms of supernatural glory, rather than in the precise terms (as in Matt. 28:18; Acts 1:6–11) of Jesus's authority over the world. In fact, the ascension, for many people, implies Jesus's absence, not his universal presence and sovereign rule. And this time it isn't only Matthew, Mark, Luke, and John who will raise objections; it's Paul, Hebrews, and Revelation as well. They all think that Jesus is already in charge of the world. (Check out, for instance, 1 Cor. 15:20–28; Heb. 2:5–9; Rev. 5:6–14.) That was what they understood by "God's kingdom."

But for the four gospels this wasn't something that simply began at the ascension. It was true, in a sense, from the moment Jesus began his public career. This was what they were trying to tell us. And most Christians have never even thought about such a thing, let alone begun to figure out what it means for us today. This is the problem, I believe, with the great majestic creeds, full as they are of solemn truth and supple wisdom. They manage not to mention the main thing the gospels are trying to tell us, and they talk about something else instead. Ought we to be worried by this? Are we missing something?

Perhaps not. Someone will no doubt point out that the creeds are the early church's clothesline. Hanging there are the clean garments that are the direct result of the "dirty linen" debates and controversies of those early centuries, the things the early Christians had to sort out and "get clean." Having formulated careful statements on these particular topics, they put them into official formulas, the creeds, to make it clear that they had arrived at those conclusions and that this was where "the church" now stood.

The point is that nobody much seemed to argue, at least within the church, about the things you find in Matthew, Mark, Luke, and John between the stories of Jesus's birth and the stories of his death. No heretics arose saying that Jesus didn't teach in parables, or didn't do miracles, or the like. Those who did write alternative so-called gospels (*Thomas* and other similar documents) or strung together collections of sayings that might or might not be from Jesus himself and those who told sharply different tales about what actually happened at Calvary and on Easter Day—in short, the Gnostics and others like them—had been firmly put in their place by Irenaeus and Tertullian. The alternative teaching of the Gnostics had proposed that one should replace the very Jewish message of God's kingdom on earth as in heaven by a very non-Jewish message about a "kingdom" that turned out to be a new form of self-help spirituality. The great second- and third-century Christian teachers insisted, against such new teaching, that God's rescue of the created order itself, rather than the rescue of saved souls *from* the created order, was central. That was part of the essentially Jewish faith, rooted in the Jewish scriptures, that the early Christians firmly maintained.

The decision on that point—that the one true God was the creator of the world who would rescue it in the end—was not itself a decision that left its mark in the creeds, except for the very first clause, which celebrates God as creator of heaven and earth. It was reflected, much more, in the church's insistence on reading Matthew, Mark, Luke, and John as the normative texts rather than any of the "alternatives." When you place the four emerging "canonical" gospels alongside the Jesus documents that others had written, again and again it appears that the canonical four are telling the story of the rescue of creation, not its abolition or abandonment—again, in other words, the essentially Jewish story. Thus, once those decisions were made, there was no need (the early Christians seem to have assumed) to say, in the creed, that the canonical gospels told the right story and the Gnostic gospels the wrong one.

The canonical gospels were, after all, read aloud in church. Christians said the Lord's Prayer day by day, asking God to establish his kingdom on earth as in heaven. One might say that the creeds and the canon were intended to stand side by side, each interpreting the other, with the Lord's Prayer as their obvious liturgical link. There was every reason to suppose that the faithful would understand the creeds as a framework within which these stories and this prayer brought everything into focus and made the sense they did. So all that material—the parables, the healings, the controversies with opponents, the great moral teaching, and above all the announcement of God's kingdom—simply wasn't mentioned in the official formulas. The gospels and their detailed teaching were taken for granted; they didn't need to be referred to in the creeds as well. If the creeds are the church's clothesline, the only clothes hanging on it would be the ones that were dirty and needed washing. If the clothes are still clean—if the gospels are being read in church day by day and week by week—you don't need to wash them and hang them out to dry.

If things had worked out like that, one might allow the point. But things didn't work out like that. The church provided a "rule of faith" by which, supposedly, to understand the scriptures. But the "rule" in question—the developing creeds and the early formulas that led up to them—turned out to ignore the central theme of the four gospels. Notice what then happens. At some point, perhaps not long after the creeds were written, the clothesline turned into a teaching aid. The list of earlier controversies became a syllabus. "These," the church declared, "are the things you need to know about God, Jesus, the Holy Spirit, and so on." And at this point we have crossed a line. Matthew, Mark, Luke, and John say, "*These* are the things you need to know about Jesus." The creeds, when taken out of their liturgical context where they belong with the gospels and the Lord's Prayer and used instead as the basis for a teaching program, say: "No, *these* are the things you need to know." And when push comes to shove the one thing you miss, when you use the creeds in that way, is the central point that Matthew, Mark, and Luke in their way and John in his own different way all say was central to the work of Jesus himself. This, they would say, is the story of *how God became king of the world.*

The great creeds, then, which have shaped and expressed the faith of millions of Christians in both Eastern and Western Christianity, simply omit the middle section, the story of Jesus's actual life and the meaning this story conveys. One could make a similar point the other way around too. All these high-flown statements about Jesus in the great creeds—all of which I endorse and say or sing *ex animo* in church (this argument is not building up to some kind of neoliberal reductionism!)—go way beyond anything even in John's gospel. The four evangelists say nothing whatever about Jesus being "begotten . . . before all worlds" or being begotten as opposed to being made. They may hint, John more openly than the others, that he is "of one substance with the Father," but they don't put it exactly like that, and for most of the time that doesn't seem to be the main thing they are talking about.

Nor, at the latter end of Jesus's life, do they mention his "descent into hell." That is hinted at in 1 Peter (3:19), but you wouldn't know it from the four gospels. Again, I am not saying that any of these ideas are wrong, or inappropriate, or unhelpful. Nor am I saying that the church was wrong to develop its teaching in different, postbiblical language to meet new challenges and settle new difficulties. That had to be done, and it created the context for further faithful and fruitful Christian living. I am simply noting that these great statements of faith, which the church has treated as foundational for its life ever since, manage not to talk about what the gospels primarily talk about and to talk about something else instead.

What I see, in other words, is a great gulf opening up between the canon and the creeds. The canonical gospels give us a Jesus whose public career radically mattered as part of his overall accomplishment, which had to do with the kingdom of God. The creeds give us a Jesus whose miraculous birth and saving death, resurrection, and ascension are all we need to know. It is not only in a historical sense that the title "Apostles' Creed" is a serious misnomer. My experience as a teenager and the one I had in my twenties were indications of something profoundly puzzling in the way we have all read the gospels. We have assumed some kind of creedal framework, and the gospels don't fit it. Have we, then, all misunderstood the gospels? Is there an emptiness at the heart of the great cloak of the creedal gospel? I fear the answer has to be yes.

Let's sharpen this up by observing an irony that follows directly from this. To this day, whenever people take it upon themselves to explore the divinity of Jesus, there is at the very least a tendency for the theme of God's kingdom, coming on earth as in heaven, to be quietly lost from view. It is as though a young man spent all his time proving that he really was his father's son and left no time or energy for working with his father in the family business—which would, actually, be one of the better ways of demonstrating the family likeness. The gospels don't make that mistake. It is by his inaugurating of God's kingdom, in his public career and on the cross, that Jesus reveals the father's glory. More of that anon. But this is a startling preliminary conclusion. It poses several additional questions for us today: about our discipleship, our preaching, our hermeneutics, and even our praying. The gospels were all about God becoming king, but the creeds are focused on Jesus being God. It would be truly remarkable if one great truth of early Christian faith and life were actually to displace another, to displace it indeed so thoroughly that people forgot it even existed. But that's what I think has happened. This book is written in the hope of correcting that distortion.

The Plot Thickens:
Twentieth-Century Scholarly Trends

So far I have confined myself to personal observations. But I believe the problem I have highlighted resonates across the whole field of Bible reading, scholarly and popular, in all the different traditions. As an American friend of mine put it, most Western churchgoers treat the gospels as the optional chips and dip at the start of the evening. They are the cocktail nibbles. Only after that do we sit down at table for the red meat of Pauline theology. I suspect—though this would take us too far afield—that this has been the case for much of the past millennium in the West, during the Middle Ages and then during and after the Reformation. That historical story, as I said in the Preface, must wait for another occasion, and probably another writer. I want, for the moment, to concentrate on one enormously influential strand of twentieth-century scholarship that both reflects the problem I am outlining and then solidifies it in the imagination and implicit understanding of the Western church at least.

The German Lutheran scholar Rudolf Bultmann (1884–1976) was one of the twentieth century's most influential New Testament scholars. For Bultmann and the generations of scholars and students who have been influenced directly or indirectly by his work, the story of Jesus himself formed no part of "New Testament theology"—it was merely the presupposition for such a thing. All that was needed was the fact of Jesus's crucifixion; that was enough. Everything else one needed to know was contained not in his teaching or public career, but in the early church's reflection on the meaning of the cross.

Bultmann therefore read the gospels not as the story of why Jesus lived, not in order to find "the gospel in the gospels" in the way I have described, but in order to observe the early Christians expressing their faith by telling and retelling stories that appear to us to be "Jesus stories," but that were, for the most part, "myth-ological" expressions of early Christian experience projected back onto the fictive screen of the history of Jesus. Bultmann's whole project of form criticism, at least in the way he practiced it, was predicated on the assumption that if you could discover the "forms," the characteristic shapes of the small anecdotes that make up much of the gospel material, you could thereby observe, as through a lens, the early church expressing its own faith. That, it was believed, was why the early gospel traditions were passed on: not to remember or celebrate something that *had* happened in the past (i.e., in Jesus's public career), but to celebrate and sustain the continuing life of faith of the early community.

Within the Bultmannian tradition—and, again, this has been very influential—it has often been assumed that the evangelists wrote from the same largely nonhistorical perspective. At least, it has often been assumed that Mark and John wrote not to tell their readers about what actually happened, but to express their own and their communities' faith and experience. Luke, how-ever, is sometimes accused of falsifying this "gospel," since he at least clearly *does* believe that "what happened" matters and has significance in and of itself. Matthew, for his part, has often been seen as a "Jewish Christian" writer (though all the New Testa-ment authors were "Jewish Christians"!) who likewise seems to have slipped up in terms of the "gospel" that one had been taught to expect (no doubt from a particular reading of Paul). This par-ticular mood, of supposing that the four gospels were not really "about Jesus," let alone "about the gospel," but, instead, "about the early Christian faith," has largely passed. Many scholars now use material from all four gospels, with appropriate critical con-trols, as evidence for Jesus himself. But the underlying problem has not been addressed.

Here we meet a telling irony. Bultmann's theology has been met, down through the years, with a stubborn and solid "No" from "conservative" quarters. Many "conservative" Christians, in both Europe and America, have been very concerned to stress the authority of the Bible, and so have been horrified by the insistence of Bultmann and his followers on the nonhistoricity of the gospels (this is not the same thing as careful critical judgment about this or that incident; it was part of Bultmann's whole agenda that the gospels, or at least the early forms of the gospels, should not as a point of principle be offering "history," since that might represent an attempt to base Christian faith on something solid and provable—in other words, to turn "faith" into a "work").

Such "conservatives," then, have stressed the historicity of the gospels as part of their insistence that "the Bible is true." But when it comes to interpretation and meaning, those same "conservatives" are regularly to be found on exactly the same page as Bultmann, reading most of the stories in the gospels as signposts toward the cross and the faith of the early church. I recall one colleague proudly telling me that his Christmas sermon was going to be on Matthew 1:21: "You are to give him the name Jesus; he is the one who will save his people from their sins." In other words, neither incarnation nor kingdom were going to be mentioned; Christmas was simply another occasion to preach the (supposedly Pauline) message of the cross. When such people claim to be "Bible Christians," I find myself saying (at least in my imagination): "If you're a 'Bible Christian,' how come you don't know what the gospels are there for? How is it that you simply treat them as somewhat random illustrative material for the thing you obviously want to focus on, the saving death and resurrection of the divine Savior?"

What I observe is this. Faced with a choice between the creed (some version of it) and the canon of scripture, in which the four gospels occupy such a central position, the church has unhesitatingly privileged the creed and let the canon fend for itself—which it hasn't always managed to do very successfully. The same is true when, in Protestantism, the great early creeds are implic-

itly replaced as the "rule of faith" by the various sixteenth- and
seventeenth-century formulas that highlight the Reformers' message of "justification by faith." This too, in its turn, becomes
the central thing, and the four gospels are valued insofar as they
illustrate it and not much beyond.

The gospels are of course so dense, so full of splendid and
vivid detail, that preachers, on the one hand, have quite enough
to do with this week's parable or miracle, and scholars, on the
other, have quite enough to do with figuring out which source
the passage comes from. Neither the preachers nor the scholars
have bothered too much about what the story in question actually *does* within the longer and larger narrative the evangelist has
constructed. (This is of course an overstatement. Many have done
and continue to do this. I am talking about the large generality
of preachers and teachers in the church and a fair proportion of
scholars as well.) In part this may stem from personality. For a
long time it has been much easier to get a Ph.D. in biblical studies if you're a "details person" rather than a "big-picture person."
This has attracted into the field people with sharp eyes for small
details; such an ability is a great asset for a scholar, but it needs to
be balanced with the vision and imagination that will ask the big
questions too, if scholarly study of the gospels is not to become
seriously distorted. The meaning of a word is its use in a sentence;
the meaning of a sentence is its use in a paragraph; *and the meaning of a paragraph is its use in the larger document to which it contributes.*
Details are vitally important, but they are important as part of the
overall picture. And the burden of my song in this book is that
we've all forgotten what the big picture actually is.

2

The Opposite Problem
All Body, No Cloak

G RANTED all we have said so far, we should not be surprised that many devout readers of the gospels have tried to redress the balance. Actually, many nondevout readers have tried to do so as well. Let's take the nondevout (perhaps, for charity's sake, we should say the less devout) first.

Jesus Without the Creeds?

Ever since the eighteenth century it has been fashionable to come at the gospels by asking the historical question: Did it really happen? And the answer that the intellectual fashions of our skeptical age have demanded has been something like this. Yes, Jesus really existed, but all that material around the edge—his miraculous birth, the saving meaning of his death, and above all his resurrection and ascension—never happened. That's what the later church added to express its own faith. But when we take that away, the bit in the middle that we're left with—the body without the cloak, if you like—is a very different story from the one the church has told. Take away the beginning and the ending, the bits you find in the creeds, the bits that people refer to today when they talk about "preaching the gospel," and the Jesus you're left with is one of three things. Either he's a revolutionary, hoping to overthrow the Romans by military violence and establish a new Jewish state. Or he's a wild-eyed apocalyptic visionary, expecting the end of the world. Or he's a mild-mannered teacher of sweet reasonableness, of the fatherhood of God and the brotherhood of "man." Or perhaps he's some combination of the above. There are plenty of possibilities.

In the first two cases, of course, Jesus was deluded. He didn't kill the Romans, but the Romans killed him. And if he was expecting the "end of the world," well, we're still waiting. In the third case he was similarly deluded, because most people, including most of his followers from that day to this, have been anything but sweetly reasonable. Instead, they have busied themselves with inventing dogmas (like the virgin birth and the resurrection), writing creeds, establishing the church, and fighting everybody else and one another, desperate to push their interpretation to the front of the line.

Those ways of telling (or not telling) the story of Jesus have been common coin among skeptics for the past two hundred years and more. The "liberal" picture of Jesus, early Christianity, and the gospels lives on in the persistent reductionism of a thousand books both scholarly and popular. For many, in fact, it is the new "orthodoxy." Unless you say something along these lines, you are likely to be sneered at. You can't be a serious thinker.

The strength of this position is that it really does try, to some extent at least, to pay attention to the bits of the church's own canon that the church's own creeds had bypassed. At its best, it produces, as we shall see, a strong "social gospel" agenda in which many of the things the gospels emphasize about Jesus—his care for the poor, the sick, the weak, and so on—are given a new energy that official "orthodoxy" has often strangely failed to supply. Its weakness is that it has neither the will nor the means to integrate that central piece, the why-did-Jesus-live bit, with the outer, creedal questions, the puzzles of Jesus's birth, death, resurrection, ascension, and second coming.

Many of us, I guess, have grown up with this liberal reductionism in the air. Books with titles like *Jesus Who Became Christ* abound. The "Jesus Seminar," which trumpeted its own "findings" ("Scholars say that . . .") while almost all New Testament scholars in America gave it a wide berth, went down very well with *Time* magazine and with liberal clergy who wanted to believe something like its reductionist teaching in the first place. The idea that Jesus came to teach a new, simple, clear ethic of being nice to people, without any "dogmatic" claims or "supernatural" elements, is so deeply embedded in Western culture that one sometimes despairs, like a gardener faced with ground ivy, of ever uprooting it. To this day there seems a ready market right across the Western world for books that say that Jesus was just a good Jewish boy who would have been horrified to see a "church" set up in his name, who didn't think of himself as "God" or even the "Son of God," and who had no intention of dying for anyone's sins—the church has gotten it all wrong. The authors of such books routinely proclaim themselves "neutral," "unbiased," "impartial," or "independent." As if.

This reductionist project suggests, in other words, that we try the picture the other way around. Instead of privileging the creeds and screening out the middle of the gospels, let's privilege the middle material of the gospels and screen out all that odd supernatural stuff at either end, the ideas that found their way into the creeds. This position remains hugely popular. As with Richard Dawkins and his ilk, people clearly still want, in fact they rather badly want, to be told that Jesus was just a great teacher, not the divine Savior. The greatly outworn phrase "the Jesus of history and the Christ of faith," which has meant many different things, naturally reflects this position.

There are of course infinite modifications within this picture. It has become commonplace to point out that these liberal portraits of Jesus have an uncomfortable habit of resembling the artists who are sketching them—or at least, the artists as they would like to imagine themselves. By itself, however, that remark is just a cheap shot, however true. We need to dig deeper and see more of what was going on.

The attempt to reconstruct a "Jesus" other than the one given by classic Christianity goes back, in the modern period, to H. S. Reimarus (1694–1768). He was writing at the height of the Enlightenment's rebellion against the classic Christianity it knew and despised. He is the equivalent, within the study of the gospels, of the great eighteenth-century French writer Voltaire, with his battle cry *Écraser l'infâme*, "Wipe out the scandal"—meaning the "scandal" of official Christianity and the posturing and hypocrisy of the church. Whereas some theologians have spoken of "faith seeking understanding," Reimarus and his later followers and imitators (up to the present day) have been more in the mode of *unfaith* seeking historical validation. That spirit is alive and well, in both the scholarly and popular markets. But the catch is this. Just like the would-be "orthodox" readings, though for almost the opposite reasons, this reductionist reading of the gospels has simply ignored the story that the gospels themselves were keen to tell. All that these movements have done is to stand the "orthodox" reading on its head, to highlight the middle at the cost of the edges rather than vice versa. But this hasn't, in fact, really advanced the understanding of the middle material itself. Nor has it begun to address the question of why the gospels told the story the way they did, with their careful and subtle integration of the edges and the middle—indeed, without any indication that they were aware of two different types of material in the first place.

Faced with these challenges, would-be "orthodox" Christian scholars and teachers have had one of two reactions. First, many—including the present writer—have accepted the historical challenge and sought to answer it. When we really study all the evidence for all it's worth, it is possible to offer a historically rooted picture of Jesus that is much fuller and more positive than the one classic liberal reductionism has constructed. Engaging in this work does not mean, as some have supposed, that one must first accept the reductionist worldview of the Enlightenment. Plenty of people were doing history before the eighteenth century; the word "history" does not simply mean "what a good eighteenth-century skeptic would allow." In the second reaction, many devout Christians, including many learned scholars and theologians, have held aloof from the "quest" and from any imperative toward actual historical inquiry concerning Jesus. Surely, they say, we simply have to go with what our great tradition has handed down to us, rather than play around with historical reconstructions offered by skeptics; we mustn't try to go behind our God-given gospels and invent something different of our own.

I still believe that the first of these positions is justifiable, though it is no part of the present book to argue the case for it. My problem with the second position is that it takes us back once again to the problem of creed and canon, or indeed "gospel" and "gospels." How can we escape this trap?

The Social Gospel of Jesus?

At this point we should turn and examine the more positive side of this middle-without-edges picture. As I hinted a moment ago, many devout Christians, without actually denying the creedal elements (virgin birth, resurrection, and so on), have glimpsed in the things Jesus did a sight of what the "kingdom of God" might look like in practice. The poor are delivered from their plight; the hungry are fed; the widows and orphans are given justice; the sick are healed; and so on. Many Christians, sustained by prayer, the sacraments, and the fellowship of the church, have given themselves energetically to these and other causes in their own day. Sometimes they have integrated, at least, the doctrine of the incarnation into what they have been attempting. In Jesus, they have said, God came and got his hands dirty in the real world, and we are called to do the same. The movement that called itself "Christian socialism" at the end of the nineteenth century worked on exactly that basis, often with a rich blend of spirituality, sacramental practice, and biblical theology, and with remarkable effect. I think, for instance, of the great biblical scholar and Bishop of Durham Brooke Fosse Westcott, who combined ferociously detailed and exact textual scholarship with zealous commitment to the poorest of the poor in the northeast of England.

Many movements of social reform at various points in the nineteenth century bear witness to this spirit, not least of course the pressure that led to the abolition of slavery. And then, around the start of the twentieth century, the movement known as the "social gospel" made its mark, not exactly by ignoring the "cloak" of ancient dogma, but by concentrating instead on the actions of Jesus and the command to his followers to behave in the same way. Matthew 25:31–46 has regularly been highlighted in this connection: "When you did it to one of the least significant of my brothers and sisters here," declares Jesus about the hungry who need feeding, the prisoners who need visiting, and so on, "you did it to me." And "When you didn't do it . . . , you didn't do it for me." The Achilles heel of the "social gospel" movement, however, was that many of its enthusiasts were, like the critical scholars of the time, focusing on the center rather than the edges, and so misreading the center itself. In trying to have a Jesus who cared for the poor without needing to be the incarnate son of God or to die for the sins of the world and be raised bodily thereafter, they falsified (so we could argue) even the bits they were highlighting.

The problem with all this, however, is not merely at the level of theory ("How come you've taken some bits of the gospel story, but left out other bits?"). The problem is that, a century after the "social gospel" was at its high-water mark, the world, including the Western world, still seems to be a place of great wickedness. Greed and corruption, oppression of the poor, violence and degradation, war and genocide continue unchecked. It isn't only the Jesus of popular imagination, then, who expected something dramatic to happen and was disappointed. The "social gospel" may have helped to clean up some slums, to reduce working hours for women and children in factories, and so on. Wonderful. But homelessness and virtual slave labor are still realities in the modern Western world, never mind elsewhere. Has anything really changed?

Faced with this puzzle, it is fair to ask: What difference might it make if the "middle" of the gospels was integrated with the "outer" bits? What would it be like if the cloak was no longer empty?

Did Jesus Talk About Himself?

One of the now standard comments from within "liberal" readings of the gospels goes like this. Jesus, it seems, went around speaking about God; but his followers, the early church, went around speaking about Jesus. This has in fact formed a central plank in the case for a liberal rereading of the gospels over against the creeds. The creeds seem fixated on defining something of which Jesus himself seems to have been innocent, namely, the precise nature of his ontological relationship to God the Father. And certainly when we read the gospels—even John's gospel—

and then look at the great creeds, this suggestion seems to have more than a grain of truth. The creeds are defining and stressing something that is never stated in that way in the gospels.

But, like many of liberalism's apparently scored points, this one disappears on closer scrutiny. It seems, of course, a clever put-down, undercutting the superiority complex of the dogmatists. But it replaces it with its own kind of modern superiority complex: "You would-be orthodox Christians stick your noses in the air, because you believe in the divinity of Jesus, whereas we modern historically conscious readers can stick *our* noses in the air, because we have discovered that Jesus himself never thought of himself that way!" The church's worship of Jesus can thus be "exposed," so it is thought, as a falsification of what Jesus himself would have said or thought. But in fact, when you get up close, the liberal salvo backfires, because Jesus was indeed talking about God, but was talking about God *precisely in order to explain his own kingdom work*. This, as we shall see, comes out again and again in the gospels' presentation.

This, however, offers no instant comfort for those "conservatives" who deny the propriety of historical investigation in the first place ("We don't want to 'go behind the canon,' so we just stick with the great tradition"). The problem with this is that it is precisely the great tradition that has always emphasized the four canonical gospels over against the Gnostic alternatives, and it is in the four canonical gospels, not in some dodgy reconstruction behind or beyond them, that we find the great emphasis on the coming of God's kingdom *in the actual events of Jesus's life, death, resurrection, and ascension*. But the coming of the kingdom is conspicuously absent not only from the great creeds, but also from "the gospel" as envisaged in the churches of the Reformation. If we want to stick to the great tradition, we should be prepared to take the gospels more seriously.

One might even state it as an axiom: when the church leaves out bits of its core teaching, heretics will pick them up, turn them into something new, and use them to spread doubt and unbelief. But the proper reaction to this, whether it's in the second century or the twenty-first, ought never to be simply to dismiss the heretical teaching outright and continue as before. The proper reaction is to look carefully to see which flank has been left unguarded, which bit of core teaching has been left out, where the canonical balance has not been maintained. Only then might one set about reincorporating that within a fresh statement of full-blown Christian faith. After all, another axiom might well go like this: when the church leaves out bits of its core teaching, it will inevitably overinflate other bits of its core teaching to fill the gap. (In other words, leave out the kingdom, and you may end up saying more than is really necessary in your "Christology" about Jesus's divine/human nature.) That doesn't mean that the overinflated core teaching is wrong. In the strange providence of God, this might even be seen as a means whereby people have been led to concentrate more intensely on vital areas. But it can only ever be a temporary move. By all means park the New Testament in a safe spot and go for a walk to pick the flowers nearby. But make sure you return to the New Testament when you want to continue your journey.

The Hidden Underlying Challenge:
Theocracy

When we examine the wider movements of thought and culture in the eighteenth century, we find something of enormous significance for understanding why the gospels were being read in the way they were. At the heart of "the Enlightenment" was a resolute determination that "God"—whoever "God" might be—should no longer be allowed to interfere, either directly or through those who claimed to be his spokesmen, in the affairs of this world. Once "man had come of age," there was no room for *theocracy.* It was as simple as that. God was pushed upstairs, like the doddering old boss who used to run the company, but has now been superseded. He has, no doubt, a notional place of "honor," a cozy office where he can sit and imagine he's still in charge. But nobody is fooled. The new generation is running the business now. They know it, and his supporters had better get used to it. Thus, for the European and American Enlightenment, God was superannuated to a position of totally ineffectual "honor."

But the whole point of the gospels is to tell the story of how God became king, on earth as in heaven. They were written to stake the very specific claim toward which the eighteenth-century movements of philosophy and culture, and particularly politics, were reacting with such hostility. Behind the attempts of Reimarus and others to suggest that the "kingdom of God" in the teaching of Jesus referred either to a violent military revolution or to the "end of the world" there lay the determination to make sure that God was kept out of real life. This was not a "result" of fresh research. It was the philosophical and theopolitical assumption that drove the research in the first place.

This is, I think, the real problem with post-Enlightenment historical skepticism. It was not simply that it begged leave to doubt all kinds of elements in the gospel stories (the "miracles," and so forth) as well as the framing dogmas of incarnation, atonement, resurrection, and so on. David Hume, the Scottish philosopher whose rejection of the miraculous still holds sway in many minds, is only one element in the picture. Alongside him are Hobbes, Rousseau, Voltaire, and, not least, Thomas Jefferson—the masterminds not only of a new "climate of opinion," but a new political agenda. The wedge they drove between faith and public life, between religion and politics, is exactly the same wedge that Reimarus and others drove between (what came to be called) the Jesus of history and the Christ of faith.

This philosophy was not new. The philosophers in question, of course, liked to present it as such, and the simultaneous advances in science and technology enabled them to suggest that this really was a wholly new era of world history. On the contrary, the mainline philosophy of the Enlightenment was simply one version of the ancient philosophy of Epicurus, who taught that the gods, if they existed at all, were a long way away from the world of humans and did not concern themselves with it. As a result, the world we know grows, changes, and develops under its own steam, as it were from within. Apply this to the scientific study of origins, and you get Darwinian evolution—again, not a new idea, but one that followed logically from the absence of divine control or intervention. Instead of "thinking God's thoughts after him," science was now studying the world as though God didn't exist. Apply it to political science, and you get democracy: society ordering itself according to its own internal wishes and whims, fears and fancies. Instead of the "divine right" of rulers, politics was now ordering the world—at least in France and America— on the strict basis of a separation between church and state.

Only when these connections and parallels are brought to light does it become clear why, from the eighteenth century onward, the massive structure of scholarly study of the gospels has asked certain questions and proposed certain answers. The choice between Reimarus's failed Jewish revolutionary and Schweitzer's failed apocalyptic visionary is, according to the gospels themselves, a choice between false alternatives. Neither Reimarus nor Schweitzer was prepared to countenance the possibility, which the gospels were strenuously proposing, that in Jesus the God of Israel, the creator God, really did confound the Epicureans and everybody else as well by becoming king on earth as in heaven. Theocracy—but theocracy of a radically different kind from anything anyone had imagined for a very long time—was the name of the game. But the post-Enlightenment world, even the devout, pious, godly, evangelical, or Catholic post-Enlightenment world, was not ready to join in. Theocracy, had the question even been raised, would have sounded far too much like corrupt and

lazy clergy trying to bully a timid population or, indeed, like
George III sending bishops to the colonies to keep them in control. Theocracy wasn't wanted either by the skeptical reformers or
by the pious "orthodox," who were content, like the rabbis after
the bar-Kochba revolt, to abandon the vision of God's kingdom
on earth and retreat into a world of private piety, of "religion."

The reason the discussion of Jesus in his historical context has
been so difficult, in other words, is not simply that the gospels
are highly complex documents, though of course that is part of
it. The underlying reason is that the wrong questions have been
asked, by "liberals" and "radicals," by "conservatives" and "orthodox" alike. Questions have been asked of the gospels that they
were not written to answer; and the questions the gospels were
addressing—questions as much political as theological—have
been ignored. It is time for a fresh look.

The Orthodox Response

Reimarus and his colleagues were not the only people reading the
gospels in the eighteenth century. Within the church, the challenge of the skeptics put the church on the defensive. Was Jesus
really divine? The eighteenth-century church was concerned to
prove that he was. This resulted in a reading of the gospels *looking
for the wrong thing*. Miracles! That's the thing, said the apologists.
Jesus did miracles, so that proves he's the divine Son of God.
For many people today, the question is still framed in the old
eighteenth-century way, and they feel themselves obliged to give
the same eighteenth-century answers. But this is a mistake. The
Old Testament has plenty of people doing "miracles" (Moses,
Elijah, and Elisha come to mind), and nobody supposed then or
supposes now that this means they were "divine," let alone "the
second person of the Trinity." This is a difficult point to make.
These questions have so dominated discussion that anything we

say about them now may be misheard. But the point has to be made nonetheless.

In addition to apologists, arguing that Jesus really did walk on water and cure the sick, thus demonstrating that he really was divine, the eighteenth century saw great movements of revival, particularly through the Methodist movement led by John and Charles Wesley and George Whitefield. Their theology and their understanding of the gospels are quite different topics upon which I am not qualified to speak. But I suspect that the Wesleyan emphasis on Christian *experience,* both the "spiritual" experience of knowing the love of God in one's own heart and life and the "practical" experience of living a holy life for oneself and of working for God's justice in the world, might well be cited as evidence of a movement in which parts of the church did actually integrate several elements in the gospels, a synthesis that the majority of Western Christians have allowed to fall apart. Even within Methodism itself, however, I do not sense that the fine instincts of the early leaders have led to an enriched, integrated long-term understanding of the church's central texts, the gospels themselves.

What I miss, right across the Western tradition, at least the way it has come through to the twentieth and twenty-first centuries, is the devastating and challenging message I find in the four gospels: *God really has become king—in and through Jesus!* A new state of affairs has been brought into existence. A door has been opened that nobody can shut. Jesus is now the world's rightful Lord, and all other lords are to fall at his feet. This is an *eschatological* message, not in the trivial sense that it heralds the "end of the world" (whatever that might mean), but in the sense that it is about something that was supposed to happen when Israel's hopes were fulfilled; and Israel's hopes were not for the demise of the space-time universe, but for the earth to be full of God's glory. It is, however, an *inaugurated eschatological* message, claiming that this "something" has indeed happened in and through Jesus and does not yet look like what people might have imagined. That is the story the gospels are telling.

But if this is so—if God has become king of the world, through Jesus—then nobody can stay indifferent. This is the point that the four gospels are making, but that the creeds appear completely to ignore and that the Reformers and subsequent "evangelical" movements have likewise normally ignored in their eagerness for "the gospel" of personal salvation. The church has gone on reading Matthew, Mark, Luke, and John, but without any clue from those great creedal and Reformed traditions as to what they are actually saying.

My case throughout this book, then, is that all four canonical gospels suppose themselves to be telling the story that Paul, in some of his most central and characteristic passages, tells as well: that *the story of Jesus is the story of how Israel's God became king.* This is how, in the events concerning Jesus of Nazareth, the God of Israel has become king of the whole world. This is the forgotten story of the gospels. We have not even noticed that this was what they were trying to tell us. As a result, we have all misread them.

A sign of how far off-track we are at this point is the natural reaction that many will already have had to the very word "theocracy." Some readers may, metaphorically or even literally, have put their hands to their mouths in dismay. "We never wanted to hear *that*! If it were true that God had become king, what on earth would it mean? The rule of the crazy and corrupt clergy? And surely it isn't true, anyway—since the world is still in a horrible mess and since indeed Jesus's followers have contributed to that mess? Wasn't the kingdom of God something having to do with the end of the world, and since that didn't happen, aren't we justified in looking at things very differently? And if in some way we believe that Jesus is exalted or enthroned, surely that is a purely spiritual reality we're talking about? Doesn't the Easter hymn say, 'Now above the sky he's king / where the angels ever sing / Alleluia' "?

Well, yes, it does. More's the pity. Actually, when I was Bishop of Durham I used to insist that we change that line to, "Now o'er all the world he's king / while the angels ever sing / Alleluia." That's what the ascension is about. But before we can get to that, we need to take several steps back and look more widely at what people have done with the "middle bits" of the gospels once they have forgotten the story that the evangelists were really trying to tell us.

3

The Inadequate Answers

S O WHAT HAVE THE CHURCHES normally done with the "middle bits," with the "body" inside the "cloak"? I have on occasion challenged groups of clergy and laity to tell me what they or their congregations might say if asked what "all that stuff in the middle" was about. What was the *point,* I have asked, of the healings and feastings, the Sermon on the Mount and the controversies with the Pharisees, the stilling of the storm, Peter's confession at Caesarea Philippi, and so on, and so on—all the mass of rich material that the gospels offer us between Jesus's birth, or at least his baptism, and his trial and death? Pastors and preachers reading this book might like to consider the question this way. If you asked your congregation about this, what do you think they would say? What, indeed, would your congregation expect *you* to say the gospels were all about?

The responses I have received have been revealing. The church's tradition has, it seems, offered at least six different types of answer. They are all, in my view, inadequate. None of them corresponds very closely to what the four gospels actually talk about.

Going to Heaven

The first inadequate answer is that Jesus came to teach people *how to go to heaven*. This is, I believe, a major and serious misunderstanding.

Don't get me wrong. The whole New Testament assumes that God has a wonderful future prepared for his people after bodily death, climaxing in the new world of the resurrection, of new heavens and new earth. I have written about all that in detail elsewhere (especially in *Surprised by Hope*).* But this is not—demonstrably not—what the four gospels are about.

The problem has arisen principally because for many centuries Christians in the Western churches at least have assumed that the whole point of Christian faith is to "go to heaven," so they have read everything in that light. To a man with a hammer, they say, all problems appear as nails. To readers interested in postmortem bliss, all scriptures seem to be telling you how to "go to heaven." But, as we shall see, they aren't and don't.

This wrong reading has gained a good deal of apparent credibility from two expressions that occur regularly in the gospels and that the Western church at least has taken to refer to "heaven" in the traditional sense. The first expression is found frequently in Matthew's gospel. Because Matthew is the first gospel in the canon and has occupied that place since early in the church's history, it exercises considerable influence on how ordinary readers understand the others as well. In Matthew, Jesus regularly speaks of "heaven's kingdom," whereas normally in the other gospels he speaks of "God's kingdom." Millions of readers, when they hear Matthew's Jesus talking about doing this or that "so that you may enter the kingdom of heaven," assume, without giving it a

---

Surprised by Hope: Rethinking Heaven, the Resurrection, and the Mission of the Church (San Francisco: HarperOne, 2008).

moment's thought, that this means "so that you may go to heaven when you die."

But that is not at all what Matthew, or Jesus for that matter, had in mind. Matthew makes it quite clear, and I think Jesus made it quite clear, what that phrase means. Think of the Lord's Prayer, which comes at the center of the Sermon on the Mount in Matthew 5–7. At the center of the prayer itself we find Jesus teaching his followers to pray that God's kingdom might come and his will be done "on earth as in heaven." The "kingdom of heaven" is not about people going to heaven. It is about the rule of heaven coming to earth. When Matthew has Jesus talking about heaven's kingdom, he means that heaven—in other words, *the God of heaven*—is establishing his sovereign rule not just in heaven, but on earth as well.

It is true that this phrase "kingdom of heaven" seems to have been understood from quite early on in the church not in that first-century sense (God's rule becoming a reality on this earth), but in the quite different sense of "heaven" as a distant place where God ruled and to which he welcomed all those who followed Jesus. That seems to be already the case in the well-known hymn we call the Te Deum Laudamus ("We Praise Thee, O God"), which dates from at least as early as the fourth century. There we find the clause (in the translation adopted by the Book of Common Prayer): "When thou hadst overcome the sharpness of death, thou didst open the kingdom of heaven to all believers." Read Matthew's gospel with *that* line in mind, and you are almost bound to see the "kingdom of heaven" as a place from which believers might have been barred because of sin, but to which now, through the death of Jesus, they have access. What's more, though the hymn does not exactly say so, it hints at a parallel: Jesus opened the "kingdom" through his death, so it is presumably through and after death that believers enter this "kingdom" themselves. That, one might risk a bet, is how generations of Christians have understood that bit of the Te Deum as they have said it or sung it. And it is a whole world away from what Matthew intended. It is as though you were to get a letter from the president of the United States inviting himself to stay at your home, and in your excitement you misread it and assumed that he was inviting you to stay at the White House.

The second expression that has routinely been misunderstood in this connection is "eternal life." Here again the widespread and long-lasting assumption that the gospels are there to tell us "how to go to heaven" has determined how people "hear" this phrase. Indeed, the word "eternity" in modern English and American has regularly been used not only to point to a "heavenly" destination, but to say something specific about it, namely, that it will be somehow outside time and probably outside space and matter as well. A disembodied, timeless eternity! That is Plato, not the Bible—and it's a measure of how far Western Christianity has drifted from its moorings that it seldom even realizes the fact. Anyway, granted this assumption, when we find the Greek phrase *zoe aionios* in the gospels (and indeed in the New Testament letters), and when it is regularly translated as "eternal life" or "everlasting life," people have naturally assumed that this concept of "eternity" is the right way to understand it. "God so loved the world," reads the famous text in the King James Version of John 3:16, "that he gave his only begotten Son, that whosoever believeth in him should not perish but have *everlasting life*." There we are, think average Christian readers. This is the biblical promise of a timeless heavenly bliss.

But it isn't. In the many places where the phrase *zoe aionios* appears in the gospels, and in Paul's letters for that matter, it refers to one aspect of an ancient Jewish belief about how time was divided up. In this viewpoint, there were two "aions" (we sometimes use the word "eon" in that sense): the "present age," *ha-olam hazeh* in Hebrew, and the "age to come," *ha-olam ha-ba*. The "age to come," many ancient Jews believed, would arrive one day to bring God's justice, peace, and healing to the world as it groaned and toiled within the "present age." You can see Paul, for instance, referring to this idea in Galatians 1:4, where he speaks of Jesus giving himself for our sins "to rescue us from the present evil age." In other words, Jesus has inaugurated, ushered in, the "age to come." *But there is no sense that this "age to come" is "eternal" in the sense of being outside space, time, and matter.* Far from it. The ancient Jews were creational monotheists. For them, God's great future purpose was not to rescue people out of the world, but to rescue the world itself, people included, from its present state of corruption and decay.

If we reframe our thinking within this setting, the phrase *zoe aionios* will refer to "the life of the age," in other words, "the life of the age to come." When in Luke the rich young ruler asks Jesus, "Good Teacher, what must I do to inherit eternal life?" (18:18, NRSV), he isn't asking how to go to heaven when he dies. He is asking about the new world that God is going to usher in, the new era of justice, peace, and freedom God has promised his people. And he is asking, in particular, how he can be sure that when God does all this, he will be part of those who inherit the new world, who share its life. This is why, in my own new translation of the New Testament, Luke 18:18 reads, "Good teacher, what must I do to inherit the life of the age to come?" Likewise, John 3:16 ends not with "have everlasting life" (KJV), but "share in the life of God's new age."

Among the various results of this misreading has been the earnest attempt to make all the material in Jesus's public career refer somehow to a supposed invitation to "go to heaven" rather than to the present challenge of the kingdom coming on earth as in heaven. Time would fail to spell out the additional misunderstandings that have resulted from this, but we might just note one. Jesus's controversies with his opponents, particularly the Pharisees, have regularly been interpreted on the assumption that the Pharisees had one system for "going to heaven" (in their case, keeping lots of stringent and fussy rules), and Jesus had another one, an easier path altogether in which God had relaxed the rules and made everything a lot easier. As many people are now aware, this does no justice either to the Pharisees or to Jesus. Somehow, we have to get our minds around a different, more challenging way of reading the gospels.

Jesus's Ethical Teaching

A second popular approach to the material "in the middle" of the gospels is to understand it in terms of Jesus's *teaching,* particularly about what we call "ethics," or how to behave. People in our culture, both inside and outside of the church, regularly invoke the Sermon on the Mount as a kind of manifesto—I have seen it recently set alongside the American Declaration of Independence and Karl Marx's Communist Manifesto—setting out Jesus's vision for what a really good human life might look like. The assumption, then, is that Jesus came as a great teacher whose career was unfortunately cut short by people who didn't like what he was saying. Indeed, I have seen it argued that, in post-Christian Britain at least, most people who think about either Jesus or the gospels assume that Jesus was a moral teacher and that the gospels offer a collection of his moral teaching. (That is why, perhaps, the philosopher A. C. Grayling could make the remarkable mistake of producing an "atheist's Bible," which is just a collection of wise moral teaching. No narrative at all. Whatever that is, it isn't a Bible.)

There is of course more than a grain of truth in this. Jesus's summons to Israel to be Israel indeed, now that he was there, turns directly into a challenge and invitation to a whole new way of being human. This way is characterized especially by forgiveness, God's forgiveness of people and our forgiveness of one another. All of that formed a quite new agenda for most of Jesus's hearers. It had to be laid out, explained, repeated, illustrated, and generally *taught*. So, yes, Jesus was undoubtedly a "teacher." Indeed, people sometimes addressed him as such, and Jesus never told them they were wrong to do so.

But, in fact, the meanings we normally associate with the word "teacher" don't come anywhere close to the reality we find in the gospels. For us, "teaching" often implies the imparting of ancient wisdom, perhaps with a new spin, but still according to a standard syllabus. But what Jesus was announcing was something much bigger, something far more startling. To use a musical illustration, Jesus is often seen as someone who can "teach" you to play the piano, so that you can perform Mozart and Beethoven. But Jesus was more like someone who had just invented an entirely new musical instrument, had written some stunning music for it, and was now "teaching" people to play the new music on the new instrument. Jesus was *announcing that a whole new world was being born* and he was "teaching" people how to live within that whole new world. To that extent, we should both embrace the idea of him as a "teacher" and radically qualify or modify it. In fact, the modification should take place before the embrace. You only understand the point of the "teaching" when you understand the larger picture of what Jesus was doing.

Without that larger picture, the word "teacher" or "teaching" can result in a severely diminished sense of what the gospels are trying to say about Jesus. The notion of "teaching" can easily collapse into the standard popular picture of Jesus as one of the world's great "religious teachers" alongside Buddha, Muhammad, and so on. In other words, there are some things called "religious truths," which some great souls have discovered and taught, and Jesus was simply one of those great souls, one of those great teachers. One often meets people who are extremely keen to insist that Jesus's teaching was "just like" that of Buddha or another great teacher—as though they are perhaps a bit too eager to make sure that the much more specific claim of Jesus, that Israel's God was launching his project of new creation in and through him, should be set aside and forgotten. Jesus as a "teacher" is much safer than Jesus as the gospels actually present him.

Most Christians today would, I suspect, see straight through that reductionism. But would they know what to put in its place? Or would they simply substitute some version of the first answer, that Jesus came to enable us to go to heaven? In the gospels, Jesus is undoubtedly a great moral teacher and exemplar. But he is much, much more. And it is that "much more" that the church has found so hard to grasp and express.

Jesus the Moral Exemplar

A third standard line people sometimes advance when wondering why the gospels tell their readers about what Jesus did in his public career is to suggest that he was offering an *example* of how to live. His utter, generous love and his fearless rebuke of wickedness and oppression make a formidable combination, especially when you add in his apparent fondness for parties, on the one hand, and prayer, on the other, and his remarkably shrewd ability to sum up situations, people, and problems in a pithy phrase or to tease out fresh meaning with a neat, telling story. What a man, we say to ourselves. Unlike many moralists then and now, his own life strikingly matched his own stringent teaching. People have sometimes accused Jesus of betraying his own standards (in cursing the fig tree, for example), but most people have accepted the gospels' portrait of him as embodying that mixture of wisdom, love, holiness, and truth that he was urging as the proper standard for human life. The idea of Jesus as "teacher" is therefore sometimes elaborated further, and Jesus is seen as "moral exemplar." Jesus came, many have said, to "show us the way," to "show us how it's done."

But that's part of the problem—with this as a theory at all, and with this as a theory about why the gospels are what they are. As

I have written elsewhere (in *After You Believe*),* it isn't actually much of an encouragement to me to read the stories about Jesus. I might as well take encouragement from watching a great athlete run a four-minute mile. Sure, it's a fine sight, but at my age and with my weight I would be lucky to do a mile in ten minutes, let alone four. I can watch a ballet dancer on stage with great delight, not because I think I can copy him, but precisely because I know I can't. Have you ever *tried* to copy Jesus, not just in his amazing generosity and kindness, but in his sharp, brightly colored little stories? Very few people throughout history have been able to tell short stories like that, so brief yet so complete. The obvious answer to this proposal, then, is that just because I see someone, even Jesus, behaving in a particular way, that doesn't necessarily make it any easier for me to do so. Only today I was reading a testimony from a leading theological teacher who lamented the fact that her own life hadn't matched up to the ideals she had assumed were the Christian norm. If Jesus came either to teach or to model a perfect way of life, hoping that people would then obey him and copy him, we would have to conclude that he was a striking failure.

And that's not the only point. Again and again in the gospels we find that Jesus is not, in fact, holding himself up as an example to follow or copy. Yes, there are times when he does say something like that. He is taking up his cross, and his followers are to take up theirs. And he expects them to share his faith and to pray in the way that he himself seems to have prayed. Ultimately, he tells them that as the Father sent him, so he is sending them. So there is an element of imitation involved, as Paul speaks of in his letters; indeed, Paul tells the Corinthians to copy him because he is copying the Messiah (1 Cor. 11:1). All that is true. But it is held within a framework where Jesus is *not simply* "an example to copy," but the one who is doing something new that will change

---

After You Believe: Why Christian Character Matters (San Francisco: HarperOne, 2010).

the way things are for everybody else. Where he is going, he tells
them, they cannot come. He is to be arrested, but they must escape. His task is unique. It cannot be reduced to that of the great
man showing his followers how it's done. Like the other suggestions we are reviewing, this one has a modicum of truth, but fails
to come anywhere close to a satisfying account of the whole.

Jesus the Perfect Sacrifice

A fourth inadequate answer has tried to tie the first and the third
together. The aim is still to get us to heaven, but Jesus is not just
the moral exemplar—his perfect life means that he can be *the perfect sacrifice*. Since it is his sacrificial death that enables our sins to
be forgiven, and since in the Old Testament the sacrifice must be
pure and without blemish, it was necessary that Jesus's life should
be sinless, so that his sacrifice would be valid, acceptable to God.
Many Christians have tried to "explain" the "middle bits" of the
gospels in this kind of way.

Once more, there is a grain of truth here. The gospels do indeed occasionally note Jesus's sinlessness (John 8:46; cf. Mark
10:18). It is also true that the same theme emerges, more strikingly, in Paul (2 Cor. 5:21), Hebrews (4:15; 7:26), 1 Peter (2:22),
and 1 John (3:5). Several of these references occur in a context in
which Jesus's death is the main subject. The idea of Jesus as the
sinless sacrifice is clearly present in early Christianity. But do the
gospels make this link?

The closest they come, I think, is in Luke's insistence that when
Jesus went to his death, he was innocent of the charges against
him. Luke makes this point quite emphatically (23:14–15, 22, 31,
41, 47), and there is good reason to think that this is a major feature
of his particular understanding of the meaning of Jesus's crucifixion. All around Jesus, in Luke, are people who, it seems, *are* guilty

of the things with which Jesus has been charged; Jesus is innocent of those charges, but he is dying the death they might have died. That is the point of the little story about Barabbas (23:18–25), and the "repentant brigand" in 23:39–43 says something very similar: we deserve this death, but "this fellow hasn't done anything out of order." So, yes, Jesus's own moral perfection does play a role in relation to his death. But, beyond these passages, the gospels show no interest whatever in making the link that much traditional teaching has employed. If that was what they were trying to say, you'd think they would have made it a bit clearer.

A subpoint in this fourth answer has been developed by some branches of Reformed theology. There we find the notion that Jesus, in fulfilling the Mosaic law (see, e.g., Matt. 5:17, where Jesus says that he didn't come to destroy the law and the prophets, but to fulfill them), acquired his own store of merit or "righteousness," which he is then able to transfer (the technical term being "impute") to those who believe in him. This has been a major theme in some expositions of Paul's theology, particularly his teaching on justification. It has therefore been assumed that the life of Jesus contributes to this result: the "active obedience of Christ," consisting of his sinless life and perfect keeping of the law, works in tandem with the "passive obedience of Christ," that is, his suffering and death. Together these constitute the "obedience" of Christ that, it is assumed, Paul is referring to in such passages as Romans 5:19.

Again we have to say, if that's what the gospels were trying to tell us, they didn't do a very good job of it. Indeed, the very striking moments when Jesus seems deliberately to flout the sabbath law or to teach things like "all foods are clean" (Mark 7:19) ought to stop us in our tracks before we simply accept that Jesus, in any straightforward sense, "fulfilled the law." He did and he didn't, and the "fulfillment" of which Matthew's gospel speaks (in such passages as 3:15; 5:17) doesn't seem to me to mean anything like what Reformed theology has said it means. As I have argued else-where (*Justification*),* it seems that, although Reformed theology has made points about grace and faith that are themselves fully justified by the biblical data, the ways it has tried to argue these points from texts, especially in Paul but also in the gospels, leaves a good deal to be desired.

Stories We Can Identify With

A fifth inadequate answer takes quite a different tack. "The gospels are written," people have said to me, "*so we can identify* with the characters in the story and find our own way by seeing what happened to them." Well, there is once again quite a lot in that. Getting inside the stories in the gospels is indeed an excellent way of coming to understand Jesus better and allowing the power of his life to transform our own.

But this is scarcely a sufficient explanation for why Matthew, Mark, Luke, and John wrote the books they did. Our small journeys may indeed overlap to some extent with the greater journey that the gospel stories as a whole are relating. We can "use" them in that way, just as one can use a beautiful crystal decanter to top off the water in a car radiator. It will work, but one should have a sense that the decanter was meant for something far more special. To change the image, just because we find that a train will take us from Coventry to Birmingham doesn't mean that that is all that the train is doing. It may well be going all the way from Southampton to Edinburgh or from London to Glasgow. The question we have to face about the gospels is the question of where they are coming from and where they are going, not simply the various things we can use them for along the way.

Justification: God's Plan and Paul's Vision (Downers Grove, IL: InterVarsity, 2009).

Proving Jesus's Divinity

The sixth standard line has been to say that the gospels were written to demonstrate *the divinity of Jesus*. This, I suspect, is what many Christians regard as the gospels' principal purpose. Some would add too the equal purpose of demonstrating his humanity. There were, after all, some people in the late first and early second centuries who thought that Jesus only "seemed" to be human and in fact was not. (Such people are the target of the warnings in 1 John 4:2–3.) Since for many centuries the main thing people wanted to say about Jesus was that he was fully divine and fully human, it has once more been assumed that this "must have been" what the gospels were "really" trying to say about him.

This way of reading the gospels was presented to me in one of the very first tutorials I attended as an Oxford undergraduate. On the reading list there was a book explaining that one could trace, in the gospels, the things Jesus did that demonstrated his divinity and the things he did that demonstrated his humanity. The miracles—especially walking on water, raising the dead, and then being raised himself—showed that "he was God." But also he was hungry, he wept, and he confessed his own ignorance (in Mark 13:32, which the early church certainly didn't make up, Jesus declares that he doesn't know the day or the hour of the cataclysmic events he is predicting). All this, I read, showed that "he was human." His death, of course, made the latter point all the more starkly.

When did people start to talk about Jesus's "humanity" and "divinity" in this way? Not, I think, in the first century. Don't misunderstand me. As we shall see, if the question were raised, the New Testament writers would be quite clear that Jesus was indeed fully human and—somehow, strangely, but definitely—truly divine. But that does not seem to be their main point. Even John, who brings his stage-setting prologue to its climax by speaking of the Word becoming flesh, does not make this the main strand in the story he is telling. It is only later, when the church moves out into the wider world of Greek philosophy, that the question gets raised like that, in the abstract. In the middle of the fifth century Chalcedonian Christology declared, in ringing, round, and frankly very paradoxical tones, that Jesus was indeed fully divine and fully human. These abstract categories were in the center of the discussion then, and no mistake. But if you compare Chalcedon with the four gospels, you'll find that they are very different sorts of documents and that the gospels, though they do indeed have Jesus doing remarkable things, on the one hand, and behaving like an ordinary human being, on the other, do not appear to be written in order to prove that point.

Sometimes people will say, making a more personal or pastoral point, that the gospels, in telling the story of Jesus, show us who God really is. That's a bit more like it. That, in fact, is precisely what John says at the end of his prologue: nobody has ever seen God, but the only son, who is intimately close to the Father, has brought him to light. Look at Jesus, and you'll see the human face of God. But even that doesn't get us far enough, because John at once goes on, as do all four gospels, to tell us *what this embodied God is now up to.* It isn't enough to know that Jesus is in some sense "divine." The question is, which God are we talking about, what is he now doing, and why? What does it mean?

As we shall see, it isn't only John who presupposes that in Jesus we see the living human embodiment of the God of Israel, returning at last to visit and redeem his people. Older scholarship used to try to present John as giving us the "divine" Jesus and the synoptic gospels giving us the "human" Jesus, but that really won't do. That idea came from within the post-Enlightenment world, which decreed that God and humankind don't mix; so scholars seized on John's rather obviously "high" Christology in order to contrast the apparently "low" Christology of the synoptics. This is a mistake, as I shall show later on and as most scholars now recognize. However, my point here is not that the gospels don't think of Jesus as divine, but that this isn't the primary thing, the point they are most eager to get across. They presuppose it. It is the key in which they write their music, rather than the main tune itself. The point, to repeat, is not *whether* Jesus is God, but *what* God is doing in and through Jesus. What is this embodied God up to?

Even John, when he tells us at the end why he has been writing his gospel (20:31: "These are written so that you may believe . . ."), may not exactly be saying what later tradition has assumed he is saying, which is "that Jesus is the Messiah, the son of God" (NRSV). This is a much more subtle and interesting sentence than most readers have assumed. First, the phrase "son of God," though certainly indicating, for John, that Jesus is in some sense "divine" (the passage follows immediately after the story in which Thomas declares of Jesus, "My Lord and my God!"), is also clearly a messianic title, as in Psalm 2. But second, the Greek almost certainly should be read with the emphasis the other way around: "that you may believe that the Messiah, the son of God, is none other than Jesus." *This Jesus,* in other words, not someone else, is the Messiah; in this man, and in him alone, we see the way the living God is establishing the kingdom spoken of in Psalm 2. And if Jesus is the Messiah, then his public career and death, and not some other way, is how Israel's God is accomplishing and establishing his kingdom on earth as in heaven. To make John 20:31 the simple statement, "I have written this book to demonstrate Jesus's divinity," is to miss the much more subtle and rich point John is making. He has written this book to show that it is in Jesus, and his death and resurrection, that Israel's God has done what he promised he would do in and through Israel's anointed king and has in this way revealed fully and finally who he himself actually is.

What has happened seems to be this. Some centuries after the gospels were written, Christians found that one of their major challenges was not only explaining, but also "proving" Jesus's "divinity." Since the gospels do indeed seem to provide some excellent material on this subject (we shall look at it in more detail in Chapter 5), and since for those Christians the kingdom agenda of the gospels seems to have receded somewhat, it was easy for them to assume that the gospel writers were trying to do exactly the same thing they were. They have therefore read the miracle stories, for instance, as contributing to that aim.

A glance at Israel's scriptures, however, shows that some of the prophets did that same kind of thing (multiplying food, raising the dead, and so on) without anyone concluding that they were "divine." In fact, one could make a case—supposing this were the thing one wanted to prove—for seeing the "powerful works" of Jesus as evidence of his true *humanity,* since it is genuine humans who are in charge of God's world, and to see his suffering and death on behalf of others as evidence of his *divinity,* since only God can rescue people from their sins. That would be stretching a point. But the fact that one can reverse the normal assumption without making total nonsense shows how unlikely it is that the gospels were written as the backstory, the historical proof if you like, for the Chalcedonian definition. The gospels do indeed exhibit a belief in Jesus's full divinity and humanity. But that is not the primary story they were written to tell.

But there is more. To speak of Jesus's divinity without speaking of his kingdom coming on earth as in heaven is to take a large step toward the detached spirituality—almost a form of Gnosticism—that the first two centuries of the church firmly rejected. Only recently did the awful realization dawn on me that a certain stance was not only possible, but actually occurring: people were affirming the divinity of Jesus—which I also fully and gladly affirm—and then using it as a shelter behind which to hide from the radical story the gospels were telling about what this embodied God was actually up to.

Or, to put it another way, doing "doctrine" out of the gospels is like joining up the dots in a child's connect-the-dots puzzle. Usually the dots are numbered, and the child can see the order in which they must be joined. But suppose they are not, and the child has to join the dots and make whatever picture seems right? There are some Christians who manage to join the dots all right, to connect all the doctrinal boxes that the great early creeds and definitions have given them—but to do so in such a way that the picture turns out to be an elephant instead of a donkey. Or vice versa. Only when the story the gospels are telling is fully integrated with the dogmas the creeds are teaching can we be sure we are on track.

Displacement Activities

The result of all this has been, I believe, that though the gospels are so rich in material of all sorts, their underlying emphasis has been quietly but thoroughly overlooked. All those parables, moral teachings, remarkable deeds, and so on—one can easily make all kinds of perfectly good theological and practical points out of them. But one may be so busy with that exercise that the main point goes unnoticed. This is what, I believe, has actually happened.

The result has been a series of displacement activities. The church has said, in effect: (a) we know the gospels are important, because they are the inspired apostolic witness to Jesus; and (b) we know what is important in Christian theology, namely, the divinity of Jesus and his saving death or, as it may be, his moral teaching and example; so (c) we assume that that is the primary message of the gospels.

In fact, to sum up the proposal toward which I have been working, the four gospels are trying to say that *this is how God became king.* We have, partly deliberately and partly accidentally, forgotten this massive claim almost entirely. Since we cannot stop reading the gospels without ceasing to be proper Christians, we have developed all kinds of strategies for making alternative sense of the gospels and so screening out the dangerous and challenging picture they are actually sketching. That is at the heart of the problem I have been trying to identify.

It has been a salutary exercise, I believe, to review in this way the different things that people have said as they face the question of why the gospels included all that material between Jesus's birth and his death. All these proposals have been advanced quite seriously, and I have tried to take them in the same serious spirit. But it is clear to me that none of them have actually taken *the gospels* seriously as they stand. They have gone to them with the wrong questions and have found answers, of a sort, to those questions. The challenge now is to accept that we have all misunderstood the gospels and to set about finding ways in which we can put this right. It is time for a fresh look at our central texts.

PART TWO

Adjusting the Volume

4

The Story of Israel

IMAGINE, IF YOU WILL, that you have set up a new sound system in your living room. You have installed a quadraphonic set of speakers, one in each corner. But you haven't yet figured out how to adjust them individually, and the sound is strange and distorted. Each of the four needs to be sorted out. Otherwise, when you're listening to orchestral music, you'll get too much violin or perhaps woodwind and no cello or brass.

Now, one of the reasons the gospels are such a challenge to read is that there are four strands, four dimensions, that contribute to what they are saying, which in much modern reading have become distorted in something like the same way. Some of them have been turned way down or even silenced altogether. Others have been turned up too loud, so that they are shrill and crackly. One way or another, the music is out of balance. Some parts are almost inaudible, and other parts are all too audible, blasting out at top volume, distorted in themselves and drowning out everything else. Of course, this isn't the same in all readings of the gospels. Different Christian traditions have twiddled the knobs on these four speakers, making this or that one louder or softer. But the point I want to make in this part of the book is that we only get the correct sound when all four are properly adjusted.

Part of our difficulty, in fact, is that so many people have become used to hearing the gospels in a distorted fashion that when the speakers are adjusted properly, they are likely to object. "We never heard it this way before," they will say. It reminds me of the time when, as a young teenager, I sat for the first time in the back row of the school orchestra (I had been drafted to learn the trombone on the quite reasonable grounds that I could sing in tune and blow hard, which are the first and principal requirements for that splendid instrument). Whereas before I had always experienced classical orchestral music through a radio or record player (this was long before any of us had stereo systems), from which the music all came out in an undifferentiated composite sound, for the first time I was able to appreciate the almost geographical as well as tonal difference between the woodwinds and the cellos, the brass and the violas, and so on. It was disconcerting to begin with, but ultimately revelatory. So, when people object that they haven't "heard" the gospels before in the way I am now going to suggest, the best answer is to invite them to listen more closely and to see if the things they have always "heard" in the gospels might actually be enhanced, given more depth and body, in this new multilayered reading. My point here is that without these four "speakers" all properly adjusted we simply won't hear the music the four gospels are playing.

The Gospels as Biographies

The tune to which we are listening, throughout all this, is of course the great tune of the life of Jesus himself. Gone are the days when scholars could confidently proclaim that the gospels are not "biographies." (This was another Bultmannism. The great but misguided German, anxious that one might turn "faith" into a "work" by anchoring it in history, was doing his best to steer people away from looking at the gospels as "biographies"—a tendentious suggestion that subsequent research has rejected.) True, the gospels are not, as C. S. Lewis pointed out tartly many years ago, what you'd expect from a Victorian *Life and Letters of Yeshua bar-Yosef* in three volumes with photographs. They omit a great deal, notably of course the silent years between age twelve (and even then we just get one story) and about age thirty. But when you compare the gospels with ancient Greek or Roman "biographies," they match up quite well.

That doesn't mean that everything is in chronological order, still less of course that they offer a straight transcription of what you'd have seen and heard if you'd set up a video camera in Nazareth or Capernaum or even in the high priest's chamber during that final fateful night. No history, no biography, ever tells you everything. All history selects and arranges, not to falsify but to highlight what is significant. And when, in Greco-Roman biography, the death of the central figure is particularly important, it is given special treatment. Think of Socrates or Julius Caesar. The four gospels, then, are not merely "passion narratives with extended introductions," as one of Bultmann's predecessors had suggested. They are not merely reflections of the faith of the later church projected onto a screen that the earliest evangelists themselves knew to be fictional. They present themselves as biographies, biographies of Jesus.

But they are biographies with a difference. One can imagine how this might work. Someone might write a biography of Abraham Lincoln that was at the same time designed to show the way in which the old America of the original revolution was passing away, never to return. Similarly, someone might write a biography of Winston Churchill that was at the same time designed to show the way in which the old British ruling class was having its final hurrah before the winds of change swept through the United Kingdom. You can read Michael Foot's biography of the great Labor politician Aneurin Bevan not simply as a window through which to view the great man, but as the description of a key moment in a much larger story that Foot was anxious to tell, a moment when British society began to embrace a socialist vision that would (Foot hoped) bring new hope to millions of poor working people. A biography can be a biography and still be a vehicle for telling a much bigger story.

Or, in the case of the gospels, four much bigger stories, which all come rushing together at this point. This, to be sure, is why the gospels, which on the surface look like such easy reads, indeed quite the page-turners, are in fact highly complex, repaying hours and years of patient thought and reflection. Let us then examine the first of our four speakers, a speaker that has, for many people, been turned right off altogether. Many people who have read the gospels all their lives have never even imagined music coming from this corner of the room.

Prequel and Sequel

In the year 1900, a book was published that changed the imagination of America. Its creator, L. Frank Baum, had stumbled into writing fantasy fiction some years before, mostly to while away time spent on the road as a traveling salesman. But *The Wonderful Wizard of Oz* was an instant hit, and Baum never looked back. Three years later, the show of the same name (but without the "Wonderful") opened on Broadway. In one form or another, the story has been delighting audiences young and old ever since.

Baum, as I said, never looked back—in more ways than one. He wrote several sequels to the *Wizard,* but never a prequel. Almost a hundred years later, in 1995, Gregory Maguire remedied this omission—and changed the way a new generation would understand the original book and the original show. He published a book entitled *Wicked,* in which the Wicked Witch of the West was not always so wicked. All sorts of new light is shed on why things were as they were when Dorothy, the heroine of the original story, came to the land of Oz. By 2003, exactly a century after the original Broadway show, *Wicked* opened as a musical and is running there and elsewhere in the world to this day.

The idea of telling the "previous history" of an already famous story is not, of course, new. J. R. R. Tolkien published his celebrated fantasy novel *The Hobbit* in 1937 and followed it with the magnum opus *The Lord of the Rings* in 1954–55. But it was left to his son, Christopher, to assemble the bits and pieces that his father had written about the far distant history of Middle-Earth in *The Silmarillion* (1977) and the massive twelve-volume *History of Middle-Earth* (1983–96).

Happily, we are not in the same position with Matthew, Mark, Luke, and John. Their backstory was written long ago, and it is readily available. But—perhaps to our surprise!—many people, reading the gospels today, read them not only as if that backstory did not exist, but as if there was a different backstory altogether. For people in that position, rediscovering the proper backstory will mean that, like those who return to *The Wizard of Oz* after reading or experiencing *Wicked,* they will see the main story itself in a whole new light.

The first speaker of our quadraphonic sound system to be turned up is this: the four gospels present themselves as *the climax of the story of Israel.* All four evangelists, I suggest, deliberately frame their material in such a way as to make this clear, though many generations of Christian readers have turned down the speaker to such an extent that they have been able, in effect, to ignore it.

In order to grasp this point we need to take a step back. We need to think about the ways in which the story of Israel was being told at the time.

The Strange Story of Israel

The story of Israel too is a subject for an entire book. But we can sum it up like this. Israel's ancient scriptures are framed with a narrative, an unfinished narrative of a certain shape and type. Whether you read the Old Testament as set out in most English Bibles from Genesis to Malachi or whether you read it in the Hebrew canon from Genesis to Chronicles with the prophets in the middle, you are still left with a sense that this story is supposed to be going somewhere, but that it hasn't gotten there yet. It is an unfinished narrative, an unfinished *agenda*. Things are supposed to happen that haven't happened yet.

What's more, the story seems to have become badly stalled. It isn't so much like the story of a journey in which the travelers have almost reached their destination and need merely to walk the last few miles down a gentle slope to arrive in fine style. It is more like the story of a journey in which the travelers have misread the map, lost their way, and become stuck in quicksand with hostile troops closing in around them. That, I suggest, is the impression we might get if we read straight through the Old Testament: great beginnings and wonderful visions of God's plan and purposes, then a steady decline and puzzling and shameful multiple failures, all ending in a question mark. Just as Genesis 1–3 tell the story of the human plight through the pattern of glorious beginnings, rich vocations, and then horrible failure and exile, so Genesis 12 through to the end of Chronicles or Malachi tell the story of Israel with tales of glorious beginnings, rich vocations, and then horrible failure and exile. Indeed, whoever put Genesis 1–3 into its present form was undoubtedly aware of, and undoubtedly intended, that resonance to be fully heard. That is itself part of the backdrop to my first main point.

The problem is that we have all read the gospels, if we haven't been careful, simply as God's answer to the plight of the human race in general. The implied backstory hasn't been the story of Abraham, of Moses, of David, of the prophets; it's been the story of Adam and Eve, of "Everyman," sinning and dying and needing to be redeemed. Israel's story sneaks in alongside, in this version, in order merely to offer some advance promises, some hints and signposts. But the story of Israel itself, for most modern readers of the Bible, is to be quietly left aside. It was part of the problem, not part of the solution. It seems, after all, to be so dark—such a failure, such a disappointment.

Here again the creeds leave an ominous gap. They don't mention Israel at all. They seem to indicate that we're going for a new start, a quite fresh beginning, reinforcing the tendency I just mentioned to see the gospels as the answer not to the story of Israel as a whole, but to the story of Adam and Eve. Can't we go back to Genesis 3, they seem to say, and begin over again? Shouldn't we just read the whole story of Genesis 12 to the end of Chronicles or Malachi as a kind of failed first attempt, God's first shot at rescuing people from their sin, full of signs and pointers no doubt, but not really as a "history of salvation" at all? Isn't it rather a history of puzzle, muddle, sin, and disaster?

Well, yes, it is. But when we turn to Matthew, Mark, Luke, and John we discover that they at least think it's important to retell the history of Israel and to show that the story of Jesus is the story in which that long history, warts and all, reaches its God-ordained climax. This is the first speaker to which we have to pay attention, and it's clear that it needs to be turned up considerably louder than most readers expect.

Matthew: The Story Reaches Its Goal

The most obvious place to begin is right at the beginning—with the genealogy with which Matthew opens his book. Most of us, I suspect, probably skip this when we decide to read the New

Testament right through for ourselves. It's exhausting, with all that begetting, but also it's full of names that mean nothing to us. But for Matthew it's vital. The story from Abraham to David, from David to the exile, and from the exile to Jesus tells us far more than we might imagine about what sort of story Matthew thinks he's telling and what meaning he expects it to have.

> The book of the family tree of Jesus the Messiah, the son of David, the son of Abraham.
>
> Abraham became the father of Isaac, Isaac of Jacob, Jacob of Judah and his brothers, Judah of Peres and Zara (by Tamar), Peres of Esrom, Esrom of Aram, Aram of Aminadab, Aminadab of Naason, Naason of Salmon, Salmon of Boaz (by Rahab), Boaz of Obed (by Ruth), Obed of Jesse, and Jesse of David the king.
>
> David was the father of Solomon (by the wife of Uriah), Solomon of Rehoboam, Rehoboam of Abijah, Abijah of Asaph, Asaph of Jehosaphat, Jehosaphat of Joram, Joram of Uzziah, Uzziah of Joatham, Joatham of Ahaz, Ahaz of Hezekiah, Hezekiah of Manasseh, Manasseh of Amoz, Amoz of Josiah, Josiah of Jeconiah and his brothers, at the time of the exile in Babylon.
>
> After the Babylonian exile, Jeconiah became the father of Salathiel, Salathiel of Zerubbabel, Zerubbabel of Abioud, Abioud of Eliakim, Eliakim of Azor, Azor of Sadok, Sadok of Achim, Achim of Elioud, Elioud of Eleazar, Eleazar of Matthan, Matthan of Jacob, and Jacob of Joseph the husband of Mary, from whom was born Jesus, who is called "Messiah."
>
> So all the generations from Abraham to David add up to fourteen; from David to the Babylonian exile, fourteen generations; and from the Babylonian exile to the Messiah, fourteen generations. (1:1–17)

To get the point, we have to understand one thing in particular. To put it simply, most Jews of Jesus's day did not believe that the exile was really, properly over. Yes, they'd come back from Babylon—well, some of them, anyway. Yes, they'd rebuilt the Temple in Jerusalem. But pagan foreigners were still ruling over them. They were still slaves even in their own land, as Ezra and Nehemiah complain: "Here we are, slaves to this day—slaves in the land that you gave to our ancestors to enjoy its fruit and its good gifts" (Neh. 9:36).

The great promises of Isaiah and Ezekiel hadn't yet come true. All this is summed up graphically in a vital passage in Daniel 9, normally assumed to have been written in the early second century BC, in which Daniel in exile in Babylon asks God whether it isn't time now for Jeremiah's prophecy to be fulfilled, the prophecy that the Babylonian exile would last for seventy years. Back comes the answer: not seventy years, but seventy *weeks of years,* in other words, seventy times seven years:

> In the first year of Darius son of Ahasuerus, by birth a
> Mede, who became king over the realm of the Chal-
> deans—in the first year of his reign, I, Daniel, perceived in
> the books the number of years that, according to the word
> of YHWH to the prophet Jeremiah, must be fulfilled for the
> devastation of Jerusalem, namely, seventy years. Then I
> turned to the Lord God, to seek an answer by prayer and
> supplication with fasting and sackcloth and ashes. . . .
>
>   While I was speaking, and was praying and confess-
> ing my sin and the sin of my people Israel, and present-
> ing my supplication before YHWH my God on behalf of
> the holy mountain of my God—while I was speaking
> in prayer, the man Gabriel, whom I had seen before in
> a vision, came to me in swift flight at the time of the
> evening sacrifice. He came and said to me, "Daniel, I

have now come out to give you wisdom and understanding. At the beginning of your supplications a word went
out, and I have come to declare it, for you are greatly
beloved. So consider the word and understand the vision:
Seventy weeks are decreed for your people and your holy
city: to finish the transgression, to put an end to sin, and
to atone for iniquity, to bring in everlasting righteousness, to seal both vision and prophet, and to anoint a
most holy place." (9:1–3, 20–24)

That sounds like a devastatingly depressing answer, and in a
way it is. That's a long time to wait. But the idea of "seventy times
seven" has a particular ring to it, more obvious to an ancient Jew
than to us today. Every seven days, they had a sabbath. Every
seven years, they had a sabbatical year. And every seven-times-
seven years, they had—or at least they were supposed to have
had, according to Leviticus—a jubilee. This was when slaves were
freed, when land sold off by the family was restored to its original
owner, when things got put back as they should be. The jubilee
is a fascinating social innovation within the legislation of ancient
Israel, a sign that relentless buying and selling of land, goods, and
even people won't be the last word.

But seventy times seven? That sounds like a jubilee of jubilees!
So, though four hundred and ninety years—nearly half a millennium—is indeed a long time, the point is this: when the time
finally arrives, it will be the greatest "redemption" of all. This
will be the time of real, utter, and lasting freedom. That is the
hope that sustained the Israelites in the long years of the centuries
before the time of Jesus.

It is normally assumed that the book of Daniel reached its final
form during the first half of the second century BC, around the
time of the Maccabean crisis, when Judas Maccabeus and his family led a successful resistance against the Syrian invasion. And so,

with Daniel 9 in mind, learned scribes were calculating and re-calculating, asking when the seventy sevens would be fulfilled. When will the real return from exile happen?

And Matthew makes it clear beyond cavil, to anyone thinking Jewishly in that period, that the moment had come with Jesus. Instead of years, he does it with generations, the generations of Israel's entire history from Abraham to the present. All the generations to that point were fourteen times three, that is, six sevens—with Jesus we get the seventh seven. He is the jubilee in person. He is the one who will rescue Israel from its long-continued nightmare. "He," says the angel to Joseph, "is the one who will save his people from their sins" (1:21). That, to any first-century Jew, didn't just mean that individuals could turn to him and find personal forgiveness, though that would obviously be true as well. Read Isaiah 40 and Lamentations 4 again and see. Exile is the payment for sin, so forgiveness of sin means the end of exile. If you have received a royal pardon, you get out of jail free. The time has come.

> *Comfort, O comfort my people,*
> * says your God.*
> *Speak tenderly to Jerusalem,*
> * and cry to her*
> *that she has served her term,*
> * that her penalty is paid,*
> *that she has received from YHWH's hand*
> * double for all her sins. (Isa. 40:1–2)*

> *The punishment of your iniquity, O daughter Zion,*
> * is accomplished,*
> * he will keep you in exile no longer;*
> *but your iniquity, O daughter Edom, he will punish,*
> * he will uncover your sins. (Lam. 4:22)*

This is perhaps the most important point to make, because it's one of the hardest for people today to grasp. We can just about take on board the idea, which Matthew also emphasizes, that the life of Jesus *recapitulates* key elements in the earlier story of Israel. For a moment, as Jesus stands on the mountain giving the famous sermon, he is Moses. For a moment, answering his critics about his actions on the sabbath, he is David. For a moment, as he calls and names the twelve disciples, he is perhaps Jacob, bringing the twelve patriarchs into the world. For a moment, healing the sick and raising the dead, he is Elijah or Elisha. And so on. In the transfiguration he actually *meets* Moses and Elijah.

All these flashbacks are important. They would have been much more readily apparent to Jesus's first followers and to Matthew's first readers than they are to us in the de-Judaized state of our secularized imagination. But far more important than flashbacks, than the picking up of detached themes and hints from long ago, is the towering sense of *a single story now at last reaching its conclusion.* For much of that time, as we said a moment ago, the story looked as if it was lost, many a mile from its destination, with night falling and enemies closing in. Suddenly, out of the blue, we discover that something is happening that will turn all that around. It isn't (we need to be very clear at this point) that things have not been as bad as we'd thought. In fact, they've been worse. But the new event that is now happening is precisely an event we might call rescue. A fresh initiative.

It hasn't come from within the story as it was—though, strangely, those with eyes to see will recognize that it is where the story *ought* to have gone all along. That's part of the complex task the gospel writers are accomplishing: describing something as *both* the fulfillment of the vocation of Israel *and* divine judgment on the mess and the muddle that Israel's story had become. Matthew, then, is telling his story in such a way as to say: "This is it! This is what we've been waiting for—even though we would never have thought it would be like this! This is where the single story of Abraham's family, of David's offspring, of the restoration from exile was going all along. We didn't think it would look like this. But now that it's happened, we can see that this is where it was supposed to be heading all along." It didn't just emerge from the story the way it was. The story was indeed stalled, stagnant, running out of hope. It required a fresh act of divine mercy to do what was needed. As later preachers would say about individual sinners, the only thing that Israel contributed to the story of Jesus that Matthew is telling was the particular set of muddle and rebellion from which God was now coming to free it.

I hope it is clear from this that, when we turn up this first speaker, the music is telling us much more than simply that all four gospels refer to the Old Testament and present Jesus as the fulfillment of prophecy. To say that sort of thing is to have the speaker turned up just far enough so that you can tell something is going on, but not far enough to be able to understand what it is. This is a point of fundamental importance for the whole New Testament and indeed the whole early Christian movement. The gospel writers saw the events concerning Jesus, particularly his kingdom-inaugurating life, death, and resurrection, not just as isolated events to which remote prophets might have distantly pointed. They saw those events as bringing the long story of Israel to its proper goal, even though that long story had apparently become lost, stuck, and all but forgotten.

But, you may say, what's the point of telling the story of Jesus as the climax of the story of Israel? What relevance has that got to the rest of the human race and to the wider world? Here we touch on another point of foundational importance for the whole of early Christian thought and life. Understand this point, and you will understand almost everything. In Israel's scriptures, the reason Israel's story matters is that *the creator of the world has chosen and called Israel to be the people through whom he will redeem the world.*

The call of Abraham is the answer to the sin of Adam.* Israel's story is thus the microcosm and beating heart of the world's story, but also its ultimate saving energy. What God does for Israel is what God is doing in relation to the whole world. That is what it meant to be Israel, to be the people who, for better and worse, carried the destiny of the world on their shoulders. Grasp that, and you have a pathway into the heart of the New Testament.

Mark: Jesus and the Breaking In of God's New World

The evangelists, each in his own way, tell the story of Jesus as the proper climax to Israel's story. This is clear right from the start. We have already glanced at Matthew. Mark indicates that the arrival and baptism of Jesus are the moments at which the prophecies of Isaiah and Malachi of the ultimate redemption, of God's returning to rescue his people, were at last coming true:

> Isaiah the prophet put it like this ("Look! I am sending my messenger ahead of me; he will clear the way for you!"):
>
> "A shout goes up in the desert: Make way for the Lord! Clear a straight path for him!" (1:2–3)

> This is how it happened. Around that time, Jesus came from Nazareth in Galilee, and was baptized by John in the river Jordan. That very moment, as he was getting out of the water, he saw the heavens open, and the spirit coming down like a dove onto him. Then there came a voice, out of the heavens: "You are my son! You are the one I love! You make me very glad." (1:9–11)

---

*See *The New Testament and the People of God* (Minneapolis: Fortress, 1992), pp. 262–68.

Mark picks up, here and throughout his gospel, a major theme from the ancient Hebrew scriptures: that when Israel's God acts in fulfillment of his ancient promises, he will do so in dramatic and radically new ways. Here, to be sure, is a paradox we meet throughout the New Testament: God acts completely unexpectedly—as he always said he would. Just because the new events are able to be seen as the fulfillment of ancient prophecy (and Mark, like the other evangelists, is clear that this is the only right way to see them), that doesn't mean that one can see a smooth, easy line from the ancient texts to the modern fulfillment. On the contrary, what is being fulfilled is precisely the promise of drastic, unexpected, and perhaps even unwelcome judgment and mercy.

But our proper emphasis on this radical, new breaking in of God's action in Jesus ought not to diminish the sense that, in Mark, this new thing that God is doing is the new thing he had always promised. "The time is fulfilled!" says Jesus in Mark 1:15. The bridegroom has arrived at last for the wedding party (2:19). The fresh seed is at last being sown, even though plenty of it will go to waste, because most of the hearers are in no condition to receive it (4:1–20). Mark allows the sequence of dramatic events to build up to the central moment in which Peter declares that Jesus is the Messiah (8:29) and witnesses this being dramatically confirmed in the transfiguration (9:2–7). Woven into this story, as we shall see in more detail, is the dark strand that warns of Jesus's impending death; yet this too is seen as part of the shocking and unexpected fulfillment of scriptural promises (10:45, alluding to Dan. 7 and Isa. 53). Jesus is fulfilling the story of Israel, even though this requires readers to understand Israel's story in a new way.

Luke: The Scriptures Must Be Fulfilled

That the scriptures must be fulfilled is precisely the point made by Luke at key points in his gospel. Luke has structured his opening so that we hear in the background the great stories of Samuel and David, all pointing forward to the arrival of the true king. The great poems we call the Magnificat and the Benedictus, the songs of Mary and of Zechariah (1:46–55; 1:68–79) speak powerfully of the fulfillment of God's ancient purposes and promises in the forthcoming births of John the Baptist and Jesus himself. This theme runs right through the gospel and is emphasized in such passages as 22:37, where Jesus declares, at table with his friends, that everything about him in the scriptures "must reach its goal."

Even Jesus's closest followers, however, cannot begin to see in the strange events of his arrest, trial, and death any kind of fulfillment. They had been living in the currently prevailing version of the Jewish story, and it certainly wasn't supposed to end with the violent death of God's anointed. "We were hoping," say the two on the road to Emmaus, "that he was going to redeem Israel!" (24:21). But he obviously hadn't.

The answer, highlighted in Luke's matchless telling both of the Emmaus story and of the larger story of Jesus as a whole, is clear:

> "You are so senseless!" he said to them. "So slow in your
> hearts to believe all the things the prophets said to you!
> Don't you see? This is what *had* to happen: the Messiah
> had to suffer, and then come into his glory!"
> So he began with Moses, and with all the prophets,
> and explained to them the things about himself through-
> out the whole Bible. (24:25–27)

In other words—as the disciples excitedly discover in going over the scene immediately afterwards—there was a new "opening of the Bible" as Jesus expounded to them the large story, which, when seen in this light, was bound to lead to the crucifixion and resurrection of the Messiah as the complex event through which, indeed, Israel and the world would be redeemed.

But, in parallel with this, there was an "opening of their minds" that had to happen as well (24:45). Luke is clear that the events involving Jesus are the events in which all of Israel's previous history has been summed up and brought to its divinely appointed goal. But this is not something that casual readers can see at a glance. It is not something that Caiaphas or the Pharisees would instantly recognize when Jesus's followers began to announce that he had been raised from the dead. People would need to "search the scriptures day by day to see if what they were hearing was indeed the case" (Acts 17:11). The point the gospel writers are eager to get across—that the life, death, and resurrection of Jesus is in fact the climax of the story of Israel, even though nobody was expecting such a thing and many didn't like the look of it when it was presented to them—is something that, like the risen Jesus himself, is visible to the eye of faith. The story makes sense as a whole or not at all.

John: Creation and New Creation

The paradox we saw in Matthew, Mark, and Luke—that the events involving Jesus are to be seen as the fulfillment of the story of Israel, but that this "fulfillment" is not what Israel was expecting or wanting—is stated sharply right at the start of John's gospel. John's prologue (1:1–18) takes us back to the first books of the Bible, to Genesis and Exodus. He frames his simple, profound opening statement with echoes of the creation story ("In the beginning . . . ," leading up to the creation of humans in God's image) and echoes of the climax of the book of Exodus ("The Word became flesh, and lived among us," 1:14, where the word "lived" is literally "tabernacled," "pitched his tent," as in the construction of the tabernacle for God's glory in the wilderness). This, in other words, is where Israel's history and with it world history reached their moment of destiny. But Israel, the people whose very backbone was Genesis and Exodus, were looking the other way: "He came to what was his own, and his own people did not accept him" (1:11). Yes, some did accept him, and they were given "the right to become God's children" (1:12), not because of human ancestry or effort, but because of God's strange mercy. So John too sees the story of Jesus as the paradoxical climax of the story of Israel.

That is why, of course, the theme of Jesus's messiahship is highlighted repeatedly—along with the constant question as to whether someone like Jesus can really be the one for whom Israel had been longing:

> "We've found him!" said Philip. "The one Moses wrote about in the law! And the prophets, too! We've found him! It's Jesus, Joseph's son, from Nazareth!"
>
> "Really?" replied Nathanael. "Are you telling me that something good can come out of Nazareth?" (1:45–46)

The theme continues through the whole book. Jesus says and does things that declare that he is in fact the one to whom Israel's scriptures all point, like many streams converging into a mighty river. But most of his contemporaries had in mind a different kind of river. "You study the Bible," Jesus says, "because you suppose that you'll discover the life of God's coming age in it. In fact, it's the Bible which gives evidence about me! But you won't come to me so that you can have life" (5:39–40). They are telling the biblical story one way, leading up to their own vision of "God's coming age." Jesus is telling it a different way, or rather he is *living* it a different way. Central to John, as to almost every New Testament writer, is the clash between two conflicting visions of how the ancient scriptural story is to be told and how, in particular, it is to reach its goal. People ask how Jesus can possibly be the Messiah, but others insist that he must be (e.g., 7:31–52; 10:22–30). Jesus persists, saying that when Moses wrote, he was writing about him, and when Abraham believed God, he was looking forward to him (5:46; 8:30–59).

This is not merely a clash of different ideas, different theories.

It becomes nakedly political. Caiaphas, the high priest at the time, suggests that the way to rescue the nation and its Temple from the Romans is to let one man—Jesus himself—die instead (11:50). It is a moment of heavy irony, because in Caiaphas's version of Israel's story the absolute priority is saving the nation and the Temple, but John sees, underneath his cold calculation, a different story being played out: Jesus will indeed "die for the nation; and not only for the nation, but to gather into one the scattered children of God" (11:51–52). The paradox of the two stories remains all the way through, and John claims that Jesus was in line with the ancient prophecies, *which always included prophecies about Israel's failure to see, hear, and understand* (12:37–41).

And all the lines draw the eye up to the final scene in which Jesus announces God's kingdom before Caesar's representative, while Israel's official leaders declare that "we have no king except Caesar" (19:15). The result—the climax of the gospel, and for John the climax of Israel's entire story—is the paradoxical "enthronement" of Jesus on the cross, the final moment of the fulfillment of the great scriptural story (19:19, 24, 28). Jesus's final word, *tetelestai,* "It's all done!" says it clearly. The story has been completed—the story of creation, the story of God's covenant with Israel. Now new creation can begin, as it does immediately afterwards with Jesus's resurrection. Now the new covenant can be launched, as the disciples are sent out into the world equipped with Jesus's own Spirit (20:19–23). This is how Israel's story has reached its goal and can now bear fruit in all the world.

Conclusion

We should note at this point that the so-called Gnostic gospels, books like the *Gospel of Thomas* and the rest, are simply in another world. They reject the story of Israel—indeed the idea that there is a "story" within which Jesus's words and deeds make sense—

and avoid any mention of Jesus's crucifixion and resurrection. This does not mean, as some have suggested, that they are earlier versions, prereflective first attempts at remembering Jesus. It means that they are later, de-Judaized, dehistoricized distortions, offering salvation not *for* the world, but *from* the world. They want nothing to do with Jewish-style creational monotheism, in which the world is God's good creation, needing to be judged and set right. They want nothing to do with Israel as the people who carry God's rescuing purposes for the world. They want a dehistoricized world, a de-Judaized world, a "spiritual" world rather than the matter-and-spirit world, the heaven-and-earth world, which Israel's God has made. They are deconstructing Genesis itself. They have no time for the God of the exodus, the God who sets the slaves free and comes to dwell in their midst.

Unless we are constantly aware, in reading the gospels, that they are telling the Jesus story in such a way as to bring out the Israel story, we will never hear their proper harmony. This is the first of the speakers in our sound system that we must turn up to its proper volume. The events of Jesus's life, death, and resurrection, to be sure, burst upon an unready first-century Jewish world, as the evangelists make clear on every page. They are the real fulfillment, even though the people weren't expecting it. All those parables about the returning master or lord come into their own. There wasn't a smooth "salvation history" in the sense of a steady crescendo, things getting better and better until the moment arrived. Rather, it was the reverse. Israel was in a mess, and God had to do something radically new. But the radically new thing God did was nevertheless the thing he'd always promised, the thing for which they'd always most deeply hoped and prayed. This is the paradox. It runs right through the New Testament, and especially through the gospels. The story reached its goal, but the story itself was looking in the wrong direction. "He came to what was his own, and his own people did not accept him." Instead of declaring that they wanted "no king except God," as their scriptures might have suggested, the chief priests, Israel's official representatives, declared that they had "no king except Caesar." But, as John makes clear, Jesus was indeed their true king, and his crucifixion was the full revelation of what that meant. Paradox upon paradox. To this we shall return.

The last point already looks ahead to the second speaker in our sound system. Israel's story was not just the story of a people. It was the story of a God, the one the Israelites believed was God, the creator of the world, the God of Israel.

5

The Story of Jesus as the Story of Israel's God

T HE FIRST SOUND SPEAKER needed to be turned up from nearly silent to its proper volume, or indeed to be turned on after being switched off altogether. People have tried to read the story of Jesus as though the only thing it had to say to the Jews of Jesus's day was that they were wrong. They were wrong about God, about God's coming kingdom, about the way to salvation. They were wrong about the idea of there being "a story of salvation" in the first place. No, "the time is fulfilled." The gospel story is the climax of Israel's story, however surprising and unexpected it may have been.

Distorted Noise

The second speaker contributing to what we hear the gospels saying is the one that enables us to hear *the story of Jesus as the story of Israel's God* coming back to his people as he had always promised. But this time the problem is the opposite one. This speaker hasn't been turned down, or off. Instead, it's been turned up so loud that the noise it makes has become distorted and has drowned out much of the rest of the music.

In much of Western Christianity down through the years, and particularly in the rather noisy conservative Christianity which has reacted (not unnaturally) to the skepticism of the Enlightenment, we have been so concerned to let the gospels tell us that the story of Jesus is the story of God incarnate that we have been unable to listen more carefully to the evangelists telling us *which God they are talking about* and *what exactly it is that this God is now doing*. We are quite happy to hear about the "God" of Western imagination, less ready to hear about the God of Israel. We are quite happy to hear that "Jesus is God," in some sense. That, we have assumed, is what the gospels are telling us. We are less ready to hear that the God of Israel had promised to do certain specific things, in particular to establish his sovereign rule over Israel and the world, and that Jesus was embodying this intention.

Within the long and sad story of Israel, the story of Israel's God is not simply, as you might think from some Christian language, the story of a distant God who wants to save people from sin and death and is trying various ways of doing so (most of which seem unfruitful). For far too long now Christians have told the story of Jesus as if it hooked up not with the story of Israel, but simply with the story of human sin as in Genesis 3, skipping over the story of Israel altogether. From that point of view, the story of Israel looks like a failed first attempt on God's part to sort out his world. "Here," he says, "you can be my people. I'll rescue you from slavery and give you my law!" But then the people find they can't keep the law and the story goes from bad to worse. Eventually, God gives up the attempt to make people (specifically, Israel) "better" by having them keep his law and decides on a different strategy, a "Plan B." This involves sending his son to die and declaring that now the only thing people need to do is to believe in him and his saving death; they won't have to keep that silly old law after all. This is a gross caricature of the actual biblical story, but it is certainly not a gross caricature of what many Christians have been taught, either explicitly or by implication.

At the same time—that is, in the Western world and church of the past two or three centuries—Christians have been aware that the very notion of "God" has been under attack. The Deism of the seventeenth and eighteenth centuries ("There may be a 'God' who made the world, but if so, he's a long way away and doesn't get involved in our world") steadily morphed into the explicit atheism of the nineteenth and twentieth centuries ("So why bother with the idea of 'God' at all?"). This ran in parallel with the historical challenges to Christian origins, noted earlier, in which Jesus was seen as just a first-century Jewish revolutionary, an "apocalypticist," or a fine teacher of morality. Faced with that double challenge, many Christians believed that they had to undertake a double counterstrategy: to "prove" the "existence of God," on the one hand, and to "prove" the "divinity of Jesus," on the other. (I put the word "prove" in quotation marks, because that same historical period saw the rise of a new way of thinking about knowledge itself: either you could "prove" something, almost like a mathematical theorem, or you couldn't be sure of it. This remains the default position for a good deal of skepticism to this day.)

Well, you may say, isn't that fair enough? If people are going about saying God doesn't exist, surely Christians have to say that actually he does? And if people are denying the divinity of Jesus, isn't it the Christian's job to reaffirm it? Put like that, yes, of course. But here we meet the paradox that Proverbs puts to us in a famous pair of apparently contradictory sayings. "Do not answer fools according to their folly, or you will be a fool yourself," and, "Answer fools according to their folly, or they will be wise in their own eyes" (26:4–5).

In the present context, two cautions are in order. First, beware, lest in giving an answer you agree to the terms of the question, which may themselves be deeply flawed. Second, beware, lest in refusing to give an answer (because of those deep flaws) you appear to let the case go by default. I honor those who have tried to do the second, but I fear—and this is the point of this whole chapter—that they have not always heeded the earlier warning. Thus the speaker has been turned up so loud—"YES! THERE IS A GOD! YES! JESUS IS GOD!"—that the much more subtle and interesting point the gospels are making has all but been drowned out, along with the messages from two of the other speakers (the first and the fourth). As I said before, it is possible for one truth, overemphasized, to drown out others with which it needs to be balanced and modulated. It is time to listen with a good deal more care to the story the Bible itself tells us about Israel's God, the world's creator.

The Biblical Story of God

The story the Bible tells about Israel's God is quite different from the stories many, including many Christians, have told. In the biblical story, the creator God calls Abraham, who lived in present-day Iraq, and bids him go wandering off as a nomad in the direction of what we now know as Israel/Palestine. This God makes a covenant with Abraham containing dramatic and grandiose promises. Through Abraham, God will cause all the families of the earth to be blessed; this follows the sorry tale of folly and wickedness in Genesis 3–11, which results in the scattering and division of the human race after the building of the tower of Babel (Babylon, also in today's Iraq). The story of God and Abraham is the starting point for the whole of the rest of the biblical narrative, and it in turn gains its meaning from what has gone before. God is now, through Abraham, going to undo the plight of the human race and will thereby enable humans to pick up again the threads of the project that had been theirs from the start (looking after God's world, making it fruitful, and peopling it), but that had been aborted through human rebellion.

There is an exciting, and often ignored, inner core to the story of God and Abraham that points all the way forward to the gospels themselves. The larger framework for the story is the narrative sweep that goes all the way from the original creation through to the end of the book of Exodus (of course, there are still larger frameworks: the whole Pentateuch, the first five books of the Bible, and then the whole Old Testament itself; but let's stay focused on Genesis and Exodus for the moment). The original creation story envisaged a God who was making a dwelling place for himself. The six "days," or "stages," of creation indicate, to those who understand the world of the ancient Near East, that creation itself, heaven and earth together, is a kind of temple, a dwelling place for God. And, as in all ancient temples (except the one in Jerusalem, for reasons that will become apparent), there was an "image" or statue of the god in question, so the creator God places into the "temple" of his heaven-and-earth creation his own "image," human beings made to reflect him, to bring his creativity to birth in his world, and to reflect the praises of the world back to the creator. That, of course, is the heart of the story, which is then spoiled by the rebellion of God's image-bearing creatures.

One might be forgiven for supposing that this original intention had been lost sight of entirely in the story that then follows. Abraham, Isaac, and Jacob find that God appears to them now here, now there, always unexpectedly, in different ways and guises. Sometimes they mark the spot with a stone, a shrine, or an altar. But then the story takes a nosedive into chaos. Joseph is sold into slavery in Egypt and, though this has the effect of saving the family from a famine, the long-term result is slavery. Israel's long servitude in Egypt is formative not only, as we have already seen, for Israel itself, but also, if one can put it this way, for God. God remembers the covenant with Abraham, passes sentence on the enslaving Egyptians, and rescues Israel from Egypt through the amazing events of Passover under the leadership of Moses. God then gives Israel the law, to be the way of life for this rescued people.

But the astonishing thing about the book of Exodus, doubly astonishing as it turns out, is that *God himself accompanies the people on their journey* and then gives instructions for the "tabernacle," the holy tent or "tent of meeting," where he will be present in their midst and where he will meet, more particularly, with Moses himself. This then precipitates a near disaster because, while Moses is up the mountain receiving the detailed commands for the construction of the tabernacle, the people rebel. They persuade Aaron, Moses's brother, to make an idol, an image, a golden statue of a calf, so they can pretend that this is the god who has brought them out of Egypt. This primal act of rebellion nearly ruins the whole plan, but—here is second astonishing thing— God answers Moses's urgent prayer for forgiveness and consents to go with his people, in their midst, despite their idolatry and rebellion. The book closes with a scene not only of pure grace, but of the completion of the long circle from Genesis 1: the tabernacle is constructed, and the glory of Israel's God comes to fill it, to live among his people as they journey to their promised land. The people of Israel are, as it were, the new humanity, on their way to take possession of their new Eden.

This pattern—God intending to live among his people, being unable to because of their rebellion, but coming back in grace to do so at last—is, in a measure, the story of the whole Old Testament. Magnify that exodus story, project it onto the screen of hundreds of years of history, and you have the larger story. Solomon builds the Temple, succeeding generations either corrupt it or try to reform it, but eventually, faced with overwhelming rebellion and idolatry, God abandons the Temple at last, leaving it to its fate when the Babylonians close in. (Note the irony: Babylon, "Babel," is the place of human pride and idolatry in contrast to which God called Abraham in the first place.) The whole of what we call the Second Temple period, roughly 538 BC onward, is characterized by this sense of divine absence; God is gone, and he hasn't come back. That is the problem faced by the prophet Malachi; the priests are bored and slack in their liturgical duties because, though they've rebuilt the Temple, there's no sense of YHWH having returned, as Ezekiel had said he would. Ah, says Malachi, but the Lord whom you seek *will* suddenly come to his Temple—"but who can endure the day of his coming, and who can stand when he appears" (3:1–2)? Are you ready, in other words, for another moment like that in 1 Kings 8 when Solomon dedicated the Temple and the glory of YHWH filled the house, or that moment in Isaiah 6 when the prophet saw YHWH high and lifted up, filling the Temple with his train and the house with smoke?

Here, then, is the great biblical theme that enables us to understand what the gospels are saying about God—not just any "god," but Israel's God, the covenant God, the creator. That YHWH will come back was the underlying theological narrative of a great deal of Second Temple literature, giving direction not only to thinkers and writers but to activists and would-be leaders, as we see in the great Temple-cleansing and Temple-rebuilding projects of the Maccabees, of Herod, of the final ill-fated would-be messiah Simon bar-Kochba. That he had not yet done so was the constant ache, the nagging sorrow both for the pious, praying the Psalms and waiting patiently, and for the pragmatists, knowing that until he came back Israel would not be free of foreign domination. The book of Exodus ends with the divine presence coming at last to dwell in the newly built tabernacle. The Hebrew scriptures as a whole end with the hope that the larger-scale story that mirrors that early, prototypical narrative will have a similar ending. The problem is that nobody knows when or how this will happen.

The story the gospels are telling, once we turn down the overly loud volume of the second speaker, which has simply been shouting, "He's divine! He's divine!" is the story of *how YHWH came back to his people at last.*

Looking for the Right Thing

At this point we have to be careful and once more get some critical distance from the main streams of our own recent traditions. It all depends on *looking for the right thing.*

It has been popular for well over a hundred years to see the explicitly high Christology of John as contrasted with the implicitly low Christology of the synoptics. According to this view, John thinks Jesus is divine, but Matthew, Mark, and Luke basically don't. True, they push the boundaries here and there, but they are still telling the story of the "human" Jesus, while John is telling the story of the "divine" Jesus.

This contrast is simply wrong—on both sides. John has been made the spokesman for the kind of "high Christology" with which devout Christians in recent centuries have been trying to oppose post-Enlightenment skepticism; and the skeptics have replied by declaring that John is late, nonhistorical, and therefore irrelevant. The skeptics, in turn, have made the synoptics their spokesmen; in them they see the human Jesus, admittedly already distorted, but still visible. But none of this dialogue of the deaf has paid attention to the biblical story of God as we have just briefly sketched it.

Both sides were, it seems, looking for the wrong kind of things. To get a genuinely biblical "high Christology"—a strong identification between Jesus himself and the God of Israel—you don't need the kind of explicit statements you find in John ("I and the Father are one," 10:30). What you need is, for instance, what Mark gives you in his opening chapter, where prophecies about the coming of God are applied directly to the coming of Jesus:

This is where the good news starts—the good news of Jesus the Messiah, God's son.

Isaiah the prophet put it like this ("Look! I am sending my messenger ahead of me; he will clear the way for you!"):

"A shout goes up in the desert: Make way for the Lord! Clear a straight path for him!"

John the Baptizer appeared in the desert. He was announcing a baptism of repentance, to forgive sins. The whole of Judaea, and everyone who lived in Jerusalem, went out to him; they confessed their sins and were baptized by him in the river Jordan. John wore camel-hair clothes, with a leather belt around his waist. He used to eat locusts and wild honey.

"Someone a lot stronger than me is coming close behind," John used to tell them. "I don't deserve to squat down and undo his sandals. I've plunged you in the water; he's going to plunge you in the holy spirit."

This is how it happened. Around that time, Jesus came from Nazareth in Galilee, and was baptized by John in the river Jordan. That very moment, as he was getting out of the water, he saw the heavens open, and the spirit coming down like a dove onto him. Then there came a voice, out of the heavens: "You are my son! You are the one I love! You make me very glad." (1:1–11)

Mark quotes that passage in Malachi about Israel's God returning at last (3:1) and couples it with Isaiah's promise about the prophet shouting to Zion that its God is coming back at last, coming back in glory (40:3–11). Mark then emphasizes John the Baptist's saying about "someone a lot stronger than me" who is "coming close behind," someone who will plunge the people in the Holy Spirit. This can only mean that Israel's God himself is arriving at last, to renew and restore his people. What Mark then shows us, in a scene in which he obviously believes that these prophecies are being fulfilled, is Jesus coming for baptism, being anointed with the Spirit, and hailed by the Father as his promised Son. That gives you, right there on Mark's first page, every bit as high a Christology as John's, though it is a high *Jewish* Christology rather than the non-Jewish variety people have for so long imagined would be necessary for the case to be made.

It is in that context that we should interpret passage after passage in Mark's gospel. When Jesus calls his first followers (1:16–20) and when he singles out the Twelve (3:13–19), he is acting in a deeply symbolic way, echoing the foundation of Israel as God's people. But he is not casting himself as first among equals. He is not the leading member of the Twelve. He is the one who calls them into existence and gives them their status and role. That, in the Old Testament, is what Israel's God had done. (Already I sense some readers slipping back into the old eighteenth-century either/or: "Ah, so Mark is saying Jesus is divine in the sense of being identified with a distant deity who is now intervening in the world." But no, that's not what I am talking about. I am talking about Israel's God, the one who created humans in his own image.) Mark's Jesus goes about doing and saying things that declare that Israel's God is now becoming king—Israel's dream come true. But Jesus is talking about God becoming king *in order to explain the things he himself is doing*. He isn't pointing away from himself to God. He is pointing to God in order to explain his own actions. In case we miss the point, Mark rubs it in by having Jesus command the wind and the sea to be still, and they obey him:

> That day, when it was evening, Jesus said to them, "Let's go over to the other side."
> They left the crowd, and took him with them in the boat he'd been in. There were other boats with him too.

A big windstorm blew up. The waves beat on the boat, and it quickly began to fill. Jesus, however, was asleep on a cushion in the stern. They woke him up.

"Teacher!" they said to him, "We're going down! Don't you care?"

He got up, scolded the wind, and said to the sea, "Silence! Shut up!"

The wind died, and there was a flat calm. Then he said to them, "Why are you scared? Don't you believe yet?"

Great fear stole over them. "Who *is* this?" they said to each other. "Even the wind and the sea do what he says!" (4:35–41)

In the Old Testament, this is what one might expect YHWH himself to do:

> *You silence the roaring of the seas,*
> *the roaring of their waves,*
> *the tumult of the peoples. (Ps. 65:7)*

> *You rule the raging of the sea;*
> *when its waves rise, you still them. (Ps. 89:9)*

> *Then they cried to YHWH in their trouble,*
> *and he brought them out from their distress;*
> *he made the storm be still,*
> *and the waves of the sea were hushed. (Ps. 107:28–29)*

This and similar passages are enough for Mark's alert readers to start asking the question: Suppose *this* is what it looks like when Israel's God returns at last? Suppose this isn't a story about a man going about "proving that he's God," but about God coming back in person to rescue his people? Part of the problem, I believe, is

not only that skeptics have sneered at the idea of "God" coming into our world. It is also that believers have found it easier to
imagine the kind of "intervening God" the skeptics have denied
and a lot harder to imagine the kind of utterly human "God"
Mark seems to be describing.

Of course, this raises huge questions that Mark doesn't really
begin to answer. What happens at the death of Jesus? What is
the relationship between Jesus himself and the one to whom he
prays—particularly, the one to whom he prays with the terrible
cry of desolation? Mark doesn't seem concerned about giving us
an answer in the form of a theory. Pay attention to the story, he
seems to be saying. Live in it and allow it to shift the ground on
which you're standing. Then maybe you won't need a theory.
Maybe you'll see everything differently:

> At midday there was darkness over all the land until
> three in the afternoon. At three o'clock Jesus shouted out
> in a powerful voice, "*Eloi, Eloi, lema sabachthani?*" Which
> means, "My God, my God, why did you abandon me?"
>
> When the bystanders heard it, some of them said,
> "He's calling for Elijah!"
>
> One of them ran and filled a sponge with sour wine,
> put it on a pole, and gave it him to drink.
>
> "Well then," he declared, "let's see if Elijah will come
> and take him down."
>
> But Jesus, with another loud shout, breathed his last.
>
> The Temple veil was torn in two, from top to bottom.
> When the centurion who was standing facing him saw
> that he died in this way, he said, "This fellow really was
> God's son." (15:33–39)

Calling Jesus "God's son" echoes, of course, the voice at Jesus's
baptism (1:11). But when a Roman centurion says those words,
we assume he didn't know what had happened on that day. For
him, the phrase "God's son" would normally have meant one

person and one person only: Tiberius Caesar, son of the "divine" Augustus. That's what the coins all said—including the coin they showed Jesus a few days before (12:15–17). This points ahead to our fourth sound speaker (Chapter 7).

For Mark, all the signs are that he was thinking, as many other early Christians were in his day, of the term "God's son" as having at least four meanings. First, in the Old Testament Israel itself is "God's son" (Exod. 4:22; Jer. 31:9). Second—and this seems to be a primary meaning in the baptism story—it is the messiah, Israel's anointed king, who is "God's son" (2 Sam. 7:12–14; Pss. 2:7; 89:26–27). Third, as we just noted, "son of God" was a regular and primary title taken by the Roman emperors from Augustus on. But fourth, looming up behind and beyond all of these was the sense we find in the very earliest Christian documents that all of these pointed to a strange new reality: that, in Jesus, Israel's God had become present, had become human, had come to live in the midst of his people, to set up his kingdom, to take upon himself the full horror of their plight, and to bring about his long-awaited new world. The phrase "son of God" was ready at hand to express that huge, evocative, frightening possibility, without leaving behind any of its other resonances. We can see this already going on in the writings of Paul. It is highly likely that Mark expected his first readers to have the same combination of themes in mind.

Matthew and Luke: Seeing Jesus, Thinking God

Once we learn, from Mark, how we might read the story of Jesus as the story of Israel's God returning at last, we may find it easier to recognize the ways in which Matthew and Luke are doing something very similar. (If, as most scholars still think, they both used Mark as a source, this is of course the more natural.) We begin with Matthew.

Matthew makes things very clear in the frame he creates for his story. Look first at the opening of the gospel, right after the genealogy, which we noted in the previous chapter. The angel tells Joseph that Mary's child is to be called "Jesus," because "he is the one who will save his people from their sins"; the name "Jesus" is here being interpreted as meaning "YHWH saves." Matthew's comment fills this in from another angle:

> All this happened so that what the Lord said through the prophet might be fulfilled: "Look: the virgin is pregnant, and will have a son, and they shall give him the name Emmanuel"—which means, in translation, "God with us." (1:22–23)

In other words, we are to look at Jesus and see in him, however strange it may seem, the personal presence of Israel's God, coming to be with his people and rescue them from the plight their sins have brought upon them—which, in ancient Jewish terms, was focused not least on the "exile" they were still suffering, the plight of being overrun and ruled by pagan nations.

Look next at the other end of Matthew's frame. Jesus has been crucified and then raised from the dead. Now he addresses his followers, in words that Matthew must have known were astonishing by anyone's standards. And the final sentence echoes that "Emmanuel" promise. "God with us" has become "Jesus with us":

> Jesus came toward them and addressed them.
>
> "All authority in heaven and on earth," he said, "has been given to me! So you must go and make all the nations into disciples. Baptize them in the name of the father, and of the son, and of the holy spirit. Teach them to observe everything I have commanded you. And look: I am with you, every single day, to the very end of the age." (28:18–20)

In Jesus himself, Matthew is saying, Israel's God has come back to be with his people and will now be with them forever.

This outer frame enables us to understand those strange scenes in which Matthew has the disciples actually worshipping Jesus after he stills the storm. Matthew makes this more explicit than Mark:

> They got into the boat, and the wind died down. The
> people in the boat worshipped him.
>
> "You really are God's son!" they said. (14:32–33)

Again, once we learn what is going on—once we think in first-century Jewish terms rather than in the terms of late modern Western skepticism and its alternatives—we begin to notice all sorts of other things too. We notice, in particular, that Jesus tells several stories about masters and servants, *to illustrate what he himself was doing,* while being aware that, within the world of his hearers, stories about masters and servants, kings and subjects, and so on, would unhesitatingly be recognized as stories about Israel's God and Israel itself.

The primary example of this is a parable found in both Matthew and Luke in slightly different versions. (Scholars have often suggested, as with other similar phenomena, that one of these versions is "original" and the other is "adapted" and have then speculated as to which is which. This is ridiculous. Jesus was a traveling teacher in the days before print and electronic media. Even today, when our words can be broadcast around the world in a split second, a politician on the campaign trail, a bishop preaching in different parishes every night of the week, or even an author doing a series of book launches will tell the same story again and again—but with local variations, either to fit a different audience or simply because he or she has decided to try a different tack.) Here is Luke's version, and Luke himself leaves us in no doubt as to what it's about, as to what Jesus intended by it. Once we get to its heart, it contains as high a Christology as anything in John, Paul, or Hebrews:

> While people were listening to this, Jesus went on to tell a parable. They were, after all, getting close to Jerusalem, and they thought that the kingdom of God was going to appear at once.
>
> "There was once a nobleman," he said, "who went into a country far away to be given royal authority and then return. He summoned ten of his slaves and gave them ten silver coins. 'Do business with these,' he said, 'until I come back.' His subjects, though, hated him, and sent a delegation after him to say, 'We don't want this man to be our king.'
>
> "So it happened that when he received the kingship and came back again, he gave orders to summon these slaves who had received the money, so that he could find out how they had got on with their business efforts. The first came forward and said, 'Master, your money has made ten times its value!'
>
> " 'Well done, you splendid servant!' he said. 'You've been trustworthy with something small; now you can take command of ten cities.'
>
> "The second came and said, 'Master, your money has made five times its value!'
>
> " 'You too—you can take charge of five cities.'
>
> "The other came and said, 'Master, here is your money. I kept it wrapped in this handkerchief. You see, I was afraid of you, because you are a hard man: you profit where you made no investment, and you harvest what you didn't sow.'
>
> " 'I'll condemn you out of your own mouth, you wicked scoundrel of a servant!' he replied. 'So: you knew that I was a hard man, profiting where I didn't invest and

harvesting where I didn't sow? So why didn't you put my money with the bankers? Then I'd have had the interest when I got back!'

" 'Take the money from him,' he said to the bystanders, 'and give it to the man who's got it ten times over!' ("Master," they said to him, "he's got ten times that already!")

"Let me tell you: everyone who has will be given more; but if someone has nothing, even what he has will be taken away from him. But as for these enemies of mine, who didn't want me to be king over them—bring them here and slaughter them in front of me." (19:11–27)

Yes, I know, some scholars have tried to make out that Jesus intended his audience to be angry with the greedy nobleman and to applaud the third servant, who refused to collaborate with his money-grubbing ways. You can just about make out a case for that—if you shut one eye to what Luke is saying. Almost at once he emphasizes the point:

When [Jesus] came near and saw the city, he wept over it.

"If only you'd known," he said, "on this day—even you!—what peace meant. But now it's hidden, and you can't see it. Yes, the days are coming upon you when your enemies will build up earthworks all around you, and encircle you, and squeeze you in from every direction. They will bring you crashing to the ground, you and your children within you. They won't leave one single stone on another, because you didn't know the moment when God was visiting you." (19:41–44)

Here is the point: "You didn't know the moment *when God was visiting you*." Actually, the Greek simply says *ton kairon tes episkopes sou,* "the day of your visitation." But the word "visitation" here has only one possible meaning. This is the time when God was coming back, coming back at last to see how his people had been doing with their centuries-old commission. This, for Luke, is the meaning of the parable. Jesus is telling a story about Israel's God coming back to his people to explain what was going on *when he himself was arriving in Jerusalem*. No wonder the immediate sequel is Jesus's expulsion of traders from the Temple, an acted-out parable of its destruction followed by several sayings, including a long discourse (Luke 21), in which the imminent destruction of the Temple is the mirror image of the arrival of Jesus. The Temple is God's house, but if God is coming in person and finds the Temple turned into a symbol of Israel's failure to be his people, there is only one possible result.

This explosive scene then makes sense of the many other hints in Luke and Matthew, hints that point the same way that we saw in Mark. I remember once studying Luke 8 and being struck by one line in particular—and then going into a high-level theological discussion where that one line became suddenly relevant. One scholar was holding forth on the notion that Luke had no thought whatever of Jesus being in any sense "divine." Luke had a human Jesus, he said, and that was a very good thing too. Somewhat daringly—I was quite young at the time—I remember pointing out Luke 8:39. It is the end of the story in which Jesus has healed the demon-possessed man, who then begs Jesus to be allowed to stay with him. As with Mark, Luke doesn't need to draw a heavy-handed "theological conclusion"; one line says it all:

> "Go back to your home," said Jesus, "and tell them what God has done for you." And he went off around every town, declaring what Jesus had done for him.

I still regard this as unassailable. If Luke was not trying to tell us that what Jesus was doing God was doing—and vice versa—then the sentence has no meaning. (It comes, in any case, as though in reply to the question at the end of the previous paragraph: "Who is this, then, if he can give orders to wind and water, and they obey him?" 8:25.) Again, once we recognize that Matthew and Luke, in line with Mark, are telling that story and making that point, we begin to see it all over—and to recognize the subtle differences between this way of "identifying" Jesus and Israel's God and the somewhat shrill and unfocused normal "apologetic" arguments for "proving Jesus's divinity." One way and another, all three synoptic gospels are clear: in telling the story of Jesus they are consciously telling the story of how Israel's God came back to his people, in judgment and mercy.

Glory Unveiled: John's Temple Christology

"The Word was God . . . and the Word became flesh." John's cards are on the table from the beginning. For him, the story of Jesus is the story of how God became human, how the creator became part of his creation. But, as we have already seen, this astonishing claim, rooted as it is in the echoing narrative of Genesis 1 in which humans were made to bear the divine image and likeness, is woven tightly together with the story of Israel.

In that story, as we saw, the God who made the world as a temple for his own possession and dwelling had deigned, as an act of unmerited fresh mercy, to pitch his tent in the midst of the Israelites, first in the wilderness tabernacle and then in the Jerusalem Temple. The Temple was the sign and focus and means of God's presence with his people, a presence at once dangerously holy and wonderfully encouraging. The regular sacrifices, day by day and hour by hour, and the regular festivals, season by season but always with a climax at Passover, gave the Temple its inner life and meaning, as the Israelites journeyed to Jerusalem to be in the very presence of the God who had promised to live there and to celebrate his promise of ultimate deliverance.

The destruction of the Temple by the Babylonians in 587 BC had been the worst possible disaster, indicating that Israel's God had abandoned his house, had left the Temple and city to their long-deserved fate. That was the verdict of Ezekiel, and it is echoed by other writers of the period. But that could not be the end of the story. God had promised to come back. He had promised one final great Passover. One day, when he returned, his people would be free forever.

And John, more clearly than the others, insists from the start that this promise has been made good in Jesus. The Word be-came flesh and *kai eskenosen en hemin*, "set up among us his *skene*," his "tent" (it's the word from which we get "scene"; a theatrical backdrop is a kind of "tent" in which the action takes place). In case there was any doubt, the Greek word *skene* is (coinciden-tally?) a close echo of the Hebrew *shakan*, which means "dwell" or "abide"; when we read of people "abiding" with Jesus or his "abiding" with them later in John, we should almost certainly catch this echo. In particular, in postbiblical Jewish writing the idea of the presence of God in the Temple was given the name Shekinah, the "tabernacling, abiding divine presence," the per-sonal presence of the glory of God. So, when John continues by saying, "We gazed upon his glory, glory like that of the father's only son, full of grace and truth" (1:14), we should get the point loud and clear.

All this means that we should be able to read John with more sensitivity to the nature of his "high Christology." Obviously he thinks Jesus was and is fully divine (as well as fully human, but he doesn't need to make that point in the same way). But this doesn't mean he is simply saying "Jesus is God" in the way of some ra-tionalist apologists. John's "high Christology" remains very, very Jewish, very much rooted in Israel's scriptures. His chosen vehicle for his matchless opening statement, the *logos*, draws not so much on Platonic or Stoic ideas as on the living Word of the Old Testa-ment, as, for instance, in Isaiah 55, where the word goes out like rain or snow and accomplishes God's work (55:10–11). This work, God's great act of rescue, rooted in the accomplishment of the "servant of the LORD" in chapter 53 and the renewal of the covenant in 54, brings about the new creation in 55, with the thorns and thistles of Genesis 3 and Isaiah 5 replaced by wonderful trees and shrubs (55:12–13). It is (in other words) the *creator* God, and it is *Israel's* God, who has become human in and as Jesus of Nazareth. Once we get the speaker turned to the right volume, we can hear this clearly and hear it in relation to everything else, rather than allowing it to drown out all other voices and strands of early Christian music.

With this as our framework, we should be able to read right through John and discern what he is actually doing. His Jesus is a combination of the living Word of the Old Testament, the Shekinah of Jewish hope (God's tabernacling presence in the Temple), and "wisdom," which in some key Jewish writings was the personal self-expression of the creator God, coming to dwell with humans and particularly with Israel (see Wis. 7; Sir. 24). But this Jesus is no mere ideal, a fictional figure cunningly combining ancient theological motifs. John's Jesus is alive; he moves from one vivid scene to another, in far more realistic dialogue with far more realistic secondary characters than in most of the synoptic gospels.

In particular, he goes again and again to Jerusalem, not least for various festivals—but in each case he appears to trump the festival itself, declaring at the Festival of Tabernacles that he is the one who provides the real living water (John 7), at Hanukkah that he is the true (royal) shepherd, and ultimately at the final Passover that he has overcome the world and its ruler, like YHWH himself overthrowing Pharaoh in Egypt, in order to liberate his people once and for all. John describes Jesus not only as the Temple in person, but as the one in whom everything that would normally happen in the Temple is fulfilled, completed, accomplished. That is why, in the incomparable final discourses of chapters 13–17, generations of readers have had a sense of entering the real Temple, the place where Jesus promises, as God promised in the ancient scriptures, to be with his people and they with him, climaxing in the prayer of chapter 17, which has often, with good reason, been called the High-Priestly Prayer. All the functions of the Temple—festival, presence, priesthood, and now sacrifice—have devolved onto Jesus. This is the heart of John's "high Christology."

All this should make it clear that we must not read John simply within the modernist frame of reference, in which a "divine" Jesus is a mere "superman" figure, striding through the world six inches off the floor. Many readers have supposed that that was what John was offering, but this is simply a massive anachronism. The gospels themselves radically deconstruct the old either/or of Jesus as *either* a human being *or* a divine being (which the creeds, and particularly the Chalcedonian formula, held together, but always with the appearance of a kind of confidence trick). The gospels offer us not so much a different kind of human, but a different kind of God: a God who, having made humans in his own image, will most naturally express himself in and as that image-bearing creature; a God who, having made Israel to share and bear the pain and horror of the world, will most naturally express himself in and as that pain-bearing, horror-facing creature. This is perhaps the most difficult thing for us to keep in mind, though the gospels are inviting us to do so on every page. And it is the failure to bear this in mind, perhaps, that makes it so difficult to hold together the idea of God's kingdom breaking into the world and God's son going to a shameful death. Insofar as the gospels do hold those things together, this isn't simply a confidence trick. It is because they have a different view of God and God's kingdom. To this we shall return in due course.

6

The Launching of God's Renewed People

THIS BRINGS US NICELY to the third speaker in our sound system. Like the second one, this third one has often been turned up far too loud. This has meant both that the music it is quite properly trying to play has itself been distorted and that the music coming from the other speakers (apart from the equally distorted second one) has been overwhelmed. In much modern biblical scholarship, in fact, this one has often drowned out *all* the others.

Here the gospels are read simply as reflections of the life of the early church, with no real connection to the narrative of Israel and (except in conservative circles) no real thought that the story of Jesus might be the story of God in person. Instead, we have the gospels as the projection of early Christian faith, reflecting the controversies and crises of the early church, which, according to the theory, placed in the mouth of a fictitious "Jesus" sayings that in fact came from early Christian prophets speaking in his name.

Before we go any farther, it is important to stress that this is at best a half-truth, and the wrong half at that. Though of course the gospels reflect the life of the early church, in which the four evangelists lived, prayed, and wrote—how could they not reflect that life?—the whole point for each of them, and for any sources they had, was that something had happened in the life, death, and resurrection of Jesus through which the world had changed, Israel had changed, humankind had changed, their vision and knowledge of God had changed, and they themselves had changed. They were reflecting the changed world, to be sure. But they were talking about the change itself, how it had come about, and what it all meant.

High-Volume, Dangerous Distortion

What has, for many generations, been passed off as "critical scholarship" has in fact regularly reflected one of two quite different prejudgments, both of which must be challenged. First, there has been the judgment of skeptics, from Reimarus to the present. They maintain that we know, in advance, that most of these stories must be fictitious, because dead people don't rise, lepers don't get healed, people don't walk on water, and not least gods do not appear in human form. That point of view, reinforced by the "spirit of the age," has enabled anyone casting doubt on the gospels to appear as sophisticated, knowing, and clever, someone who isn't going to be taken in by a lot of religiously motivated claptrap. People have thus assumed that it is a mark of intellectual maturity to be able to question the historical truth of any and every statement in the gospels. (Curiously, the historical critics are often much more generous when they read Josephus, Tacitus, or other non-Christian first-century sources.) Those who accept things at face value ("Matthew says Jesus said this, so Jesus said it") are scorned as naive, uncritical, or perhaps fundamentalist. Or all of the above.

When asked the point of the stories if it is not that "they happened," the skeptics answer that these stories reflect the faith of the early Christians. The stories are, as it were, coded statements of the faith of the "early church." They are, in that sense, "myths," stories told not in order to say "what happened," but in order to provide a narrative basis for present existence. Though the philosophical basis for this way of thinking has steadily been eroded over the past half century, many New Testament scholars still insist on the skeptical reading as a mark of intellectual maturity or academic credibility.

Well, skeptics must be allowed to have their say. But serious historical arguments can be mounted in favor of a much more positive account. I and plenty of others have offered such accounts, and there has been remarkable little attempt at serious refutation.

The second prejudgment has been that made from within the dominant school in New Testament studies in the early part of the twentieth century, namely, the radical Lutheranism of some elements in the German academy, represented particularly by Rudolf Bultmann. As we saw earlier, Bultmann and others believed that it was in the very nature of authentic Christian faith that it should rest on nothing outside itself, no human achievement or status, no historical events. The bare fact of the cross was enough; almost, for some of Bultmann's followers, more than enough. It would therefore falsify the essence of Christian faith to suppose that the evangelists were telling us about *things that actually happened as though those things mattered*. It has become an either/or question: *either* this story is about Jesus, *or* it is about the early church. A story about Jesus doing something on the sabbath and making a comment about it is thus assumed to reflect not so much an actual incident in the life of Jesus, but a sabbath controversy in the early church (not that we have much other evidence of controversy on this topic). The sound from this speaker has therefore been turned up to deafening point. Some people haven't been able to hear anything else.

Many readers, not least in Britain and America, who were not particularly up on existentialist Lutheranism, but were susceptible to the mood of the times—the "spirit of the age"—found this idea very congenial. Of course Jesus didn't really walk on water; of course he didn't really say "I and the Father are one"; of course he didn't rise bodily from the dead, but what marvelous expressions of early faith! Now how can we, who know these things didn't happen, express our faith in appropriate terms for today?

These prejudgments have simply falsified the entire gospel tradition. This isn't a matter of "proving" that this or that element in the gospels is in fact historically reliable. History has, in any case, a type of "proof" different from that in many other disciplines. Science studies repeatable phenomena; an experiment can be replicated on the other side of the world. History studies unrepeatable phenomena; you cannot step twice into the same river. "Proof" in history must therefore reside in the balance of probabilities, not in the repeated experiment or the analytical mathematical truth. It's more a matter of recognizing that the gospels were indeed intended as "biographies" in some sense or other, even though they are biographies that carry all kinds of other stories, as we are seeing in this part of the present book. And my judgment as a historian is that, once we think our way into the world of Jesus's day, they convey the mood and flavor of the times and of its toweringly central character with remarkable precision.

Having said all that, it is vital that we do not therefore miss the point that, in addition to referring back to Jesus himself, the gospels were telling his story in such a way as to say that this was indeed the moment when "our movement," the early Christian "Way," as it was sometimes called, was launched. Like Americans retelling the story of the brave pioneers who crossed the ocean and settled in a difficult and dangerous land, and doing so not merely for the sake of a good tale but in order to reinforce the sense of modern America as a country with a particular kind of risky, can-do attitude toward life, so the gospel writers told the story of Jesus in order to undergird and reinforce the Christian determination to follow him, to go on following him, to live as he lived and, if necessary, to die as he died, believing that God's kingdom, established through his work, was becoming a reality in more and more of the world through their own lives, work, and costly witness. Once we adjust the volume on this speaker so that we can lose the distortion introduced by radical skepticism, on the one hand, and radical Lutheranism, on the other, we should be able to hear the more nuanced and distinctive notes of the early Christians celebrating the life, death, and resurrection of Jesus as the moment when, and the means by which, their own work took its flying instructions and got off the ground.

The gospel writers were not, then, simply telling the story of Jesus in some "neutral," "objective," fly-on-the-wall kind of reportage. Actually, as I and others have often pointed out, there is no such thing as "neutral" reportage. All stories are told from a point of view; without that, you have no principle of selection and are left with an unsorted ragbag of information. No, the gospel writers were telling the story of Jesus, quite deliberately, in such a way as to put down markers for the life and witness of their own communities. The thing to bear in mind, though, as we adjust the volume on this third speaker, is this: just because the gospel writers were consciously telling the story of Jesus as the foundation story of the church, that doesn't mean they weren't telling the story of Jesus himself. Just because the sports reporter is a thoroughly biased supporter of one team rather than the other, that doesn't mean he is allowed to get the score wrong.

Another distorting pressure, however, must also be named. This is the tendency, which we have already observed, for people in our generation, both inside and outside the church, to assume that the gospels are basically about "moral teaching," that Jesus was a moral teacher and that the gospels record his wise words. Any serious readers of the gospels will see the flaw—Jesus was not less than a "moral teacher," but he was certainly much, much more. But for many preachers and teachers this exerts an insidious pressure, helped on its way by the need to produce yet another sermon (or two or three) for yet another Sunday. How much easier to produce moral musings than present the fresh challenge of the kingdom!

Hence, once more, this speaker gets turned up far too loud. The resounding refrain is that the gospels are about Jesus founding the church, so we, the church, can read them straightforwardly as "Jesus's rules for us to obey." Thus, for instance, the Sermon on the Mount has been read as Jesus's set of instructions to the church—not, as we might have thought from the actual setting in Matthew, as Jesus's challenge to his Jewish contemporaries. Preachers have routinely bracketed out the specific first-century context and meaning of Jesus's words and deeds and indeed of his death and resurrection. They have "universalized" all of that.

This is hardly surprising, in that there is little evidence, after the first four or five centuries of the church, that the Jewish context of Jesus's public career was playing any role in theological or pastoral reflection. To this day there remains a strong prejudice against any such thing. If we really put Jesus back in his first-century Jewish context, people feel (and I mean "feel"—I'm not sure "thinking" really comes into it), we risk making him irrelevant, awkward, and distant. So Jesus becomes the "founder of Christianity," with the type of Christianity varying according to the predilections of the preacher or teacher.

So, whether at a scholarly or a popular level, the gospels have been perceived and read as the story of Jesus launching the Christian movement, teaching the early Christians (and by implication their successors), and then dying and rising to save them. The speaker carrying these notes has been up at full volume. And this has prevented us from hearing the much more subtle point that all four gospels, each in its own way, are making.

Foundational Documents

One good way to get this third speaker adjusted to its proper volume is to think of the four gospels as deliberately composed *foundational documents* for the new movement. They are, in this quite proper sense, "myths"—not in the sense of "stories that didn't happen," but in the sense of "stories communities tell to explain and give direction to their own lives." In my country, the story of the Battle of Britain has become, in that sense, a "myth," not because it didn't happen (it did), but because the way it has been told is designed not only to remember things that happened in the early 1940s, but to celebrate something of the character of Britain as it understands itself, a little embattled offshore European island standing pluckily against tyranny and barbarism. The great debates about Darwinian evolution that have continued to be such a feature of American public life are not about the question of whether Darwinian evolution is a "myth"; there is no doubt about that. It is a powerful story told again and again in order to reinforce one particular view of the world and human life. The question is whether the "myth" corresponds to reality.

Well, the question of the gospels is whether the "myth" that they convey corresponds to reality. Early Christians would have said that the test of this was the reality not simply of their historical memories, but of their community life. When they told the stories in the gospels, they told them not simply as a way of reminding one another of things that had happened, however interesting. They were reminding one another of things that had happened through which the new movement of which they were a part had come into being and through which it had gained its sense of direction. Their whole raison d'être depended on these stories.

If, then, with the sound coming from the first speaker, we observed the church telling the story of Jesus as the story of how

Israel's story came to fulfillment, part of the reason for that was that this is the very foundation of the new movement that then sprang up. The early Christians believed that Jesus was Israel's Messiah, not, as some Jewish apologists today have absurdly said, "the Christian Messiah." There was, and is, no such independent thing. The fulfillment of Israel's story in the story of the Messiah is the foundational charter of the church.

That is why I speak of the gospels as telling *the story of the launching of God's renewed people.* It is wrong to imagine that the gospels (or Jesus, for that matter) were concerned with "founding the church," which is the way some people have said it. There already was a "people of God." We saw, with the first speaker, that the gospels were telling the story of Jesus as the climax of that people's story. Jesus came, they indicate, to rescue and renew that people, not to destroy it and replace it with something else. Israel is to be fulfilled, not replaced. (There is of course a lot of sensitivity about this question just now, but it does no good to pretend that things are other than they are.) This phrase about "renewal" is therefore much more than a mere alternative way of saying "found the church." The earlier story was certainly not, as far as the gospel writers were concerned, cut off without remainder and replaced with something quite different. It is precisely because the gospels tell the story of how Israel's long history reached its surprising climax that they become "foundational documents." Think again of the poems at the start of Luke's gospel. God has fulfilled the promises to Abraham; now things can proceed in a new way.

What's more, it seems to me clear that the four canonical evangelists were deliberately writing the story in such a way as to be the foundation for the whole church, not just for their own part of it. Despite the tendency of scholars a generation or so ago to suppose, for example, that Matthew was writing simply for "Matthew's church" or John for the "Johannine community," I am strongly inclined to agree with those who have insisted that all four gospels were written at a time when the early Christian movement was quite mobile with the intention of addressing all followers of Jesus, wherever they might be. It is important that we get the sound from this third speaker adjusted as precisely as possible. The music is getting quite complicated, and we need to be sure we can hear it all.

Signposts of the Future Church

All this encourages us to reread the gospels once more with a view to seeing the ways in which they were sketching out the ground for the life of the church. The most obvious passages, I suppose, are the commissionings of the disciples, both during the course of Jesus's public career and after his resurrection. Thus we find the famous passage in Matthew 10, which, despite some clauses that seem to have been only temporary, can hardly have been intended to refer to a mission entirely restricted to the time of Jesus's own ministry:

Jesus sent these Twelve off with these instructions.

"Don't go into Gentile territory," he said, "and don't go into a Samaritan town. Go instead to the lost sheep of the house of Israel. As you go, declare publicly that the kingdom of heaven has arrived. Heal the sick, raise the dead, cleanse people with skin diseases, cast out demons.

"It was all free when you got it; make sure it's free when you give it. Don't take any gold or silver or copper in your belts; no bag for the road, no second cloak, no sandals, no stick. Workers deserve their pay.

"When you go into a town or village, make careful inquiry for someone who is good and trustworthy, and stay there until you leave. When you go into the house, give a solemn greeting. If the house is trustworthy, let your blessing of peace rest upon it, but if not, let it return

to you. If anyone won't welcome you or listen to your
message, go out of the house or the town and shake the
dust off your feet. I'm telling you the truth: it will be
more bearable for Sodom and Gomorrah on the day of
judgment than for that town.

"See here," Jesus continued, "I'm sending you out like
sheep surrounded by wolves. So be as shrewd as snakes
and as innocent as doves.

"Watch out for danger from people around you. They
will hand you over to councils, and flog you in their
synagogues. You will be dragged before governors and
kings because of me, as evidence to them and to the nations. But when they hand you over, don't worry how to
speak or what to say. What you have to say will be given
to you at that moment. It won't be you speaking, you
see; it will be the spirit of your father speaking in you.

"One brother will betray another to death; fathers
will betray children, and children will rebel against their
parents and have them put to death. You will be hated
by everyone because of my name. But the one who holds
out to the end will be delivered.

"When they persecute you in one town, run off to the
next one. I'm telling you the truth: you won't have gone
through all the towns of Israel before the son of man
comes." (10:5–23)

We can see here both the specific and unrepeatable elements
in the commission and the shape of a much longer-lasting missionary movement. The time-bound elements include the restriction on territory (not going to Gentiles, as in v. 5—a restriction
specifically lifted in 28:19, for which see below) and the restriction on time (an urgent mission that won't have been completed
before "the son of man comes," which seems to be a reference to

the climactic events at the end of the gospel story). Equally, there are elements here that we would be right to assume relate to the period after Jesus's public career is over. We have no reason to suppose that his followers were "dragged before governors and kings" because of him, and their witness before them "and to the nations" does seem to presuppose a time after the "no Gentile" rule of verse 5 has been lifted. So too the promise of "the spirit of your father" in verse 20 would seem to indicate a postresurrection time. Matthew seems to be saying, then, that Jesus launched a mission that continues, in changed circumstances, through into the ongoing life of the church, even though it was rooted in the very specific and particular situation of his own day.

We then find the mission "translated" into the postresurrection setting:

> Jesus came toward them and addressed them.
>
> "All authority in heaven and on earth," he said, "has been given to me! So you must go and make all the nations into disciples. Baptize them in the name of the father, and of the son, and of the holy spirit. Teach them to observe everything I have commanded you. And look: I am with you, every single day, to the very end of the age." (28:18–20)

It isn't just that Jesus has lifted a temporary ban on going to the Gentiles. The point is that now, with Jesus's death and resurrection, the rule of the king of the Jews has been established over the nations, as in Isaiah 11 and Psalms 2, 72, and 89. His followers are therefore to go and put that rule into effect.

This, like the closing of all the gospels, is obviously thought of by its author as a specific charter for the life and mission of the church. Yet the point we have made by the juxtaposition of this with chapter 10 (and there is of course plenty more that we could have added) is that the postresurrection commissionings are

firmly rooted in the earlier ministry of Jesus and his commission-
ing, then and there, of the Twelve and their associates to be Jesus's
colleagues in his kingdom work.

And of course this is just the tip of the iceberg. Think about
Jesus's constant emphasis on the reversal of power and prestige in
which the first would become last and the last would become first.
Sometimes this flickers out, a little hint on the edge of something
else. At other times it is a substantial statement, firmly rooted
in the specifics of Jesus's own public career, but equally firmly
relevant, as far as the evangelists are concerned, to the life of the
early Christian community:

> James and John, Zebedee's sons, came up to him.
>
> "Teacher," they said, "we want you to grant us what-
> ever we ask."
>
> "What do you want me to do for you?" asked Jesus.
>
> "Grant us," they said, "that when you're there in all
> your glory, one of us will sit at your right, and the other
> at your left."
>
> "You don't know what you're asking for!" Jesus re-
> plied. "Can you drink the cup I'm going to drink? Can
> you receive the baptism I'm going to receive?"
>
> "Yes," they said, "we can."
>
> "Well," said Jesus, "you will drink the cup I drink;
> you will receive the baptism I receive. But sitting at my
> right hand or my left—that's not up to me. It's been as-
> signed already."
>
> When the other ten disciples heard, they were angry
> with James and John. Jesus called them to him.
>
> "You know how it is in the pagan nations," he said.
> "Think how their so-called rulers act. They lord it over
> their subjects. The high and mighty ones boss the rest
> around. But that's not how it's going to be with you.

Anyone who wants to be great among you must become
your servant. Anyone who wants to be first must be
everyone's slave. Don't you see? The son of man didn't
come to be waited on. He came to be the servant, to
give his life 'as a ransom for many.'" (Mark 10:35–45)

Think, then, about the other challenges Jesus gave to his followers, not least in the Sermon on the Mount, and consider the
process by which what started off as Jesus's challenge to his contemporaries to live as the true Israel ("the light of the world,"
"the salt of the earth," "a city on top of a hill," 5:13–16) was
transformed, by Jesus himself, into the agenda he would act out in
person and then bequeath to his followers. Think, in particular,
about the challenge of forgiveness and the way in which the little
groups of Jesus followers that sprang up in the towns and villages
he visited and that became the nucleus of the early Palestinian
church had to wrestle in a new way with questions of corporate
family life and discipline. Imagine how they would have read passages like this:

"If another disciple sins against you," Jesus continued,
"go and have it out, just between the two of you alone.
If they listen to you, you've won back a brother or sister.
But if they won't listen, you should take with you one or
two others, so that 'everything may be established from
the mouth of two or three witnesses.' If they won't listen
to them, tell it to the assembly. And if they won't listen
to the assembly, you should treat such a person like you
would a Gentile or a tax-collector. I'm telling you the
truth: whatever you tie up on earth will have been tied
up in heaven; and whatever you untie on earth will have
been untied in heaven.

"Again, let me tell you the truth: if two of you come
to an agreement on earth about any matter that you want

to ask, it will be done for you by my father in heaven.
Yes: where two or three come together in my name, I'll
be there in the midst of them." (Matt. 18:15–20)

If the little groups that were left behind in the towns and villages during Jesus's public career needed that kind of assurance, how much more would the communities that grew up in the aftermath of Jesus's death and resurrection? Here, again and again, the evangelists are telling the story of Jesus with an eye, rightly and properly, toward the communities they know will be reading these books as the foundational documents of their corporate life. The needs of the developing church were many and varied, and we can see the four gospels meeting those needs in different ways. (We may at this point note, once again, how different all this is from the Gnostic and semi-Gnostic gospels. For them, individual "enlightenment," rather than the communal life of Jesus's followers, is paramount.)

But when we adjust the sound from this speaker to its correct volume, we find out that there is more to listen for from this corner of the room than simply the early examples of what the church is supposed to be doing and the teaching of Jesus that gives direction and order to its life. Rather, the gospels are consciously telling the story of how God's one-time action in Jesus the Messiah *ushered in a new world order* within which a new way of life was not only possible, but mandatory for Jesus's followers.

It isn't just that the church finds itself doing a few of the things that Jesus's first followers found themselves doing. It is that the story of the gospels, reaching its unique climax in the death and resurrection of Jesus, is told in such a way as to indicate that Jesus's followers now have a mission, indeed a mission that goes way beyond anything they had had during Jesus's lifetime. We have already seen that Matthew suggests a transition from a limited mission in Jesus's lifetime to a worldwide one after the resurrection.

Something similar is true in John's gospel (not that the disciples have as much of a "mission" there during Jesus's lifetime).

In John, until Jesus is "glorified," the Spirit is not given (John actually says, starkly, that up to that point "there was no spirit," 7:39); but once Jesus has died and has been raised—once, in other words, Israel's God has been glorified in him, in the "new Temple" sense that permeates John's gospel—then the Spirit is given, so that the disciples can at last be for the world what Jesus was for Israel. "As the father has sent me, so I am sending you" (20:21) is one of the most demanding of mission charges, but also a key moment in gospel hermeneutics. That passage explains how, in the gospel writers' own telling of the story, the unique and unrepeatable mission and achievement of Jesus becomes the mandate and pattern for the mission of the church. Thus:

> On the last day of the festival, the great final celebration,
> Jesus stood up and shouted out, "If anybody's thirsty,
> they should come to me and have a drink! Anyone who
> believes in me will have rivers of living water flowing
> out of their heart, just like the Bible says!"
>
> He said this about the spirit, which people who believed in him were to receive. The spirit wasn't available yet, because Jesus was not yet glorified. (7:37–39)

> "Peace be with you," Jesus said to them again. "As the father has sent me, so I'm sending you."
> With that, he breathed on them.
> "Receive the holy spirit," he said. (20:21–22)

Here is the heart of it. The more you tell the story of Jesus and pray for his Spirit, the more you discover what the church should be doing in the present time. Because the gospels are the foundational charter for the church's life, they *must be* stories primarily about Jesus; otherwise the church would be rooted in itself. Here we find, in fact, the mirror image of the Bultmannian position: *unless* the church's life and mission is rooted in the historical accomplishment of Jesus, all Christian life would be either arrogance or folly, or both. (As I write this paragraph, an e-mail comes in from Christian friends working among refugees and trafficked women in one of the toughest corners of the world. Why do we do this unless it's the work of Jesus?)

But perhaps the most mysterious and powerful thing about the way the gospels are written is the way they end. Or do they?

The End Is the Beginning

The gospels, in fact, do not really "end" in the way many stories do. Or rather, their ending is framed as, in a sense, a new beginning. Even if we suppose (as I do not) that Mark meant his gospel to end with the women saying "nothing to anyone, because they were afraid" (16:8, where our best manuscripts now break off), there are plenty of hints earlier in the story that this would just be the start of a whole new phase of life and work for Jesus's disciples. Jesus has, after all, already declared that the gospel of the kingdom must be announced to all the nations (13:10) and has repeated the point in relation to the woman who anointed him with ointment in Bethany:

> Jesus was in Bethany, at the house of Simon (known as "the Leper"). While he was at table, a woman came up with an alabaster pot containing extremely valuable ointment made of pure spikenard. She broke the pot and poured the ointment on Jesus's head.
>
> Some of the people there grumbled to one another.
>
> "What's the point of wasting the ointment?" they asked. "That ointment could have been sold for three hundred dinars, and given to the poor."

And they were angry with her.

"Leave her alone," said Jesus. "Why make trouble for her? She has done a wonderful thing for me. You have the poor with you always; you can help them whenever you want to. But you won't always have me.

"She has played her part. She has anointed my body for its burial, ahead of time. I'm telling you the truth: wherever the message is announced in all the world, the story of what she has just done will be told. That will be her memorial." (14:3–9)

Clearly Mark did not envisage that 16:8 would be the real and final "end" to the story. He would hardly have been writing his gospel if it had been. He has led us at a brisk pace all through his story, peppered as it is with "immediately," hurrying on from one place and scene to another. The story hasn't stopped just because his words have run out. He assumes that it continues—and that it continues in the ways already hinted at.

Matthew, for his part, ends his gospel with Jesus sending his followers out on a mission, secure in the knowledge that he was already enthroned as the world's rightful Lord. To this we shall return.

John, most poignantly, ends the narrative proper with a sentence that, if we were publishing it today, we might well want to conclude with a trick of punctuation available to us though not to John, namely, an ellipsis pointing ahead into the unknown. Peter has asked Jesus about the vocation of the "beloved disciple," and Jesus's only answer is this: "If it's my intention that he should remain here until I come, what's that got to do with you? You must follow me . . ." (21:22). Readers are left to look ahead, to ponder the strange new world of mission, and of suffering, that the risen Jesus was opening up in front of his followers. And they would then expect to go back and read the whole story through once more, this time reflecting that *this was how it all began*. These are not merely antiquarian documents telling a strange story about a powerful but now long-gone moment of history. They are the moment of sunrise on a new morning, casting a strange glory over the landscape and inviting all readers to wake up, rub the sleep from their eyes, and come out to enjoy the fully dawned day and give themselves to its tasks.

The sound from the third speaker is heard to particularly good effect—not least in relation to the first one—in Luke's story of the two disciples on the road to Emmaus:

> That very day, two of them were going to a village called Emmaus, which lay about seven miles from Jerusalem. They were discussing with each other all the various things that had taken place. As they were discussing, and arguing with each other, Jesus himself approached and walked with them. Their eyes, though, were prevented from recognizing him.
>
> "You're obviously having a very important discussion on your walk," he said; "what's it all about?"
>
> They stood still, a picture of gloom. Then one of them, Cleopas by name, answered him. "You must be the only person around Jerusalem," he said, "who doesn't know what's been going on there these last few days."
>
> "What things?" he asked.
>
> "To do with Jesus of Nazareth," they said to him. "He was a prophet. He acted with power and he spoke with power, before God and all the people. Our chief priests and rulers handed him over to be condemned to death, and they crucified him. But we were hoping that he was going to redeem Israel!
>
> "And now, what with all this, it's the third day since it happened. But some women from our group have astonished us. They went to his tomb very early this morning, and didn't find his body. They came back saying they'd

seen a vision of angels, who said he was alive. Some of
the folk with us went off to the tomb and found it just as
the women had said, but they didn't see *him*."

"You are so senseless!" he said to them. "So slow in
your hearts to believe all the things the prophets said
to you! Don't you see? This is what *had* to happen: the
Messiah had to suffer, and then come into his glory!"

So he began with Moses, and with all the prophets,
and explained to them the things about himself throughout the whole Bible.

They drew near to the village where they were heading. Jesus gave the impression that he was going further,
but they urged him strongly not to.

"Stay with us," they said. "It's nearly evening; the day
is almost gone." And he went in to stay with them.

As he was sitting at table with them he took the bread
and gave thanks. He broke it and gave it to them. Then
the eyes of both of them were opened, and they recognized him; and he vanished from their sight.

Then they said to each other, "Do you remember how
our hearts were burning inside us, as he talked to us on
the road, as he opened up the Bible for us?"

And they got up then and there and went back to
Jerusalem. There they found the eleven, and the people
with them, gathered together.

They were saying, "The Lord really has been raised!
He's appeared to Simon!" Then they told what had happened on the road, and how he was known to them in
the breaking of the bread. (24:13–35)

The story is full of echoes. Think, for instance, of Mary and
Joseph looking for Jesus in the Temple and finally finding him
about his father's business (2:41–52). "Didn't you know," says the
twelve-year-old boy, "that I would have to be getting involved

with my father's work?" (2:49). This sense of what *had to happen,* of Jesus's sense of a purpose to be fulfilled, is exactly echoed in his words to the two sad and puzzled disciples on the way to Emmaus: "Don't you see? This is what *had* to happen: the Messiah had to suffer, and then come into his glory!" (24:26). But the echoes go much farther back as well. Think of Genesis 3, where the first two humans ate the forbidden fruit and found that their eyes were opened, so that they knew their condition. Now this sad pair, heavy with the sorrow and shame of Jesus's death, pour out their tale of woe, only to be answered by a fresh reading of scripture and then, wonderfully, the moment of breaking bread in which "the eyes of both of them were opened, and they recognized him" (24:31).

Luke, telling the story, is keen that we should not miss the point. The one-time, unrepeatable moment will nevertheless serve as a paradigm, a template, for all subsequent Christian experience. He is telling the story of Jesus as the story of the launching of God's renewed people. The two disciples, in their excited astonishment, at once discuss the way in which this new exposition of the Bible caused their hearts to burn inside them, sending them back to Jerusalem to tell the others that he had been "known to them in the breaking of the bread" (21:35). A glance ahead at Acts 2:42 (where Luke highlights the marks of the church as "the teaching of the apostles and the common life, the breaking of bread and the prayers") will confirm what we had already guessed. Luke, telling the story of the Emmaus road from one point of view as a unique moment of extraordinary joy and revelation, is telling it from another point of view in such a way as to say that this resurrection appearance of Jesus sets the pattern for the way in which he will be known from now on. Again and again, he will come to surprise, comfort, and commission his puzzled and anxious followers through the opening of the scriptures and the breaking of the bread. Luke is telling the story of Jesus in such a way that his hearers are bound to reflect on these as the central features of the life of the community that celebrates Jesus as its risen Messiah and Lord.

When we ponder this, and the many other moments in all four gospels that have the same kind of effect, we realize that the scholars' instincts were in this way right on target: the four gospels were never meant as "historical reminiscence" for its own sake. Just because we are (in my view) right to insist that, in supporting and sustaining the life of the early church, the gospels are precisely telling the story of Jesus, we are not for that reason to swing the other way and imagine that their writers are not aware, constantly, of their task of writing foundational documents for God's renewed people. The gospels are, and were written to be, fresh tellings of the story of Jesus designed to be the charter of the community of Jesus's first followers and those who, through their witness, then and subsequently, have joined in and have learned to hear, see, and know Jesus in word and sacrament.

7

The Clash of the Kingdoms

S PEAKERS TWO AND THREE NEED, as we have seen, to be turned down a bit. Their volume has been too shrill over the past few generations, and we lose thereby not only the real music they are playing—the gospels really are telling the story of Jesus as the story of the God of Israel coming in human form, and they really are telling that story as the story of the launching of God's renewed people—but also the music from the other two speakers themselves, which have been drowned out, in some cases completely. This has not been helped by the fact that the fourth speaker has often not merely been turned down, but never switched on in the first place. Maybe, to extend the metaphor, it's even worse; maybe the speaker needs to be retrieved from its lonely spot in the attic, dusted off, put in its place, and plugged in. Many readers of the four gospels, it appears, have managed to ignore this element altogether. The fourth element in the music to which we must pay proper attention, along with everything else, is the story of Jesus told as *the story of the kingdom of God clashing with the kingdom of Caesar.*

God and Caesar

Before we explain, a word about the shadowy powers that stand behind even Caesar. The gospels are very much aware of the dark forces that ultimately owe their origin and strength to the power sometimes called "the satan," "the accuser." The gospel writers have plenty to say about those dark forces, that dark power. They are quite clear where the ultimate enemy lies. Jesus reminds us not to fear people who can kill merely the body, because there is a more dangerous power lurking behind (Matt. 10:28; Luke 12:4–5). We must never imagine that in dealing with "political" forces we have gotten to the heart of it. As we shall see, it is only when we take fully into account the gospel writers' belief that Jesus was involved in the ultimate battle against the ultimate forces of evil that we can begin to see how their combination of kingdom and cross—and, looking wider, of incarnation, kingdom, cross, and resurrection—makes sense.

But that doesn't mean that the conflict between God and Caesar is only relative or secondary. Unless we are prepared to factor this element into the story, we are one speaker short of full polyphony. We can be quite sure the gospel writers themselves had this element clearly in mind. The music from the first speaker always hinted at it: whenever Jews of the period told their story, one key element was always the question of how their God would deliver them from wicked and powerful pagan empires (echoing, of course, God's rescue of his people from Pharaoh's Egypt).

The music of the second speaker, when heard in proper balance with the first, made the same point: throughout the Old Testament Israel's God had shown himself to be more than a match for pagan rulers and authorities (the Egyptians, the Amalekites, the Philistines, the Assyrians; and think of the majestic revelation of Israel's God in Isaiah 40–55, set over against the silly little human-made gods of Babylon). If the story of Jesus was to be seen, somehow, as the story of Israel's God come in person, one would automatically assume that this element, of triumph over the nations and their gods, would play a significant role.

And the music we hear from the third speaker, the story of Jesus told as the story of the launching of God's renewed people, was being played out in a world where Caesar was Lord and didn't take kindly to other "lords" claiming a similar universal sovereignty. We can be sure that the first readers of the gospels would be listening eagerly for any telltale signs of how to navigate this new and dangerous situation. How did following Jesus relate to living in Caesar's empire?

God and the Powers in Jewish Tradition

Come back, for more detail, to the first of our four speakers. The entire story of Israel, on one level at least, is the story of how Israel's God is taking on the arrogant tyrants of the world, overthrowing their power, and rescuing his people from under its cruel weight. Think back quickly through the great stories. Here is Babel—ancient Babylon—building a tower. Ever since Cain's vain attempt to repair the damage of sin and murder by building a city (Gen. 4:17), that's what humans have done by way of organizing themselves, and doing so, as often as not, out of willful pride (Gen. 11:1–9). Humans, even after the disaster of Genesis 3, simply can't help planting gardens and creating communities; it's in their DNA as God's image-bearers. The problem is that they now do these things, and much else besides, with a fatal twist of self-serving arrogance, producing at best one parody after another of the ultimate Garden City, the new Jerusalem (Rev. 21–22). So at Babel God confuses their tongues; and he then begins, instead, in Genesis 12 the family through which all the nations will, after all, be blessed. What humans want to do by their own arrogance God will do by his own grace. The call of Abraham is God's answer to the arrogance of human power.

We next find Israel in Egypt, forced by Pharaoh to build other sorts of cities (Exod. 1:11), but then rescued by God in his mighty act of overthrowing the tyrant and bringing his people out through the shed blood of the lamb and the crossing of the sea. We jump forward swiftly to the sad sight of Israel under the heel of the Philistines, rescued by David's dramatic defeat of Goliath, and later not only of the Philistines, but also of other surrounding nations. Only then, once the pagan threat had been taken care of, was David's son Solomon able at last to provide a safe home for God's tabernacle in the city where God had promised to dwell. But the fatal twist in human nature reappears even in David and Solomon themselves, and much more in their descendants.

The strange climax (or perhaps we should say the anticlimax) of the ancient scriptural story sees the Jewish people in Babylon, back in Babel once more, unable to sing God's song in a strange land. The heart and thrust of the two great books that reflect that period, Isaiah 40–55 and Daniel—both, significantly, books on which the early Christians drew a great deal—is the clash of the kingdoms. In both cases the theme is the same: the kingdoms of the world versus the kingdom of the true God. Israel's God confronts the pagan idols and the petty princelings who worship them. They are at present lording it over God's people; but when God acts, as he will, he will show them in no uncertain terms that he is God and that they and their puny little human-made idols (and cities) are not. He will vindicate his people, rescuing them from their exile (Isa. 52; Dan. 9), exalting them to his right hand (Dan. 7), setting up a kingdom that cannot be shaken (Dan. 2), the true Davidic kingdom, which, built on the renewal of the covenant, will be nothing less than new creation (Isa. 54–55). In Isaiah this will be accomplished through the work of the "servant of the LORD"; in Daniel it will be accomplished through the suffering and faithfulness of God's people. It's the same story all the way through. And there is no doubt that this is the story the gospel writers intend, in their different ways, to retell in the basic story of Jesus himself.

Isaiah and Daniel do indeed provide something of a climax to this much larger narrative. But then, growing within that soil, we find all kinds of fresh plants: a continual stream of people, movements and, writings in the postbiblical period, up to and including the revolt of bar-Kochba in the 130s, that draw on and develop the same beliefs and hopes. It's not difficult to imagine the Judaean people, all the way through this period, singing psalms like Psalm 2, where the nations rage but God installs his king on Mount Zion and summons the nations to bow down before him:

> *Why do the nations conspire,*
>   *and the peoples plot in vain?*
> *The kings of the earth set themselves,*
>   *and the rulers take counsel together,*
> *against YHWH and his anointed, saying,*
> *"Let us burst their bonds asunder,*
>   *and cast their cords from us."*
>
> *He who sits in the heavens laughs;*
>   *YHWH has them in derision.*
> *Then he will speak to them in his wrath,*
>   *and terrify them in his fury, saying,*
> *"I have set my king on Zion, my holy hill."*
>
> *I will tell of the decree of YHWH:*
> *He said to me, "You are my son;*
>   *today I have begotten you.*
> *Ask of me, and I will make the nations your heritage,*
>   *and the ends of the earth your possession.*
> *You shall break them with a rod of iron,*
>   *and dash them in pieces like a potter's vessel."*

Now therefore, O kings, be wise;
  be warned, O rulers of the earth.
Serve YHWH *with fear,*
  with trembling kiss his feet,
or he will be angry, and you will perish in the way;
  for his wrath is quickly kindled.

Happy are all who take refuge in him.

It doesn't take a higher degree in ancient Jewish history to guess, accurately, what they would be thinking as they read Psalm 89, with its glorious vision of God's whole world ruled over by the Davidic king and its mystified sorrow at the way in which that hope seems to have been dashed yet again:

I will sing of your steadfast love, O YHWH, *forever;*
  with my mouth I will proclaim your faithfulness to all
    generations.
I declare that your steadfast love is established forever;
  your faithfulness is as firm as the heavens.
You said, "I have made a covenant with my chosen one,
  I have sworn to my servant David:
'I will establish your descendants forever,
  and build your throne for all generations.'"

Then you spoke in a vision to your faithful one, and said:
  "I have set the crown on one who is mighty,
  I have exalted one chosen from the people.
I have found my servant David;
  with my holy oil I have anointed him;
my hand shall always remain with him;
  my arm also shall strengthen him.
The enemy shall not outwit him,
  the wicked shall not humble him.

I will crush his foes before him
  and strike down those who hate him.
My faithfulness and steadfast love shall be with him;
  and in my name his horn shall be exalted.
I will set his hand on the sea
  and his right hand on the rivers.
He shall cry to me, 'You are my Father,
  my God, and the Rock of my salvation!'
I will make him the firstborn,
  the highest of the kings of the earth.
Forever I will keep my steadfast love for him,
  and my covenant with him will stand firm.
I will establish his line forever,
  and his throne as long as the heavens endure. . . .

His line shall continue forever,
  and his throne endure before me like the sun.
It shall be established forever like the moon,
  an enduring witness in the skies."

But now you have spurned and rejected him;
  you are full of wrath against your anointed.
You have renounced the covenant with your servant;
  you have defiled his crown in the dust.
You have broken through all his walls;
  you have laid his strongholds in ruins.
All who pass by plunder him;
  he has become the scorn of his neighbors.
You have exalted the right hand of his foes;
  you have made all his enemies rejoice. . . .

How long, O YHWH? *Will you hide yourself forever?*
  How long will your wrath burn like fire? . . .

Lord, where is your steadfast love of old,
  which by your faithfulness you swore to David?
Remember, O Lord, how your servant is taunted;
  how I bear in my bosom the insults of the peoples,
with which your enemies taunt, O YHWH,
  with which they taunted the footsteps of your anointed.
  (89:1–4, 19–29, 36–42, 46–51)

But the hope persists, and psalm after psalm brings it to expression. The gods of the nations are but idols, but Israel's God made the heavens. God reigns over the nations, God sits on his holy seat; the princes of the people gather as the people of the God of Abraham, who has subdued peoples and nations. God has established his city, and the powers of wicked pagans will not prevail against it. Again and again it comes, shaping the hearts and imaginations of God's people even in the many centuries when these songs of praise and triumph bore no relation to the sociopolitical reality in which they were living. This is the world in which we are to hear what the gospels are trying to tell us about the story of Jesus seen as the focal point of the story of God and Caesar.

God and Caesar in the Gospels

But, you say, surely Caesar is only mentioned once in the gospels, and there Jesus says that there's a clear division between God and Caesar, a split of church and state, so that never the twain shall meet. Well, not so fast. We'll get to that. It sounds suspiciously modern. Did Jesus really anticipate post-Enlightenment Western ideology so exactly? And the objection is forgetting, in any case, the wonderful passage in John 18–19 (to which also we shall return), in which Jesus, representing God's kingdom, confronts Pilate, representing Caesar's. They go at it together, arguing about kingdom, truth, and power until Pilate proves Jesus's point by having him executed with the words "King of the Jews" above his head. And once we recognize that confrontation for what it is—part of the very climax of John's astonishing gospel—there is more. Much more.

But I would rather begin at the beginning, the beginning of Luke's gospel (not least because Luke, quite wrongly, is often supposed to have been uncritically friendly toward Rome). After his opening chapter, which evokes the opening of 1 Samuel—and thereby already reminds his hearers of the long story that eventually led to Samuel anointing David as king and David defeating the Philistines—Luke begins again, as it were, in chapter 2, by declaring portentously that a decree went out from Caesar Augustus that all the world should be registered for the purpose of taxation:

> At that time a decree was issued by Augustus Caesar:
> a census was to be taken of the whole world. . . . So
> everyone set off to be registered, each to their own
> town. Joseph too, who belonged to the house and family
> of David, went from the city of Nazareth in Galilee to
> Bethlehem in Judaea, David's city, to be registered with
> his fiancée Mary, who was pregnant. (2:1–5)

A census! Everyone in Palestine knew what *that* meant. It meant not only that the people were going to have to pay up, but that they were being enlisted as subject members in a kingdom ruled by a foreign power. Not for nothing does Josephus tell those stories about the revolutionary movements that arose spontaneously because of the various censuses the Romans took and about the numerous violent deaths that followed:

> But a certain Judas, a Gaulanite from a city named Ga-
> mala, who had enlisted the aid of Saddok, a Pharisee,
> threw himself into the cause of rebellion. They said that
> the assessment [i.e., the census] carried with it a status

amounting to downright slavery, no less, and appealed to
the nation to make a bid for independence. . . .

They have a passion for liberty that is almost uncon-
querable, since they are convinced that God alone is their
leader and master. They think little of submitting to
death in unusual forms and permitting vengeance to fall
on kinsmen and friends if only they may avoid calling
any man master. . . . I have no fear that anything reported of them will be considered incredible. The danger
is, rather, that report may minimize the indifference
with which they accept the grinding misery of pain.*

We should also remember that when Luke narrates how the
chief priests went to Pilate to bring charges against Jesus, one of
the key things they said, untruthfully of course, was that he had
been forbidding people to give tribute to Caesar:

The whole crowd of them got up and took Jesus to
Pilate.

They began to accuse him. "We found this fellow,"
they said, "deceiving our nation! He was forbidding
people to give tribute to Caesar, and saying that he is the
Messiah—a king!" (23:1–2)

The opening of Luke 2, in other words, isn't simply a chronological note or a bit of incidental history. Augustus, at the height
of his power and glory in Rome, signs a decree, and far away, off
at the other end of his empire, a baby is born in the place where
David's son ought to be born. Augustus's signature on the decree
was Rome signing the ultimate death warrant for its classic pagan
power. We should not be surprised when, at the end of Luke's
second volume, we find Paul in Rome, announcing God as king
and Jesus as Lord right under Caesar's nose "with all boldness

---

*Josephus, *Jewish Antiquities*, 18.4, 23–24, trans. L. H. Feldman, Loeb Classical Library.

and with no one stopping him" (Acts 28:31). Luke intends that to be the fulfillment, albeit in a new sense, of the ancient dream of God's people, the dream that went back to Samuel and David and beyond. One day, one day, the nations would be summoned to pay allegiance to great David's greater Son. And the fulfillment of Israel's ancient dream would always involve the overthrow, at least by implication, of the pagan power that had exalted itself, like Babel, against the creator God.

We could go on about Luke, but we find equivalent features in Matthew and Mark. For Matthew, ever conscious of the immediate Jewish surroundings, it is the Herod family who loom darkly on the horizon. Matthew's equivalent of the opening of Luke 2 is the start of his second chapter, where Herod the Great, nearing the end of his increasingly paranoid reign, receives an unexpected and unwelcome visit from eastern sages who claim that the stars are proclaiming the birth of the Jews' rightful king. Herod's instant suspicions and subsequent overreaction indicate well enough the way that pagan power always behaves when confronted with news of the true God and the true king. His son, Herod Antipas, then looms over Jesus's public career, killing his cousin John and providing the threatening backdrop for Jesus's own (implicitly messianic) work (11:1–14; 14:1–12).

This points forward to the larger power, Rome itself, which will close in at the end, only to be symbolically overthrown as the Roman guards at the tomb fail to prevent Jesus's resurrection. Luke has Herod in Jerusalem at this time as well, in league at last with Pontius Pilate (23:1–12). The sense is the same: the powers of the world are waiting there, in the wings, mostly offstage, but ready to pounce at a moment's notice. If this really is the story of God's kingdom arriving on earth as in heaven, sooner or later there will be a confrontation. Again, it doesn't take a Ph.D. in political psychology to know what the world's powers will do to those who act and speak to bring about God's kingdom. As well as all the other elements in the gospel story, we must recognize this for what it is, a telling of the story of Jesus as the clash between the kingdom of God and the kingdoms of the world.

Mark is a bit sharper, perhaps more obvious. We might highlight the response Jesus gives to James and John in the famous passage in chapter 10:

> James and John, Zebedee's sons, came up to him.
>
> "Teacher," they said, "we want you to grant us whatever we ask."
>
> "What do you want me to do for you?" asked Jesus.
>
> "Grant us," they said, "that when you're there in all your glory, one of us will sit at your right, and the other at your left."
>
> "You don't know what you're asking for!" Jesus replied. "Can you drink the cup I'm going to drink? Can you receive the baptism I'm going to receive?"
>
> "Yes," they said, "we can."
>
> Well," said Jesus, "you will drink the cup I drink; you will receive the baptism I receive. But sitting at my right hand or my left—that's not up to me. It's been assigned already."
>
> When the other ten disciples heard, they were angry with James and John. Jesus called them to him.
>
> "You know how it is in the pagan nations," he said. "Think how their so-called rulers act. They lord it over their subjects. The high and mighty ones boss the rest around. But that's not how it's going to be with you. Anyone who wants to be great among you must become your servant. Anyone who wants to be first must be everyone's slave. Don't you see? The son of man didn't come to be waited on. He came to be the servant, to give his life 'as a ransom for many.'" (10:35–45)

There it is. The kings of the earth exercise power one way, by lording it over their subjects, but Jesus's followers are going to do it the other way, the way of the servant. You might almost think Mark thought Jesus had been reading Isaiah 40–55, where the "servant of the LORD" and his shameful death are the means by which, somehow, the gods and rulers of Babylon are overthrown, Israel is rescued, and God himself returns to Zion to renew not only the covenant, but the whole creation. And Mark (followed by Matthew) also highlights Jesus's words about the vindication of the "son of man," which by its evocation of the whole narrative of the book of Daniel declares, as powerfully as any statement to a scripture-soaked audience could do, that, despite present suffering and disappointment, Israel's God is indeed going to take his seat and, in vindicating the one who represents his suffering people, pass judgment on the monsters, the pagan powers, that have arrogantly taken charge of the world.

There is, in other words, a clear line all the way from Genesis 11, via Isaiah 40–55 and Daniel 7, to Mark 10, and thereby in turn to Mark 14–15, where Jesus meets his captors, his judges, and his death. He not only theorizes about the difference between pagan power and the kind of power he is claiming; he enacts it. The passage just quoted is not a "political" statement (about different types of power) followed by an "atonement" statement (about how sins would be forgiven), as though the two were entirely separate things. As we shall see in the next part of the book, when we put together "kingdom" and "cross" in a way few readers of the gospels have even tried to do, Jesus establishes the new kind of power—God's kingdom as opposed to Caesar's, on earth as in heaven—precisely through his (scripturally interpreted) death. And, to put it the other way around, God rescues his people from their sins, through the work of the Isaianic "servant," precisely in order to establish his rule, his own very different kind of power, in all the world.

It should already be clear from this that the music we are now hearing from the fourth speaker harmonizes very well indeed with the music we heard from the first (the story of Israel). Indeed, once we understand that, we may also glimpse one possible reason why both have been turned down so low or even off altogether. If this story of Jesus is the story of Israel reaching its climax, it is inescapably political and will raise questions the Western world has chosen not to raise, let alone face, throughout the period of so-called critical scholarship. The post-Enlightenment world was born out of a movement that split church and state apart and has arranged even its would-be historical scholarship accordingly; and that same Enlightenment insisted that Judaism was the wrong kind of religion, far too gross, too material. Rejection, from the start, of a "political" reading of the gospels and of a "Jewish" reading went together. Fortunately, genuine history—the actual study of the actual sources—can sometimes strike back and insist that what a previous generation turned off this generation can at last turn back on. It is time, and long past time, to reread the gospels as what we can only call political theology—not because they are not after all about God and spirituality and new birth and holiness and all the rest, but precisely because they are.

What, then, about John? There is a whole book to be written on the implicit and sometimes explicit undermining of Caesar's empire in John's gospel. But for the moment we can at least say this. In the midst of the dozens of other major Johannine themes, we begin to hear in chapter 12 a note of where it's all going. Some Greeks come to the festival and ask to see Jesus, and Jesus, to our surprise, speaks about a grain of wheat that will fall into the earth and, dying, bear much fruit:

> Some Greeks had come up with all the others to wor-
> ship at the festival. They went to Philip, who was from
> Bethsaida in Galilee.
> "Sir," they said, "we would like to see Jesus."

Philip went and told Andrew, and Andrew and Philip went together to tell Jesus.

"The time has come," said Jesus in reply. "This is the moment for the son of man to be glorified. I'm telling you the solemn truth: unless a grain of wheat falls into the earth and dies, it remains all by itself. If it dies, though, it will produce lots of fruit." (12:20–24)

The scene then gains an extra dramatic element when Jesus prays that God will glorify God's name, and the crowds think they hear thunder in reply:

"I have glorified it," came a voice from heaven, "and I will glorify it again."

"That was thunder!" said the crowd, standing there listening.

"No," said others. "It was an angel, talking to him."

"That voice came for your sake, not mine," replied Jesus. "Now comes the judgment of this world! Now this world's ruler is going to be thrown out! And when I've been lifted up from the earth, I will draw all people to myself."

He said this in order to point to the kind of death he was going to die. (12:28–33)

Here we have a very similar train of thought to the one we just observed in Mark 10. The world's rulers and the way the world's rulers rule are going to be overthrown, and the result will be, through the death of Jesus, that people from all over the world will be drawn to Jesus himself. Here is the answer—a bit late, we might think, but that is how John's gospel often works!—to the question asked by the Greeks. Jesus is no mere tourist attraction for pilgrims to come and gawk at. Jesus is to be the true world ruler, dismissing all other pretenders with a wave of the hand and inviting people from all over the world to come to him and find new life. But for that to happen he must first overcome the present ruler of the world. The Greek's request, in other words, is taken by Jesus himself as a sign that the age-old messianic dream of the Psalms and the prophets is starting to come true. The powers that have ruled the world are being overthrown, and Jesus's death, the strange means by which that victory will be accomplished, will therefore be the means by which the world is drawn to him, and so to the one true God.

How will this come about? The "accuser," working through Judas, will draw the enemy fire onto Jesus (John 13:2, 27). But that, strangely, seems to be part of the plan. Jesus knows what's coming and declares twice, in the Farewell Discourses (John 13–17), that he is winning the victory. The first of these is brief and to the point:

> "I haven't got much more to say to you. The ruler of the world is coming. He has nothing to do with me. But all this is happening so that the world may know that I love the father, and that I'm doing what the father has told me to do." (14:30–31).

In other words, Jesus's followers are to understand the horrible events of the next twenty-four hours as the battle reaching its height, a battle with the real enemy who is working through the treachery of Judas and the callous power of Rome. And they are to understand Jesus's involvement in this battle, up to and including his apparent losing of it, as under the hitherto unimagined command of the one Jesus refers to as "father." Once again, Jesus's embrace of the hideous vocation to die on a cross is seen as the overthrow of the world's powers, the world's way of power.

This, no doubt, will already take many modern Western Christians way outside their normal backyard. But there is more. In chapter 16, Jesus declares that when the "helper" comes, the "spirit of truth" of whom he has been speaking, this Spirit will have an extraordinary, complex, and dangerous-sounding task to perform. The Spirit, says Jesus, "will prove the world to be in the wrong on three counts: sin, justice, and judgment" (16:8). Jesus goes on to explain each of these—though the explanations themselves will leave many readers today equally puzzled by the dense, almost cryptic way he says it:

> "In relation to sin—because they don't believe in me. In relation to justice—because I'm going to the father, and you won't see me anymore. In relation to judgment—because the ruler of this world is judged." (16:9–11)

We can perhaps add our own brief further explanations. First, the world (which includes, tragically, most of Jesus's fellow Jews at the time) doesn't believe in Jesus. It is therefore heading off on the wrong track, missing the mark. The technical term for that is "sin." Second, Jesus is going to be vindicated, dramatically proven to be in the right. This will be God's great act of "justice," putting everything right and so showing up the injustice, the not putting right or the active putting wrong, of the rest of the world. The world, in other words, is deeply and radically out of joint, with all sorts of things going wrong; God will put it all right. Third, God will pass a sentence of condemnation on the "ruler of this world" ("judgment").

How will all this happen? Through the work of the Spirit, whom Jesus is promising to send to his disciples. In other words, it will happen *through the Spirit-led work of Jesus's followers*. This is another place where the third speaker is heard (the story of God's renewed people), its music balancing the fourth one to which we are currently paying attention. John is telling the story of Jesus in such a way as to show how its implicit confrontation between God's kingdom and Caesar's kingdom (speaker four) will be played out in the explicit life and witness of Jesus's followers (speaker three).

These are vital strands of what John is doing throughout his gospel. When, after the final prayer (chap. 17) and the arrest and the Jewish trial (18:1–27), we find Jesus standing before Pilate (18:28–19:16), we ought to know, because John has set it up, what is actually going on. This is the point at which the ruler of the world is being judged. Caesar's kingdom will do what Caesar's kingdom always does, but this time God's kingdom will win the decisive victory.

Jesus explains (18:36) that his kingdom is not the sort that grows in this world. His kingdom is certainly *for* this world, but it isn't *from* it. It comes from somewhere else—in other words, from above, from heaven, from God. It is God's gift to his world, but, as John already pointed out in the prologue, the world isn't ready for this gift. The key is this: if Jesus's kingdom were the regular sort, the kind that grows all too easily in the present world—the sort of kingdom, in fact, that James and John had wanted!—then Jesus's followers would be taking up arms:

> "If my kingdom were from this world, my support-
> ers would have fought to stop me being handed over to
> the Judaeans. So then, my kingdom is not the sort that
> comes from here." (18:36)

The difference between the kingdoms is striking. Caesar's kingdom (and all other kingdoms that originate in this world) make their way by fighting. But Jesus's kingdom—God's king-dom enacted through Jesus—makes its way with quite a different weapon, one that Pilate refuses to acknowledge: telling the truth:

> "So!" said Pilate. "You *are* a king, are you?"
> "You're the one who's calling me a king," replied
> Jesus. "I was born for this; I've come into the world for
> this: to give evidence about the truth. Everyone who
> belongs to the truth listens to my voice."
> "Truth!" said Pilate. "What's that?" (18:37–38)

The point about truth, and about Jesus and his followers bearing witness to it, is that truth is what happens when humans use words to reflect God's wise ordering of the world and so shine light into its dark corners, bringing judgment and mercy where it is badly needed. Empires can't cope with this. They make their own "truth," creating "facts on the ground" in the depressingly normal way of violence and injustice. Pilate's cynical retort leads to another exchange with the crowd, who ask for Barabbas (18:40). Pilate's soldiers dress Jesus up as a king in order to mock him; the sight of him thus attired provokes the chief priests to make fresh demands for his death and to offer a fresh twist in the accusation: "He deserves to die," because "he made himself the son of God" (19:7).

This prompts a new set of questions from Pilate. "Son of God" in his world, of course, meant Caesar; but he seems to sense that there may be a different sort of claim going on. It brings up the question of power: the Greek is *exousia,* which carries the notion of "authority" or "right," as in the prologue where John says that those who believed in Jesus were given the *exousia* ("right," "power," or "authority") to become God's children (1:12). Here we find an astonishing thing: Jesus recognizes that Pilate has power over him, power given him from God:

> Pilate addressed him again.
>
> "Aren't you going to speak to me?" he said. "Don't you know that I have the authority to let you go, and the authority to crucify you?"
>
> "You couldn't have any authority at all over me," replied Jesus, "unless it was given to you from above. That's why the person who handed me over to you is guilty of a greater sin." (19:10–11)

Even the rule of Caesar and his subordinates, it seems, has its place within the larger providence of God; the only sense we can make of this is the standard Jewish sense that God, as creator, intends his world to be looked after by humans, and that even when the humans who are supposed to be exercising that vocation are self-serving brutes, the mandate still stands, though they will be judged more severely for what they have done with their commission. Jesus's affirmation of Pilate's subordinate but God-given authority is of course itself related to his sense that God is in overall control of the process now under way. This is the way by which the rulers of the world will overreach themselves and, doing their worst, be overthrown by the triumphing power of God's creative love.

And it is at this point that the Judaean leaders make their final double move. Like their forebears in 1 Samuel 8:4, 20, they want to be "like the nations." They want to be part of Caesar's empire. They have grown tired of waiting for the "son of man" to be vindicated and will cut a deal with the fourth monster. They have glimpsed the servant vocation held out to Israel and are content to accept the rule of Babylon. Jesus came to his own, and his own didn't want to know him. "If you let this fellow go," they say, "you are no friend of Caesar" (19:12). And when Pilate challenges them one more time about whether he should, after all, crucify "their king," they answer, chillingly, with the words that exactly reverse the ancient Jewish dream of God's kingdom. Instead of "no king but God," they sell their birthright for a mess of imperial pottage. "We have no king," they reply, "except Caesar" (19:15).

And so Jesus goes to his death, with the royal claim above his head: "JESUS OF NAZARETH, THE KING OF THE JEWS" (19:19). Pilate knew it was provocative, but went ahead. From his point of view, it was a slap in the face for the Judaean rulers as well as additional mocking of the utterly unkinglike Jesus. But from John's point of view this means that Pilate, like Caiaphas eight chapters before (11:49–53), is saying far more than he knows. Jesus is enthroned as king of the Jews, and from now on he is also king of the world.

The cross in John, which we already know to be the fullest unveiling of God's, and Jesus's, love (13:1), is also the moment when God takes his power and reigns over Caesar. From now on, the ruler of this world is judged.

This great scene, to which we shall return in more detail, summarizes the dimension we begin to hear in the music when we have turned the fourth speaker up to its proper volume, so that all four are balanced. But what then did Jesus mean in that strange but world-famous little saying about rendering unto Caesar what is Caesar's and unto God what is God's?

Render unto Caesar?

All three synoptic gospels record Jesus's short exchange on the subject of paying tribute to Caesar. Here is Mark's version (Matt. 22:15–22 and Luke 20:20–36 have more explanatory detail):

> They sent some Pharisees to Jesus, and some Herodians, to try to trick him into saying the wrong thing.
>
> "Teacher," they said, "we know you are a man of integrity; you don't regard anybody as special. You don't bother about the outward show people put up; you teach God's way truly.
>
> "Well then: is it lawful to give tribute to Caesar or not? Should we pay it, or shouldn't we?"
>
> He knew the game they were playing. "Why are you trying to trap me?" he said. "Bring me a tribute-coin; let me look at it."
>
> They brought one to him.
>
> "This image," he asked, "whose is it? And whose is this superscription?"
>
> "Caesar's," they replied.

"Well then," said Jesus, "give Caesar back what belongs to Caesar—and give God back what belongs to
God!"

They were astonished at him. (12:13–17)

The saying about Caesar and God presents a famous puzzle. For
those who have not been able to recognize any other "political"
allusion throughout the gospel story (showing that our fourth
speaker has indeed been unplugged), this constitutes "Jesus's
teaching on church and state." And that "teaching" is taken to
be that they are two distinct spheres, to each of which Jesus's
followers must give their due, in quite separate compartments of
life, without confusing the two. I think it is safe to say that nobody until the late eighteenth century ever took it like that; in
other words, we are hearing in that interpretation the echo of a
very different set of voices, those of the European and American
Enlightenment and the theory of "church and state" that they
developed. In that theory, "religion" and "politics" are simply
two quite different sides of life; one must not bring the one into
the other. This is trotted out by those who write angry letters to
the newspapers every time somebody from the church ventures
a comment on a political question. "Stick to your own patch,"
we are told. "Jesus separated Caesar and God and so should you."
But within Jesus's own world the echoes would have been very
different.

For a start, there is no question about this being a set piece
of "teaching" on a particular "topic." Jesus is faced with an extremely dangerous question. Everybody knows that he is leading
a kingdom-of-God movement. In his day, in Palestinian Judaism,
that meant political independence; and political independence
meant, beyond a doubt, no longer being under Caesar's heel.
People had been crucified, in living memory, for staging antitax
rebellions. Jesus's accusers, as we saw, tried to pin the same charge
on him (Luke 23:2).

No doubt many of his hearers were hoping that he was going to lend his powerful support to their anti-Roman revolution. No doubt too many of his opponents were rather hoping he *would* come out and declare himself on the subject; it would give them just the ammunition they wanted. (Interestingly, in Mark's telling of the incident, it was a combination of Pharisees and Herodians who came together with the trick question, the same combination that Mark observes in a much earlier plot in 3:6.) Perhaps, at the same time, the hard-line independence movements were already regarding Jesus as a bit too soft, not revolutionary enough. This question would smoke him out one way or another.

But when you are faced with a potentially hostile crowd, it is no time for nuanced, balanced teaching. It's time for a one-liner. They show Jesus a coin. He asks the obvious question, with its obvious hint of criticism: whose is this *image* (Jews weren't supposed to use or possess "images" of human beings), and whose is this *inscription* (declaring Caesar to be "son of god" and "chief priest"—how blasphemous can you get?)? "Caesar's," comes the reply. Already the tables are half turned. Jesus sounds as though he's taking the hard line: "What are you doing with this horrible stuff in your purses?" But then comes the short, double command, which in context has nothing to do with a church-state split and everything to do with the fact that God trumps Caesar on all fronts.

When I translated the New Testament, I didn't quite have the courage to let this verse say what I suspect it says: "So, you'd better *pay Caesar back in his own coin*—and pay *God* back in *his* own coin!" This saying would then echo a saying that had already become famous in Jewish circles following the Maccabean revolt two centuries earlier. "Pay back the Gentiles in full," said old Mattathias to Judas Maccabeus and his brothers, "and obey the commands of the law" (1 Macc. 2:68). And he wasn't telling them to pay the Gentile taxes. The Greek in question uses the same root word for "pay back," *antapodote,* cognate with the *apodote* we find in all three synoptic gospels at this point. I suspect that Mattathias's double command may already have been proverbial. Jesus may well have been deliberately echoing it.

His one-liner was, of course, a trick. Some have speculated, guessing rightly that the context demanded a bit of street theater, that Jesus, borrowing a coin, may have performed some friendly sleight of hand, perhaps even pretending to make the coin disappear. That's not important. What is important is that the quizzical saying, highlighted by Matthew, Mark, and Luke alike, indicates that Jesus is refusing to collude either with the pro-Roman party in Jerusalem or with the would-be violent revolutionaries. His comment can be taken either way. And that's not just a trick. It's a way (almost like a Buddhist koan, certainly like his parables) of breaking open the either/or in which his hearers were stuck and pointing toward a deeper reality. Perhaps it's time for God— whose image is on every human being and whose "inscription" is written across the pages of creation and the story of Israel—to receive his due.

This is the message of God's kingdom, all right, but it doesn't play out in either of the obvious, simplistic ways, either as an "otherworldly" kingdom completely separate from that of Caesar or as a straightforward, old-fashioned violent revolution. For Matthew, Mark, and Luke the story is one of the key pointers, following Jesus's triumphal entry into Jerusalem and prior to his arrest and death, to what is "going on" throughout: this is the story of how God truly became king, as Jesus offered back to God what was his own, in his obedient suffering and death. And within the new world that was thereby created, the question of Caesar, his power, and his coins looks completely different. There may be a time for confrontation; there may be a time for appropriate collaboration. But all is to be done within the bounds of God's kingdom. It cannot be otherwise. That kingdom is universal, all-present, and all-powerful. That is, after all, the message of all four gospels, and once we have turned all four speakers to their proper volume, we will not be able to miss the challenge they presented in the first century and could perhaps present again in the twenty-first.

The Four Speakers Together

What can we say, at the conclusion of this second part of the book, about these four speakers and about the music that the gospels want us to hear when all four speakers are properly adjusted?

Let me point out one feature of what we have seen in this second part. Think back to the story of the exodus in its many elements. All first-century Jews knew this story well, just as most twenty-first century Jews do, because it was and is celebrated in song and symbol every Passover. The New Testament is full of echoes of the exodus, either as a whole or in this or that feature. Listen to the way this emerges when we adjust the volume on the speakers and pay attention to the full music of the four gospels.

From the first speaker, the long narrative of Israel, we hear of the exodus in terms of rescue and journeying. The people celebrate God's liberation, but they then wander for forty years through the wilderness before reaching their promised land. The long narrative, say the evangelists, has come to an end, a goal. Here, with John the Baptist down by the Jordan, we discover that this is where it was all going all along. It is time for the promises to be fulfilled. In the original exodus, they were fulfilled by Joshua (Yeshua in Hebrew) leading the people across the river and into their new territory. Now here is Jesus (Yeshua) doing the same.

During the exodus, according to the second speaker, the story of YHWH, Israel's God, the living God reveals his identity to his people in a new way, and then goes with them on their journey, in the pillar of cloud by day and fire by night. Their idolatry very nearly makes him withdraw from them, but then, in response to Moses's intercession, he consents to go with them after all and ultimately to dwell in the Temple in Jerusalem. The second speaker tells us (if we learn to listen to it) that in Jesus the living God has once again come into the midst of his people in person. Jesus has dramatically upstaged the Temple as the place where God now dwells. This is the fulfillment of Isaiah's vision of the returning glory of God. This is the fulfillment of Ezekiel's promise of the restored Temple. And this time God in person takes the weight of the people's sin and rebellion upon himself.

The third speaker, the gospel story as the story of the renewed people of God, reminds us of two other elements of the exodus story: Israel's vocation to be the royal priesthood (Exod. 19:5–6) and the gift of the Torah, through which that vocation might become a reality. When we listen to the story with the speaker properly adjusted, we hear at last the gospels describing Jesus as not only a great moral teacher, but as the one who gives to God's people their new vocation and way of life. The gospel story, and the teaching of Jesus within it, is not simply a new "Torah," as though replacing the old one with a new one. The whole situation is now different. Jesus's way of life, and the renewed heart that he promises goes with it, partake already of the new creation, which enables this people to be God's people indeed.

When, thinking of the exodus, we read the gospels with the fourth speaker adjusted properly, we are reminded of God's dark and solemn victory over Pharaoh, first in the plagues and then in the Red Sea. The story of the exodus is of course an exciting, dramatic rescue operation. When you relive it at a Passover celebration, you tend to identify with the people as they dream of freedom while living under a cruel regime, as they begin to dare to hope for it when Moses confronts Pharaoh, as they start to taste it when the plagues fall on Egypt and they are allowed to leave, as they experience it vividly in the crossing of the Red Sea—and then as they find that freedom poses its own new challenges in the wilderness. But with all this we are still focusing, naturally enough, on the experience of the people. Behind this, underneath this, is the deeper and darker story that makes sense of it all. The powers of this world exalt themselves against the creator God, the God of Israel, and God will not be mocked forever. The kingdoms of this world are to become the kingdom of our God, and he will reign forever and ever. The story of the exodus is the story of "how God became king." That is what Moses and the Israelites sang about after the Red Sea had returned to drown the pursuing imperial army:

> *I will sing to YHWH, for he has triumphed gloriously;*
>   *Horse and rider he has thrown into the sea.*
> *YHWH is my strength and my might,*
>   *And he has become my salvation.*
> *This is my God, and I will praise him,*
>   *My father's God, and I will exalt him.*
> *YHWH is a warrior;*
>   *YHWH is his name. . . .*
> *YHWH will reign for ever and ever. (Exod. 15:1–3, 18)*

The four gospel writers, each in his own way, tell the story of Jesus as the story of the new and ultimate exodus. What our present fourfold exercise has done is to draw out the various dimensions of that new exodus and to highlight their significance.

The gospels all insist that it was Jesus's own choice to make Passover the moment for his decisive action. This, they are saying, was his own chosen grid of interpretation. And all four gospels together, once we have learned to listen to their four dimensions, bequeath to Jesus's followers the task of being the people in and through whom the achievement of Jesus is implemented in the world. That is why the story told by the gospels is not only incomplete without two millennia of backdrop (the story of ancient Israel), which they assume we will know and which we in our generation often have to supply with considerable pedagogic effort. The story is also incomplete because it points forward to a future yet to come. "What's that got to do with you?" Jesus asks

Peter when he inquired about someone else's future. "You must follow me" (John 21:22). John's gospel ends, as they all do, with a forward look; and it is that forward look to which we shall return presently.

Before then, however, we must, in Part III of this book, bring together the threads of our argument as we look at the central challenge posed by the gospel, the dramatic and explosive combination of the kingdom and the cross.

PART THREE

The Kingdom
and the Cross

8

Where We Get Stuck

Enlightenment, Power, and Empire

W E ARE NOW APPROACHING the heart of the four gospels, the dense and complex center of their world of meaning. We should allow ourselves, on a regular basis, to be struck anew by the thick, rich, multilayered nature of these four documents, so full of vivid human scenes, but so evocative in their resonance of meaning about the world, God, life and death, and pretty much everything else. As I read the gospels and think what the church has done (and hasn't done) with them, I am reminded of a wonderful scene in Peter Shaffer's play *Amadeus*. There, the cynical old court composer Salieri contrasts his own operas, telling and retelling great tales of legendary heroes but through stale and tedious music, with Mozart's astonishing ability to take characters off the street and create something truly magical. "He has taken ordinary people," says Salieri, "ordinary people—barbers and chambermaids—and he has made them gods and heroes. I have taken gods and heroes . . . *and made them ordinary.*"

Making the Gospels Ordinary

Near the heart of my purpose in this book is to suggest that not only have we misread the gospels, but that *we have made them ordinary,* have cut them down to size, have allowed them only to speak about the few concerns that happened to occupy our minds already, rather than setting them free to generate an entire world of meaning in all directions, a new world in which we would discover not only new life, but new vocation.

It is not easy to escape the trap of "making the gospels ordinary." There are habits of thought and of the practice of the church (some lectionaries, for instance) that are so ingrained that we don't realize they're there. But habits of thought, especially when we are not aware of them, have the capacity to keep us imprisoned in small-minded readings unless we name them, smoke them out of their hiding places, set them aside, and take steps to prevent their return. This chapter is, in one sense, a digression, because in it we turn aside to examine these habits, these patterns of thought and imagination, so that we can at least reduce their powerful influence. Only then can we return to the gospels themselves with some hope of seeing more clearly what they are actually saying.

The gospels are telling us that the whole story belongs together: the kingdom and the cross are part of one another (and both, together, are part of the larger whole that includes incarnation, on the one hand, and resurrection, on the other). We have become stuck in habits of thought that pull these apart. Once you lose the kingdom theme, which is central to the gospels, everything else becomes reinterpreted in ways that radically distort, that substitute a subtly different "gospel" message for the one Matthew, Mark, Luke, and John are eager to convey. We must address and, it is hoped, break the bad habits of thought before we can proceed to read the gospels for all they're worth.

The Separation of Kingdom and Cross

To begin with, we must recognize that the four gospels effortlessly draw together, into a rich unity, many things that later tradition split apart. I don't just mean the point I made in the first part of the book, that we have allowed the creedal content, Jesus's birth, death, and resurrection, to drown out the message of the kingdom, or in some cases vice versa. That split comes out in the title of this third part of the book, "The Kingdom and the Cross."

We have lived for many years now with "kingdom Christians" and "cross Christians" in opposite corners of the room, anxious that those on the other side are missing the point, the one group with its social-gospel agenda and the other with its saving-souls-for-heaven agenda. The four gospels bring these two viewpoints together into a unity that is much greater than the sum of their parts, and that is mostly what Part III is about. In fact, what we call "politics" and what we call "religion" (and for that matter what we call "culture," "philosophy," "theology," and lots of other things besides) were not experienced or thought of in the first century as separable entities. This was just as true, actually, for the Greeks and the Romans as it was for the Jews.

Here's an obvious example. I wrote in my book *Evil and the Justice of God** about the way in which what modern philosophers call the "problem of evil" has been split off from what modern theologians think of as the "atonement"—as though the cross of Jesus were not, in the New Testament, God's ultimate answer to the "problem of evil." We have allowed "atonement" to be narrowed down to "forgiving sins so people can go to heaven," leaving unaddressed the (to us quite different) problem of "evil" as an abstract thing. That was a dangerous mistake. What then happened was that when something unmistakably "evil" happened

---

Evil and the Justice of God (Downers Grove, IL: InterVarsity, 2006).

in our comfortable Western world—I'm thinking of course of September 11, 2001—our politicians reacted as though they could "solve" this new (political) "problem of evil" by dropping bombs on it.

That kind of dangerous naïveté could only have arisen when theology, philosophy, and politics had become detached from one another. We should know by now that this simply won't do, but because we haven't got an alternative framework to offer, we seem unable to break out of the trap. We still seem to think that bombs and bullets can deal with "evil," liberating people who, once the "evil" has been thus obliterated, will turn out to be nice liberal Western democrats after all. This is just one of the many traps into which Western culture has allowed itself to sleepwalk. I believe the gospels can help us to break out of all such traps and to see the world and its multilayered continuing "problem of evil" through new eyes.

But the problem we face lies deeper within the mind-set of the critical scholarship of the past two hundred years. As I said earlier, it was axiomatic for early modern biblical scholars that the kingdom of God, as announced by Jesus, did not arrive. Those scholars who thought that when Jesus spoke about God's kingdom he was referring to the usual kind of armed revolution were able to point out that that hadn't happened. Those who supposed that Jesus was referring to the end of the world were able to point out that that hadn't happened either. Whichever way you went in the scholarly debates, it seemed that Jesus had promised something that hadn't arrived. Either way, the theory then ran, the church found itself obliged to shuffle the cards of Jesus's deeds and words and to deal them out in a new pattern to make something fresh and lasting out of Jesus's failed vision. "Some people standing here," says Jesus in Mark, "won't experience death before they see God's kingdom come in power" (9:1). Well, say the critics, that didn't happen for a start.

Well, of course it didn't—if you think Jesus meant either a military coup or the end of the world. And of course it didn't—if, with the same critical scholarship, you bracket out the resurrection as a later self-justifying bit of ecclesial mythology. What the critics failed to realize, not because it was obscure, but because the philosophy of the European Enlightenment demanded that they close their eyes to it, was that Jesus announced and inaugurated a vision of God's kingdom that he was constantly redefining, through actions and parables, and that would be inaugurated by his own *vindication*. The importance of Daniel 7, of the exaltation and vindication of the "one like a son of man," cannot be overstressed here—and of course it is at that very point that critical scholarship has again done its best to neutralize a central element of the evidence.

At the risk of repeating something that alert readers will have picked up already (but that remains enormously important), the critical scholarship of the past two hundred years was born in a world (that of the European Enlightenment) where it was felt vitally important to separate religion and politics. Critical biblical scholarship was then nurtured in a world (that of German Lutheranism) where the "two kingdoms" theory, which separated the kingdom of religion/faith and the kingdom of the state, was all but set in stone. Thus, for philosophical, cultural, and theological reasons the inner core of the gospels—the message of God becoming king—remained impenetrable. The story the gospels tell, of a Jesus who embodied the living God of Israel and whose cross and resurrection really did inaugurate the kingdom of that God, remained not only incomprehensible, but unheard.

The New Testament writers did their best to make it heard and to make it understood. Matthew believed that Jesus had already accomplished it: "All authority," declares Matthew's Jesus, "in heaven *and on earth* has been given to me" (28:18). Paul believed Jesus was already reigning; you can't understand Romans or 1 Corinthians or Philippians unless you take that as basic. Revelation celebrates the sovereignty of Jesus from first page to last. But of course neither Matthew nor Paul nor Revelation supposed for a minute that this meant that utopia had already arrived, that the vision of Isaiah 11 was already fully in place. Christians were being persecuted, facing violent opposition, celebrating the lordship of Jesus in a world where Caesar and his type of power still seemed to be solid and unshaken.

The early Christian writers were, of course, setting forth an eschatology that had been inaugurated, but not fully consummated; they were celebrating (Paul is quite explicit on this point in 1 Cor. 15:20–28) something that *has already happened,* but at the same time something that *still has to happen in the future.* They believed themselves to be living between Jesus's *accomplishment* of the reign of God and its full *implementation.* But the eschatology in question was not just the personal or "spiritual" eschatology of so much Western thought ("going to heaven" in the future, but with a taste of "heaven," of "eternal life," already in the present), but the social, cultural, political, and even cosmic eschatology of Matthew, Paul, Revelation, and of course—perhaps above all— the fourth gospel. New creation itself has begun, they are saying, and will be completed. Jesus is ruling over that new creation and making it happen through the witness of his church. "The ruler of this world" has been overthrown; the powers of the world have been led behind Jesus's triumphal procession as a beaten, bedraggled rabble. *And that is how God is becoming king on earth as in heaven.* That is the truth the gospels are eager to tell us, the truth the past two hundred years of European and American culture has been desperately trying to stifle.

And of course, as we've seen already, the world of the Enlightenment has been ready with its counter-Christian polemic. "What good," it asks, "has the church ever done for us? It's produced nothing but squabbles, crusades, inquisitions, and witch burnings. The church is part of the problem, not part of the solution." Well, of course you have to tell the story that way if you are Voltaire, eager to wipe out the "scandal" of the church, or indeed if you are a postmodern journalist ready to sneer at God's apparent representatives (the often muddled clergy) to stop yourself from having to take God himself seriously. But the failure of Christianity is a modern myth, and we shouldn't be ashamed of telling the proper story of church history, which of course has plenty of muddle and wickedness, but also far more than we normally imagine of love and creativity and beauty and justice and healing and education and hope. To imagine a world without the gospel of Jesus is to imagine a pretty bleak place, the cultural and ideological equivalent of those horrible 1960s buildings that were structures without spirit, boxes without beauty, all function and no flourish.

And of course the reason the Enlightenment has taught us to trash our own history, to say that Christianity is part of the problem, is that it has had a rival eschatology to promote. It couldn't allow Christianity to claim that world history turned its great corner when Jesus of Nazareth died and rose again, because it wanted to claim that world history turned its great corner *in Europe in the eighteenth century.* "All that went before," it says, "is superstition and mumbo-jumbo. We have now seen the great light, and our modern science, technology, philosophy, and politics have ushered in the new order of the ages." That was believed and expounded in America and France, and it has soaked into our popular culture and imagination. (George Washington contrasted the "gloomy age of ignorance and superstition" up to that point with the new epoch ushered in by the great revolutions of the late eighteenth century, when "the rights of mankind were better understood and more clearly defined.")

So of course Christianity is reduced from an eschatology ("This is where history was meant to be going, despite appearances!") to a religion ("Here is a way of being spiritual"), because world history can't have *two* great turning points. If the Enlightenment is the great, dramatic, all-important corner of world history, Jesus can't have been. He is still wanted on board, of course, as a figure through whom people can try to approach the incomprehensible mystery of the "divine" and as a teacher of moral truths that might, if applied, actually strengthen the fabric of the brave new post-Enlightenment society. But when Christianity is made "just a religion," it first muzzles and then silences altogether the message the gospels were eager to get across. When that happens, the gospel message is substantially neutralized as a force in the world beyond the realm of private spirituality and an escapist heaven. That, indeed, was the intention. And the churches have, by and large, gone along for the ride.

Meanwhile—to continue the picture—the philosophy that had driven God upstairs out of sight, and so produced the modernist "problem of evil," had also produced a new kind of politics. The democracies that were born at that time were tending, with varied success, toward the same kind of Deism that was all the rage in science; now that God was no longer involved, the world would get on and develop under its own steam. The divine right of kings went out with the guillotine, and the new slogan, *vox populi vox Dei* ("The voice of the people is the voice of God"), was truncated; God was away with the fairies doing his own thing, and *vox pop,* by itself, was all that was now needed. Like all new movements, this one called itself "justice" and "freedom," however many injustices it then colluded with and however many new slaveries it introduced. Our own present rhetoric about democracy and legitimacy, about systems of voting and reforms of institutions, still sloshes around in the muddy waters left behind by the receding tsunami of the eighteenth-century revolutions. We would do better, philosophically speaking, to clear the whole area and rebuild from scratch.

Christian Reactions

So what has been the Christian reaction to all this? How have those who habitually read Matthew, Mark, Luke, and John responded to the challenge of modernity? In very mixed fashion. There have of course been great and powerful moments and movements, from that of William Wilberforce two centuries ago to Desmond Tutu's two decades ago, and many more besides. There have been great Christian thinkers who have wrestled mightily with the gospel, on the one hand, and the ambiguities of the modern Western world, on the other. William Temple comes to mind, as do Reinhold and H. Richard Niebuhr. Dietrich Bonhoeffer continues to stand out as someone who read the Bible quite differently from most of his tradition and had the courage to take it seriously. But by and large the churches have lapsed into one of four (to my mind) unhelpful reactions.

The first is to say that all this doesn't matter, because we're going to heaven and we'll leave this old world behind once and for all. That stance, interestingly, became increasingly popular throughout the nineteenth century, when "heaven" became the ultimate home and "resurrection"—with all its political overtones of new creation and new society—was quietly shelved or reduced to the status of an ineffective dogma or even metaphor. I have written about this extensively elsewhere (*Surprised by Hope*),* and I trust it is becoming increasingly clear to people now that such a position simply won't do. This isn't what the four gospels are about. It's actually closer to Gnosticism.

The second thing that Christians have done is to say, with the neo-Anabaptists, that the church must simply put its own house in order, keep its own nose clean, and live as a beacon of light, but without actually engaging with the world. It must construct a parallel society in which the kingdom values of Jesus are lived out for all to see. Now I'm all for the church cleaning up its act and shining like a light in the world. But the strong sectarian separatism that all this implies seems to pay no attention to the great

---

Surprised by Hope: Rethinking Heaven, the Resurrection, and the Mission of the Church (San Francisco: HarperOne, 2008).

statements of Jesus's cosmic lordship in the New Testament, not
least to the claim of Matthew 28 that Jesus already possesses all
authority on earth as well as in heaven. It is always in danger of
dualism, of cutting off the creational branch on which all Christian thinking ought to be sitting.

The third and fourth reactions among Christians, which are
all too powerful today (particularly in the United States), have
simply baptized the right-wing and left-wing politics of a deeply
divided society and claimed this or that one as Christian, to
be implemented and if possible exported. Listening to the sub-
Christian language on display among those exultant at the killing
of Osama bin Laden in the early summer of 2011 was an example
of the right-wing tendency; anything that advances the worldview of Fox News is assumed to be basically Christian, wise, and
automatically justified. But listening to many on the left, I have
a similar problem. The left claims the high Christian and moral
ground of a concern for the poor and the marginalized, but again
this regularly parrots the elements of liberal modernism, not least
its new sexual ethic, without any attempt to scale the true heights
of the gospel vision in the New Testament.

Meanwhile we in the United Kingdom, hearing all this going
on from our cousins across the ocean, tend to be grumpy pragmatists. We don't much care for theory, and we don't, for the most
part, want anything too drastic to disturb our uneasy peace. (It
has often been pointed out that, in response to the communist
chant, "What do we want? Revolution! When do we want it?
Now!" the classic English protest movement might be imagined
chanting, "What do we want? Gradual change! When do we
want it? In due course!") No, we English mostly just want to get
on with our lives, grumble about our politicians but still vote for
them, watch some cricket, and go to Choral Evensong now and
then when we feel like it.

In the middle of all this, more and more scholars, particularly
in America and among its left-leaning thinkers, have rediscovered

the New Testament as a book full of political philosophy, of subversive critique of empire. That's fine; this really is the case. But,
as often happens when a long-sustained vacuum suddenly im-
plodes, a lot of explosive hot air is emitted, and often (to my
mind) in the wrong direction. In particular, there is a danger of
anachronism. As an example, in Pauline studies we are now used
to the claim, whether or not we agree with it, that the sixteenth-
century Reformers read Paul as though he were addressing the
problems of the late fifteenth century, whereas in fact he was addressing the significantly different problems of the mid-first century. That debate is still rumbling on. I am anxious lest, in our
own new eagerness for political relevance, we assume that the
early Christians were addressing the sociopolitical problems of
the late twentieth century, whereas in fact they were addressing
the significantly different sociopolitical problems of the mid-first
century.

In the first case, the Reformers assumed that when Paul talked
of "justification" and "salvation," he meant what a late-medieval
theologian might have meant by those terms and was giving a
new answer ("justification by faith" in the Lutheran or Reformed
sense). But when we read Paul in his proper first-century setting,
we get to keep all the liberating power of that doctrine, but within
a quite different framework. In the second case, today's would-be
"political" readers of the New Testament often assume that when
the gospels, Paul, and Revelation, speak of "power," "empire,"
"lordship," and things like that, they meant what we mean by them
today. (This then divides into various debates: for some, it's a matter
of the rather obvious global economic empire of the early twenty-
first century; for others, it's thought of in relation to the Continental debates about politics and the state that have recently done their
best to revive elements of the teaching of Friedrich Nietzsche, on
the one hand, and Carl Schmitt, on the other.)

No doubt these are all important questions and points of
view. No doubt we could, eventually, offer a historically faithful

exegesis of the New Testament that would engage with these and with many other perspectives on what we now call "politics." But—as we can see from some of the extreme manifestations of this phenomenon—it simply won't do to assume that, because the New Testament contains some quite radical critiques of Caesar's empire, we can pick them up, as Luther picked up Galatians, and make them serve our particular contemporary agendas, whether American, British, or Continental—not to mention those of the rest of the world (which is often squeezed out of the conversation in another breathtaking act of post-Enlightenment "superiority": perhaps we'll get around to thinking about Africa when its countries get around to copying our now rather threadbare political institutions). We owe it to ourselves, to the gospels, to the church, and, not least, to the poor and oppressed in the world not simply to produce a vaguely biblical echo of today's fashionable left-wing critique, but to read the New Testament afresh and to try to discern the deeper and more powerful pathways it offers through the morass of social and political uncertainty. Perhaps we have been looking for hope in the wrong places.

All this is still by way of introduction. We shall shortly return to the four gospels themselves. But before we can do so with any hope of advancing the argument, it will be necessary to spend a few moments longer thinking about the way in which power and empire were thought of within first-century Judaism, not least in contrast to the way the same issues are often addressed today.

Power and Empire Within First-Century Judaism

As we saw earlier, the Judaism of the postexilic period had quite a well-developed narrative of God and empire. Even though many Jews longed for God to become king in the full, complete way he'd promised, they still believed that in the interim he was in fact already in some sense sovereign over the nations. Yes, he allowed pagan kings to rule; as the creator, he didn't want his world to collapse into anarchy. But he judged rulers severely, cutting them down to size, as with Nebuchadnezzar and Belshazzar in the book of Daniel. The Jews assumed, on the basis of their strong creational theology, that the creator had made the world in such a way as to be properly ordered and run by human beings. The Jewish vision of theocracy, of God being in charge, was always one of a rule mediated through his image-bearers, that is, through human beings.

The problem as the Jews saw it was not, then, that of the modern European and American political left. That kind of movement tends to assume that some kind of near anarchy is the ideal. The fewer the rules, the less top-down organization and interference, the better. (Of course, once the "revolution" has happened, what then tends to follow in short order is a new and fiercer top-down legalism in which the "revolutionary" values are imposed by a new sort of dictatorship.) Equally, the problem was not that of our modernist conservative politics, in which traditional values are either to be imposed from above or, as in the "small government" movements, allowed to grow (as it is assumed they will) where "state intervention" is reduced to a minimum.

None of this bears much relation to the way first-century Jews saw the organization of society. In a genuinely creational monotheism, the world works best when ruled by wise stewards, human beings who are humble before God and hence effective in bringing fruitful order to his world. (My Anabaptist friends may gnash their teeth at this, but I submit that I am simply thinking scripture's thoughts after it on these topics. Saying that the creator God wants his world to be ordered under the rule of human beings is not saying that whatever human rulers do must be right. Far from it. All it means, at that level, is that human rulers are answerable to God for what they do with the power he has lent them. That is a very different thing.)

The Jews didn't, it seems, care very much how rulers became rulers; so much for our modern ideals of "legitimacy through voting." They cared very much what the rulers did once they were in power. Power itself wasn't the problem; it was what you did with it that counted. In our eagerness, today, to affirm the "legitimacy" of *vox populi,* we have allowed a system of voting to hand a government the power to do, effectively, what it wants, with the only check on power being the implicit threat that we may vote in a different direction next time—a threat that, with many seats utterly "safe" and with so many issues at stake that a single vote can never reflect them, looks increasingly irrelevant. Most people in the ancient world, in fact, not just Jews, would have supposed that legitimacy came, ultimately, from what you did in office, not from the method by which you got there.

But that's only the immediate and rather obvious political problem. There are deeper issues afoot as well. In today's muddled thinking we find, on the one hand, some people who are almost ready to deny the Fall, imagining that the world is a nice, safe place and that nobody needs any "power" to look after it (hence the anarchist dream and its right-wing small-government equivalent). On the other hand, there are other people who are ready to produce a doctrine of total depravity when it comes to anyone who actually has power, so that power is automatically, ipso facto, bad. Both of these viewpoints result in suspicion of actual rulers: the first, because they're not really needed, and the second, because they are bound to abuse their power. You could of course run the argument the other way, with the charitable assumption attaching itself to rulers and the doctrine of depravity going with the mob. (Another contemporary irony is that the libertarians, who are all for cutting back on police powers and making prisons more comfortable, are often the first in line to call for harsh penalties when violent mobs rampage through their own neighborhoods.)

And, in the middle of this, the word "theocracy" is not one that many people like to hear. It makes them think of Fascist states in Europe in the first half of the twentieth century or fundamentalist states in the Middle East in the first half of the twenty-first. If God is in charge, then—so people suppose—there will be a hard-line "clerical" elite or near equivalent (the Party bosses in Communist or Fascist systems) who claim to be channeling God's will. No room, then, for dissent or even debate. God says it; they enforce it; that settles it. But does this square with first-century Jewish views of what "theocracy" might look like, and perhaps should look like?

First-century Jews knew all about bad rulers, both pagan and Jewish. But when they longed, as many did, for God alone to become king, this vision, rooted as it was in the great biblical kingdom texts, usually envisaged that the *way* God would become king would be through the appropriate human agency. This, in the Psalms, Isaiah, and many other texts both biblical and postbiblical, meant of course the messiah, the anointed king. And we must never forget, though many today do, that in the ancient scriptural picture of the messiah he is king not only of Israel but, like David and Solomon (at least in principle and in rose-tinted memory), of the whole world. Here again the Psalms are central; Psalms 2, 72, and other similar ones made sure the vision remained fresh in a liturgically oriented worshipping people.

But, in the texts that first-century Jews read, prayed, sang, and pondered, there were various visions of how God's "theocracy," his worldwide kingdom, would come into reality and (not least) what it might look like when it did. Some people, it seems, really did want a "theocracy" not too far removed from what we see in some parts of the world today. Simeon ben Kosiba (a.k.a. bar-Kochba), the great would-be messiah of the 130s AD, seems to have tried to establish that kind of divine rule. Others were not so sure. But because the Jews believed that (as we find in books such as Daniel and Jeremiah) God's will for his people in exile was that they live wisely within the pagan world where they found themselves, and because they believed that God was ultimately sovereign (in ways that are normally invisible) over those nations, they were able to develop a theological account of the comings and goings of pagan nations and their rulers as well as a subversive literature and lifestyle designed to critique the pagan rulers, to encourage the faithful, and to warn of God's ultimate judgment. (That literature included what may be called "apocalyptic," coded and symbolic writing about the powers of the world and the powers of God, intending to "reveal" or "unveil" the hidden divine truth behind the outward realities of power and empire.)

But within Israel itself there were problems too. The corrupt pseudoaristocracy of the high-priestly family, the fake monarchs of the Hasmonean and then Herodian families, and different movements of reform and revolution and various stages in between—none of this offered a real sense of completion, of God's best will for the world coming into view at last. That sense of incompleteness, of an unfinished story, was not simply a matter of texts. It was a matter of a whole society struggling to see its way forward, clinging to the institutions of Temple and Torah and the festivals that embraced both, hoping that somehow the sovereign creator God would take his power and reign in the way he had always promised. Hoping, in fact, for a new exodus.

So, to sum up this very long but necessary introduction. Judaism always assumed that the creator God wanted the world to be ordered and ruled by his image-bearing humans. The world, heaven and earth, was created as God's temple, and his image-bearers were the key elements in that temple. But the world was out of joint through the failure of humans in general and Israel in particular, so God the creator would have to act in judgment and justice to hold them to account. And the sign of that coming judgment was that at the heart of the world God had placed his covenant people, gathered around the Temple, which was the microcosm of creation, to celebrate his true order and to pray for it to come on earth as in heaven.

The significance of the Temple as the fulcrum of ancient Jewish theocracy, actual and eschatological, cannot be overemphasized. And with the Temple we find, of course, the priests who offered worship in it and the king who was to build and restore it. Israel's institutions thus instantiated, however imperfectly, the vocation, named in Exodus 19, to be God's royal priesthood. And the Torah—given, of course, in Exodus 20—went with the Temple as the other central symbol of Jewish life. These elements are central, not incidental, to the whole vision, precisely because it is the Temple that joins heaven and earth together and so makes possible the sovereign rule of God on earth as in heaven, just as it is Torah that, given from heaven to earth, is designed (so a devout first-century Jew would have said) to order the lives of God's people so that they can be the truly human people they were called to be. It is, of course, the absence of any equivalent to Temple or Torah in our contemporary culture that makes our own way of posing the political questions so very different from those of the Jews of Jesus's day.

And it was, of course, to those first-century Jews that the evangelists saw Jesus coming with his message of God's kingdom. As we turn now, none too soon, to consider the themes of kingdom and cross, we note that for all the evangelists, as for Paul, there is no sense of the kingdom not after all having appeared. Yes, it has been redefined. Yes, there is still more to do, as long as evil continues to stalk the earth. But the early Christians all believed that with Jesus's death and resurrection *the kingdom had indeed come in power,* even if it didn't look at all like they imagined it would. The hope had been realized, even though it had been quite drastically redefined in the process. A new theocracy had indeed been inaugurated, because the Temple where God lived among his people had been radically redefined. A new empire had been launched that would trump Caesar's empire and all those like it, not by superior force but by a completely different sort of power alto-gether. And the place where this vision is set out is, to the great surprise of many who at one level know these documents well, the collection of the four gospels we find in the New Testament. This chapter has, I think, been a necessary digression. We now return to our main theme.

9

Kingdom and Cross in Four Dimensions

WE COME NOW to the central claim of this book. All four gospels are telling the story of *how God became king* in and through this story of Jesus of Nazareth. This central theme is stated in a thoroughly integrated way, again in all four gospels (though not at all in the so-called gospels that were produced later within the Gnostic and similar movements). This integrated theme, with the kingdom and the cross as the main coordinates, flanked by the question of Jesus's divine identity, on the one hand, and the resurrection and ascension, on the other, is one that most Christians, right across the Western tradition, have failed even to glimpse, let alone to preach. The story Matthew, Mark, Luke, and John tell is the story of *how God became king—in and through Jesus both in his public career and in his death.* The present chapter and the one that follows will do their best to show what this means and why it seems to me so central and vital.

I showed in Part I that the way the gospels have been read, not least through the lens of the great early creeds, has quite accidentally pulled this tightly coherent story apart. This has come through into contemporary readings in which "kingdom" and "cross" have been played off against one another. Sometimes this has been done (as in some nineteenth-century "lives" of Jesus) by presenting Jesus's ministry as composed of two periods, an early period (the so-called Galilean springtime), in which the kingdom movement seemed to be going well, followed by a quite different period, during which, for whatever reason, storm clouds gathered and Jesus found himself compelled to go to Jerusalem to force the issue. Sometimes, without stating any such narrative, different Christians have found that they want to highlight one element or the other, whether the "kingdom," to validate a contemporary social agenda (and to leave a question mark as to why the cross mattered at all), or the "cross," to emphasize the mechanism by which God rescues sinners from this world and enables them to go to "heaven" (leaving a question mark as to why either Jesus or the evangelists would think it mattered that much to do all those healings, to walk on water, or to give such remarkable teaching).

The anomalies in these views can, of course, be addressed and the shaky structure shored up, whether by inappropriate use of other "orthodox" motifs (so that, for instance, "all those things in the middle" between incarnation and cross can be interpreted, as we saw, as "proofs" of "Jesus's divinity"). But anomalies they will remain. Forcing other bits of the jigsaw to fit together despite their actual shape may produce a picture of sorts. But it isn't the one originally intended.

The story the gospel writers all tell thus brings together, into close fusion, the two major themes of kingdom and cross. But what sense does this make? How can the suffering and death of Israel's Messiah somehow bring about his worldwide sovereign kingdom? Or, conversely, what can the establishment of God's sovereign rule on earth as in heaven have to do with the brutal and unjust execution of Jesus, however "high" a Christology we may espouse?

Centuries of atonement theology since Anselm, Luther, Calvin, and the rest have explored ways in which we might say that Jesus's death delivers us from our sins, but this seems to be an altogether wider theme. That, perhaps, is why traditional atonement theologies have, bizarrely to my mind, failed to draw on the gospels for their primary source material. (Yes, Paul has plenty to say on the subject, but when "biblical" theologies ignore the gospels, something is clearly very wrong.) Again, conversely, traditional kingdom theologies (with an emphasis on God's liberation of the oppressed and the "option for the poor") have regularly held aloof from speaking too much about the cross. That, perhaps, is why they have, to their own great loss, not looked to Paul for primary source material.

But now that we have, over the past two generations, rediscovered all four evangelists as sophisticated and thoroughgoing theologians in their own right, we can hardly avoid the question. How do they relate these two central themes?

Beyond that again, of course, there are wider questions. Even if we bring together kingdom and cross, how does this combination relate to the "incarnation" or the "divine identity" of Jesus, on the one hand, and to his resurrection—and, farther off again, his ascension? Those themes too seem to be in one form or another an equally important part of the story the gospel writers are telling. (Yes, Matthew and Mark do not talk about the ascension, but the vindication of Jesus, not least modeled on the vindication of "the son of man" coming to the "Ancient of Days" is crucial in both of them.) As we have already seen, the incarnation is vital for all the gospels. They all saw, in Jesus, the living embodiment of Israel's God, returning to live among his people and to rescue them from their ultimate plight. And, however much they highlighted kingdom and cross, none of them supposed that there would have been anything to write about unless it had been for the resurrection from the dead of the crucified, God-embodying kingdom-bringer. Approaching things like this will seem strange to those brought up with "traditional," creed-shaped formulations about Jesus. When

we insert "kingdom" into the creedal sequence (incarnate, crucified, raised, enthroned), we don't just add another item to a list. We
alter the meaning of all the other terms as well as the shape and balance of the whole implicit narrative. And it is that implicit narrative
that becomes explicit in Matthew, Mark, Luke, and John.

Let us begin where we left off in the previous section, with the
four speakers of our sound system that together, when properly
adjusted, allow us to hear the music the four evangelists are playing. The gospels do not ask us to figure out the integration of
kingdom and cross simply from the top-level story they are telling
(i.e., the story of Jesus's own public career). They encourage us
to think it through in the light of the larger stories that together
contribute to the sheer density of their respective presentations.
How does paying attention to these larger stories enable us to
tune in to the integrated story of kingdom and cross?

Kingdom, Cross, and Israel

Take the first speaker, the gospels as the climax of the story of
Israel. Israel, we recall, is God's royal priesthood, God's servant
people, the chosen light to the nations. But the world, though it is
God's good creation, has become a place of darkness and gloom,
of rebellion and wickedness, of sorrow and pain. What is more,
Israel itself, entrusted with the high vocation to bring God's rescue to the world, is itself in need of rescue. Prophet after prophet
says so; the psalmists sometimes join in the complaint. Israel, the
people who bear God's solution for the world's problems, is itself
part of the problem.

The result is that the long and winding story of the people of
God appears to run into the sand. Exile in Babylon is about as bad
as it gets, symbolically and actually; and though of course some
Jews return and rebuild the Temple, there is a strong sense that
all is still not resolved. The postexilic writings bear witness to

the crushing disappointment; even among the leading Jews there is rebellion and folly, as Ezra and Nehemiah found out and as Malachi makes alarmingly clear. If, then, the gospel writers are, as we suggested earlier, offering the story of Jesus as the completion of the story of Israel, in what sense is it now complete? How has it been fulfilled?

The answer seems to lie, for the gospel writers themselves, in the dark strand that emerges at various stages of the tradition of ancient Israel. As the psalms and prophets sharpen up their vision of how God's kingdom is to come to the world, there emerges a strange and initially perplexing theme: Israel itself will have to enter that darkness. The songs and oracles focus, from time to time and often mysteriously, on the idea that Israel's own suffering will not simply be a dark passage through which the people have to pass, but actually part of the means whereby they will—perhaps despite themselves!—fulfill the original divine vocation.

Sometimes the suffering seems to be focused on a particular representative figure. Endless debates about whether the suffering psalmists are specific individuals or poetic representatives for the people should not obscure the fact that they are there, solidly, within the tradition and that in almost all cases (Psalm 88 being the obvious exception) they turn the corner and move through intense suffering to celebration of God's victory and kingdom. Psalm 22 is perhaps the best-known example:

> *My God, my God, why have you forsaken me?*
> > *Why are you so far from helping me, from the words*
> > *of my groaning?*
> *O my God, I cry by day, but you do not answer;*
> > *and by night, but find no rest.*
> *Yet you are holy,*
> > *enthroned on the praises of Israel.*
> *In you our ancestors trusted;*
> > *they trusted, and you delivered them. . . .*

> *But I am a worm, and not human;*
>> *scorned by others, and despised by the people. . . .*
> *I am poured out like water,*
>> *and all my bones are out of joint;*
> *my heart is like wax;*
>> *it is melted within my breast;*
> *my mouth is dried up like a potsherd,*
>> *and my tongue sticks to my jaws;*
>> *you lay me in the dust of death. . . .*
> *I will tell of your name to my brothers and sisters;*
>> *in the midst of the congregation I will praise you;*
> *You who fear YHWH, praise him! . . .*
> *For he did not despise or abhor*
>> *the affliction of the afflicted;*
> *he did not hide his face from me,*
>> *but heard when I cried to him. . . .*
> *All the ends of the earth shall remember*
>> *and turn to YHWH;*
> *and all the families of the nations*
>> *shall worship before him.*
> *For dominion [hammelukah, i.e., "the kingdom"]*
>> *belongs to YHWH,*
>> *and he rules over the nations.*
>> *(22:1–4, 6, 14–15, 22–24, 27–28)*

Here the whole sequence is laid out. The sufferer goes all the way down to death, and somehow he is rescued, not only for his own sake, but also so that YHWH's "kingdom," that is, his sovereignty over the nations, might become a reality. We hardly need to add that both Matthew (27:46) and Mark (15:34) put the opening words of this psalm on the lips of Jesus as he hangs on the cross, leaving generations of interpreters to puzzle over whether they meant it as a cry of dereliction or, remembering how the psalm continues, ultimate hope. Perhaps it was both; perhaps

Matthew and Mark might have said that for Jesus it was the former, but that they were hinting at the latter as well. It hardly matters. The point is that in the story they are telling the crucial moment when Israel's king is executed is highlighted as the fulfillment of one of the clearest kingdom-and-suffering passages in the whole scripture.

The same could be said, of course, about the "servant" passages in Isaiah. It is ultimately futile to inquire whether the "servant" is Israel or Israel's representative. In all sorts of ways it must be both, even though in the end it appears that the sufferer is one upon whom the faithful within Israel (those who "obey the voice of his servant," 50:10) gaze in a mixture of horror and gratitude. The "servant" is at one moment "Israel, in whom [God] will be glorified" (49:3) and the one who stands in for Israel, doing for the people (in vicarious suffering) what they cannot do for themselves. Interpreters have, of course, regularly noted the hints (such as Mark 10:45) in the direction of Isaiah 53, the climax of the "suffering servant" theme. Fewer have noted the way in which the servant's suffering, in that chapter in particular, is framed by the promise of the kingdom. The messenger who announces the fall of Babylon and the liberation of enslaved Israel brings this simple, two-word announcement of the good news: *malak elohayik,* "Your God reigns" (52:7). Your God has become king. In other words, he has overthrown the tyrant (the actual tyrant and the dark spiritual forces that stand, as ever, behind him) and has demonstrated to the world that he, Israel's God, is also sovereign over the nations:

> yhwh *has bared his holy arm*
>   *before the eyes of all the nations;*
> *and all the ends of the earth shall see*
>   *the salvation of our God. (52:10)*

There then follows almost immediately the graphic Fourth Servant Song (52:13–53:12), in which the onlookers say, in amazement:

> *Surely he has borne our infirmities*
>   *and carried our diseases;*
> *yet we accounted him stricken,*
>   *struck down by God, and afflicted.*
> *But he was wounded for our transgressions,*
>   *crushed for our iniquities;*
> *upon him was the punishment that made us whole,*
>   *and by his bruises we are healed.*
> *All we like sheep have gone astray;*
>   *we have all turned to our own way,*
> *and* YHWH *has laid on him*
>   *the iniquity of us all. (53:4–6)*

This poem too eventually emerges into a triumphant conclusion (53:10–12).

But the real triumph comes in the following two chapters, with the almost delirious joy and incredulity at the renewal of the covenant (chap. 54) and then God's solemn promise to extend his "steadfast, sure love for David" to anyone, anyone at all, who hears the message and comes, hungry and thirsty, for the food and drink that Israel's God will now supply (55:1–3). Here again is the note of the kingdom, the worldwide dominion of Israel's God, now becoming a reality:

> *See, you shall call nations that you do not know,*
>   *and nations that do not know you shall run to you,*
> *because of* YHWH *your God, the Holy One of Israel,*
>   *for he has glorified you. (55:5)*

The result will be nothing less than new creation, the replacement of the thorns and thistles with beautiful flowering shrubs (55:12–13).

Kingdom and cross are thus woven tightly together in some of the very texts that the gospel writers themselves highlight in their interpretation of the story of Jesus. There are of course many, many more. The prophet Jeremiah finds that his personal pain embodies and focuses the pain of the nation. Farther back (and not so often noted in this connection), the combination of victory and intense personal pain of Elijah (1 Kings 18–19) tells a similar story, as he resolutely opposes the wickedness of Ahab and Jezebel and has to bear the cost in his own experience. Later on we find the suffering of Daniel and his friends and God's vindication of them set out as the quintessential Jewish vocation, as the kingdom of God confronts and eventually overthrows the kingdoms of the world.

All of these and more point to the following conclusion. When we see the story of Jesus as the climax of the story of Israel, we should not be surprised to discover that the suffering of Israel and of Israel's supreme representative is to be understood as part of the longer and larger purposes of Israel's God, in other words, the establishment of his worldwide healing sovereignty. Conversely, we should not be surprised to discover that when this God finally claims the nations as his own possession, rescuing them from their evil ways, the means by which he does it is through the suffering of his people—or, as in the story the gospels themselves are telling, the suffering of his people's official, divinely appointed representative.

All this is brought out brilliantly by Luke as, drawing together the threads of his whole narrative, he tells the story of the road to Emmaus:

> "You are so senseless!" said Jesus to them. "So slow in your hearts to believe all the things the prophets said to you! Don't you see? This is what *had* to happen: the Messiah had to suffer, and then come into his glory!"
>
> So he began with Moses, and with all the prophets, and explained to them the things about himself throughout the whole Bible. (24:25–27)

This is then followed, in the Upper Room, with a further emphasis of the same point:

Then he said to them, "This is what I was talking to you about when I was still with you. Everything written about me in the law of Moses, and in the prophets and the Psalms, had to be fulfilled." Then he opened their minds to understand the Bible.

"This is what is written," he said. "The Messiah must suffer and rise from the dead on the third day, and in his name repentance, for the forgiveness of sins, must be announced to all the nations, beginning from Jerusalem. You are the witnesses for all this." (24:44–48)

"To suffer, and then come into his glory"—in other words, cross and kingdom. The very word "Messiah" already implies kingdom; now it is clear how that kingdom is attained. This is how the story of Israel comes to its climax. The suffering of Israel's representative has drawn the sting of the world's evil; Luke made it clear that Jesus's betrayal, arrest, and death were the point at which the powers of darkness were doing their worst (22:53). Now the original vision for Israel can at last get back on track. The other three evangelists have their own ways of getting at the same point, but we have every reason to suppose they would have agreed. The first reason we can be sure that kingdom and cross belong tightly together in mutual interpretation is that this is the way the gospel writers saw the story of Israel reaching its climax in the story of Jesus.

Kingdom, Cross, and God

The same is true, in naturally quite a different way, with the music coming from the second speaker. God himself would be the savior of his people, according to Isaiah's glance back at the exodus. It was his own presence that saved them:

> For he said, "Surely they are my people,
>   children who will not deal falsely";
> and he became their savior
>   in all their distress.
> It was no messenger or angel
>   but his presence that saved them;
> in his love and in his pity he redeemed them;
>   he lifted them up and carried them all the days of old.
>   (63:8–9)

A similar point emerges in the "shepherd" passage in Ezekiel 34. When the official leaders of God's people fail in their task and begin to prey on the flock rather than looking after them, YHWH will come himself to do the job instead. But, although this is quite unambiguous and emphatic, the prophet moves on quite quickly to introduce a parallel motif:

> For thus says the Lord YHWH: I myself will search for my sheep, and will seek them out. As shepherds seek out their flocks when they are among their scattered sheep, so I will seek out my sheep. I will rescue them from all the places to which they have been scattered. . . . I will set up over them one shepherd, my servant David, and he shall feed them: he shall feed them and be their shepherd. And I, YHWH, will be their God, and my servant David shall be prince among them; I, YHWH, have spoken. . . . You are my sheep, the sheep of my pasture, and I am your God, says the Lord YHWH. (34:11–12, 23–24, 31).

So is it YHWH who will be the shepherd or David? Ezekiel seems content to leave it open. It seems to be both. YHWH will do the rescuing, but David will look after the flock, which will remain YHWH's own flock (as, of course, in passages like Pss. 23:1; 80:1; 100:3).

The natural place to go in the gospels to follow up this strand is John 10 (though the "shepherd" theme is found elsewhere, e.g., Luke 15:3–7). Any with scriptural echoes in their heads and hearts could hardly fail to pick up the resonances from this:

> "I am the good shepherd," Jesus continued. "The good shepherd lays down his life for the sheep. . . .
>
> "I am the good shepherd. I know my own sheep, and my own know me—just as the father knows me and I know the father. And I lay down my life for the sheep. And I have other sheep, too, which don't belong to this sheepfold. I must bring them, too, and they will hear my voice. Then there will be one flock, and one shepherd."
> (10:11, 14–16)

We should remind ourselves of the setting and the sequel. The setting is at the Dedication Festival (Hanukkah), the commemoration of the cleansing of the Temple by Judas Maccabeus in 164 BC and (by implication) of his founding of a new royal dynasty as a result. The sequel is that the Judaeans, confronted with these echoes of Ezekiel, ask Jesus, "How much longer are you going to keep us in suspense? If you are the Messiah, say so out loud!" (John 10:24). But Jesus, of course, cannot simply give them the answer they want. Jesus is redefining the notion of messiahship around his own sense of particular vocation; we can see this elsewhere in the story, as we already noted in the exchange with Pilate, and as is apparent in 6:15, where Jesus has to escape from the crowd because they want to make him king, according to their aspirations for kingship. But the same sense of parallel tracks, of God and David being somehow fused together in this shepherd work and yet also remaining separate, is exactly focused in the extraordinary claim a few verses later:

> "My sheep hear my voice. I know them, and they follow me. I give them the life of the coming age. They

will never, ever perish, and nobody can snatch them out
of my hand. My father, who has given them to me, is
greater than all, and nobody can snatch them out of my
father's hand. I and the father are one." (10:27–30)

This is as clear a statement as we find anywhere in the four gospels. When we are watching the story of Jesus unfold, we are also
watching the story of Israel's God coming back, as he had long
promised, to rescue and "shepherd" his people.

To be sure, neither John nor any of the others makes the mistake one often encounters in popular parlance, of saying "Jesus is
God" without remainder. Jesus constantly refers to "the father"
both as distinct from himself and as bound with him in a tight
bond of love and obedience. And the point to be made here for
our present purposes is that in this central "incarnational" passage we find the themes of cross and kingdom once more tightly
interwoven. This reinforces the warning we gave earlier, that it is
possible to state the doctrine of Jesus's "divinity" in such a way as
to let it float loose from both kingdom and cross, but this is what
the New Testament never does. The "God" who has become
human in Jesus is the God who, as he had always promised, was
returning to claim his sovereignty over the whole world (note the
"other sheep" in John 10:16) and would do so by himself sharing
the pain and suffering of his people, "laying down his life for the
sheep." It is all too possible to "believe in the divinity of Jesus"
and to couple this with an escapist view of salvation ("Jesus is God
and came to snatch us away from this world") in a way that may
preserve an outward form of "Christian orthodoxy," but that has
left out the heart of the matter. God is the creator and redeemer of
the world, and Jesus's launch of the kingdom—God's worldwide
sovereignty on earth as in heaven—is the central aim of his mission, the thing for which he lived and died and rose again.

How can we even begin to understand this? Perhaps we should
say that, with the hindsight the evangelists offer us, God called

Israel to be the means of rescuing the world, so that he might himself alone rescue the world *by becoming Israel in the person of its representative Messiah*. This explains the place of David in the story. He is, in some respects at least, the man after God's own heart, the man whose Temple-building son would be God's own son, as God says to David through the prophet Nathan:

> "When your days are fulfilled and you lie down with
> your ancestors, I will raise up your offspring after you,
> who shall come forth from your body, and I will estab-
> lish his kingdom. He shall build a house for my name,
> and I will establish the throne of his kingdom forever.
> I will be a father to him, and he shall be a son to me."
> (2 Sam. 7:12–14)

This text, highlighted elsewhere in first-century Judaism as well, was very important for the early Christians as they strug-gled to understand the enormous thing that had just happened in their midst. There is a very tight nexus between God, David, the Temple—and the purposes of establishing the kingdom. The early Christians also saw that in the word "I will raise up" there was a hint of something else: resurrection.

This rich, dense combination of themes reappears in a passage we looked at a moment ago, namely, Isaiah 53. In the previous section of the book, the prophet has invoked "the arm of YHWH" as a way of talking about YHWH himself, coming in person to do what he had promised, namely, to defeat the enemy and rescue his people:

> Awake, awake, put on strength,
>   O arm of YHWH!
> Awake, as in days of old,
>   the generations of long ago! . . .
> Was it not you who dried up the sea,
>   the waters of the great deep,

> who made the depths of the sea a way
>   for the redeemed to cross over? . . .
> YHWH has bared his holy arm
>   before the eyes of all the nations,
> and all the ends of the earth shall see
>   the salvation of our God. *(51:9–10; 52:10; cf. 40:10)*

This means that when we arrive at 53:1, there is only one possible interpretation:

> *Who has believed what we have heard?*
>   *And to whom has the arm of* YHWH *been revealed?*
> *For he grew up before him like a young plant,*
>   *and like a root out of dry ground. (53:1–2)*

The prophet looks on in horror at the "servant," battered and bruised beyond recognition, and says in wondering tones, "Who would have thought that *he* was 'the arm of YHWH'?" Looking at him, at this "servant," you'd never have guessed it. But the point of the larger poem, of Isaiah 40–55 as a whole, is that *the servant is the one through whose representative work Israel's God will accomplish his purposes for Israel and the whole world.* The "servant" is a role made for YHWH's own use. The purpose is to establish the kingdom; the means is the obedient suffering of Israel's representative. This role and the accomplishment of this purpose are tasks that only YHWH himself can undertake. Here is the mystery at the heart not only of the New Testament (which went back again and again to these texts in the quest for understanding what had just happened), but of the Old as well.

What we call "incarnation" thus lies at the heart of, and gives depth and meaning to, the kingdom-and-cross combination that, in turn, lies at the heart of all four gospels. And—to develop a point we hinted at a moment ago—this means that one "normal" reading of the creeds and of the whole Christian tradition at this point has to be challenged. The "divinity" of Jesus is not to be separated from his kingdom work, his cross-accomplished kingdom work. It does not, as a dogma, "come away clean."

So too with the "one like a son of man" in Daniel 7. To be sure, this strange visionary figure represents "the people of the holy ones of the Most High" (7:27). There seems no reasonable doubt that the one who is brought before the "Ancient of Days" in that great judgment scene is to be understood in this way. The passage offers two "interpretations," one shorter and one longer, but in both this point is clear. (Some have speculated that an earlier form of the vision in 7:1–16 had a different meaning, but the text that was being read in the first century was the one we now have.)

This is how it works. First, the vision. Daniel has a dream of four monsters trampling the earth in great wickedness and violence. Then a court scene develops in heaven: "Thrones were set in place, and an Ancient One took his throne" (7:9). This is clearly God himself, calling the world to account at last. The last great monster speaks its final arrogant words and is then put to death. Then something quite different takes place:

As I watched in the night visions,

> I saw one like a human being [Aramaic kebar enash,
>   "like a son of man"]
>   coming with the clouds of heaven.
> And he came to the Ancient One [Aramaic 'atiq yomaya,
>   "Ancient of Days"]
>   and was presented before him.
> To him was given dominion
>   and glory and kingship,
> that all peoples, nations, and languages
>   should serve him.
> His dominion is an everlasting dominion
>   that shall not pass away,
> and his kingship [Aramaic malkutheh] is one
>   that shall never be destroyed. (7:13–14)

Daniel, as is common in such literature, asks an attendant to interpret the vision. This is the first response:

> As for these four great beasts, four kings shall arise out
> of the earth. But the holy ones of the Most High shall
> receive the kingdom and possess the kingdom forever—
> forever and ever. (7:17–18)

It is already clear. As regularly in "apocalyptic" writing, the elements of the vision are symbolic and need decoding. The monsters represent human empires, but the "one like a son of man" represents Israel, or at least the righteous within Israel. They have suffered long under the rule of the monsters, but they are to be rescued—and not only rescued, but given sovereignty over the world. Then Daniel, still curious, asks his question again, describing the crucial element in the scene once more:

> As I looked, this horn made war with the holy ones and
> was prevailing over them, until the Ancient One came;
> then judgment was given for the holy ones of the Most
> High, and the time arrived when the holy ones gained
> possession of the kingdom. (7:21–22)

This makes it even clearer. It is indeed a court scene, with the "holy ones"—God's true people—in the position of vindicated defendant, while the "horn"—the final king of the fourth great empire—is condemned. What is most interesting here, for the secure interpretation of the whole passage as it stands, is that in repeating his description of the scene Daniel does not speak, this time, of "the coming of the son of man" to the "Ancient One," but already interprets that as "the holy ones gaining possession of the kingdom." We are then prepared for the restated and amplified interpretation at the end of the chapter:

> *Then the court shall sit in judgment,*
> *and [the horn's] dominion shall be taken away,*

> *to be consumed and totally destroyed.*
> *The kingship and dominion*
> > *and the greatness of the kingdoms under the whole heaven*
> > *shall be given to the people of the holy ones of the Most High;*
> *their kingdom shall be an everlasting kingdom,*
> > *and all dominions shall serve and obey them. (7:26–27)*

By now we should be in no doubt whatever. The history and the future of Israel are being interpreted through a heavenly court scene. At the moment the "monsters" are running the world, speaking arrogant words against God and making war on his people (7:21). But the time is soon approaching when God himself will set up his throne for judgment and will pronounce against the "horn" and in favor of "the people of the holy ones of the Most High."

In the first century (when the book of Daniel was, not surprisingly, a popular text among those longing for Israel's redemption), if someone were to evoke the theme of "the coming of the son of man," people would naturally hear three things. First, this would be about *representation:* "the son of man," or "one like a son of man," could of course refer to a single human being, but within the implicit narrative of Daniel 7 that was being evoked this human being would be seen as a literary or apocalyptic symbol standing for "the people of the holy ones of the Most High." Second, it would be about *vindication:* the scene being evoked is focused on the vindication of Israel over the nations that had hitherto been oppressing it. It is, quite explicitly, a courtroom scene, in which the judge finds in favor of one party and against the other. Third, it would be about *kingdom:* with increasing volume as the chapter progresses, Israel (or the righteous within Israel) will end up ruling the world on God's behalf. This would be how God's kingdom, his sovereignty over the world, would be established. This is not, in other words, simply about the rescue, or salvation, of God's people from their present plight. It is about their being rescued in order to be enthroned.

But for them to be enthroned implies thrones. Yes, as the text already indicated, there were *thrones,* plural, placed in heaven at the start of the judgment scene (7:9). God, the "Ancient One," takes his seat on one of these thrones. And though it is not explicitly stated that, in the vision, "one like a son of man" ends up sitting on the other, what is said indicates that this in fact is what has happened. "To him was given dominion and glory and kingship. . . . The holy ones of the Most High shall receive the kingdom and possess the kingdom forever. . . . The time arrived when the holy ones gained possession of the kingdom. . . . The kingship and dominion and the greatness of the kingdoms under the whole heaven shall be given to the people of the holy ones of the Most High." It could hardly be clearer. *The "one like a son of man" ends up sitting on the throne beside the "Ancient One."* The "people of the holy ones of the Most High" are exalted to a place right beside God himself.

So thought one of the greatest rabbis of a century after the time of Jesus. "One throne for God," said Rabbi Akiba, "and one for David," in other words, for the Messiah. This was no esoteric speculation; Akiba had a candidate. He believed that Simeon ben-Kosiba was the Messiah and would sit on that throne. Akiba got into trouble for saying such a thing. Was he not compromising Israel's cherished monotheism? Clearly he didn't think so. He died with the Shema, Israel's great monotheistic prayer, on his lips ("Hear, O Israel, YHWH is our God, YHWH alone," Deut. 6:4). But the point for our present purposes—listening to the second speaker in relation to the whole story of the gospels—ought now to be clear. It may help to set this out in a sequence:

a. There is no doubt that Matthew and Mark, and to a lesser, but still significant extent Luke and John, are

telling the story of Jesus in such a way as to evoke
Daniel 7. The key passages (Mark 13:26; 14:62, and the
parallels in Matthew) ought not to be controversial at
this point. Whatever the phrase "son of man" means
elsewhere in the gospels (a topic for another time), these
are clear quotations of Daniel 7 and fit very closely
within the whole theme of suffering, vindication, and
kingdom, which all four gospels are building up to a
climax as Jesus approaches Jerusalem and plunges into
his final days.

b. All the signs are that the evangelists are encouraging us
(as we hear from the first speaker) to think of Jesus as
the individual in whom the fate and the hopes of "the
people of the holy ones of the Most High" are now
summed up. He is the bearer of Israel's vocation, of
Israel's destiny, and in his suffering and vindication that
destiny will be fulfilled. The phrase "son of man" does
not, by itself, mean "messiah" in pre-Christian Judaism, but the narrative, even in visionary symbol, of an
individual who represents God's holy people lent itself
easily and naturally to the "messianic" meaning.

c. This links the suffering of Jesus (when the "monsters,"
i.e., the Judaean rulers, on the one hand, and Rome,
on the other, appear to have triumphed over him) very
closely to his coming exaltation as the world's true
king, exactly as we find, for instance, at the end of
Matthew's gospel.

d. But the one who is thus exalted to worldwide sovereignty
after his suffering is the one who then *sits on the second
throne in heaven*. This is a huge claim, but it is exactly cognate with the implicit claim we saw in all four gospels in

Chapter 5. The messianic vocation of suffering and kingship appears to be a vocation marked out in scripture for
God's own use. When we understand the ancient Jewish
roots of the gospels' "incarnational" vision of Jesus, we
understand more fully that this vision belongs intimately
and inextricably with the establishment of God's kingdom, through the figure who now shares his throne,
across the whole world. We understand, in other words,
that the "gap" in the classic creeds—the gap between
incarnation and atonement—is filled by the evangelists
with their claim that in Jesus, and particularly through his
suffering, Israel's God was becoming king of the whole
world. Daniel 7 is about the establishment not just of a
radical and total theocracy, but of the rule ("-cracy")
of the God ("theo-") who calls the cruel powers of the
world to account and exalts those who have been crushed
under their arrogance.

That theme, of course, resonates with every corner of Matthew, Mark, Luke, and John. It chimes with the song of Jesus's
mother: "Down from their thrones he hurled the rulers, up from
the earth he raised the humble" (Luke 1:52). It fits exactly with
the Beatitudes: "Blessings on people who hunger and thirst for
God's justice! You're going to be satisfied" (Matt. 5:6). It dove-
tails precisely with Jesus's own great redefinition of power and
kingdom; the rulers of the earth behave in one way, but we're
going to do it the other way: "Anyone who wants to be first must
be everyone's slave. . . . The son of man didn't come to be waited
on. He came to be the servant, to give his life 'as a ransom for
many'" (Mark 10:42–45). Kingdom and cross belong exactly and
profoundly together. And both gain their astonishing depth of
meaning from the music we hear in the second of our speakers.
The one who goes to the cross to establish God's kingdom is none

other than "the arm of YHWH," Israel's God in human form, the one who shares the throne of the "Ancient One."

All this is bringing us nearer, I think, to understanding the evangelists' atonement theology. It highlights too the distortions that result when people construct an "atonement theology" that bypasses the gospels. God himself will come to the place of pain and horror, of suffering and even of death, so that somehow he can take it upon himself *and thereby set up his new style theocracy at last.* The evangelists tell the story of Jesus in such a way that this combination of Israel's vocation and the divine purpose come together perfectly into one. This, I suggest, is the reality behind the later abstractions of "humanity" and "divinity." The humanity is the humanity of Israel, the divinity is the divinity of Israel's God.

Kingdom, Cross, and Church

The third speaker invites us to listen to one particular dimension of the music of the gospels. This dimension, we recall, highlights the story of Jesus heard as the story of the launching of God's renewed people. The gospels, in telling the story of Jesus (including the fulfillment of Israel's long narrative and the remarkable claim that this is also the story of God in person), declare in a thousand ways that Israel is hereby transformed, through its Messiah, Jesus, into a new community, based on him but shaped by the Twelve, whom he called as one of his initial great symbolic actions.

Many in Jesus's day were seeking to renew God's people this way and that. The gospels present Jesus as fitting exactly into that context and culture, with his prophetic ministry aimed, like all prophetic ministries over the previous centuries, at challenging Israel to turn from its wayward folly and to embrace once more its true vocation. The gospels themselves were written from and to communities of Jesus's followers, who believed that in Jesus as Israel's Messiah this renewal had become actual. Israel had not been abandoned. It had not been "replaced." It had been transformed. That, indeed, was the source of many of the early Christians' problems (should pagan converts get circumcised and keep the food laws?) as well as the root of their self-understanding.

Of course, this transformation was anything but a smooth progression, a steady "development" from one phase to another. The story retains its thoroughgoing "apocalyptic" overtones all the way through: a veil is ripped back; things previously hidden are now unveiled, making the world a radically different place; events occur that change Israel and the world for ever. All of this, in its meaning for the early Christian community, is right there in the way the evangelists tell the story.

At the center of it all, we find once more the themes of kingdom and cross. Jesus announces the kingdom and summons his followers to share in the work of announcing and inaugurating it. Yet the kingdom confounds their expectations; they don't understand what's going on, and they fail to pick up the significance of his strange stories and his powerful deeds. The story of the "foundation of the church" in the gospels does not show Jesus's first followers latching right on to his message and his meaning and being sensibly and easily "trained" to follow Jesus in putting the kingdom into effect. The two disciples on the road to Emmaus were still shocked and sad because, despite the rumors of the resurrection, as far as they were concerned the crucifixion of their friend and master meant the dashing of all their hopes. "We were hoping that he was going to redeem Israel!" (Luke 24:21). *Part of the meaning of the kingdom, in the four gospels, is precisely the fact that it bursts upon Jesus's first followers as something so shocking as to be incomprehensible.*

That is why Jesus told so many parables. His kingdom vision was so unlike that of his contemporaries that this was the only way to get through, to launch his followers upon the strange new vocation that would continue, energized by another dramatic and life-changing event (Pentecost), after his death, resurrection, and ascension. And part of the meaning of the kingdom, seen as the launching of God's renewed people, is particularly that the launching itself involved the death of Jesus, something again for which his first followers were completely unprepared and that, indeed, they refused at first to countenance:

> From then on Jesus began to explain to his disciples
> that he would have to go to Jerusalem, and suffer many
> things from the elders, chief priests, and scribes, and be
> killed, and be raised on the third day.
>
> Peter took him and began to tell him off. "That's the
> last thing God would want, Master!" he said. "That's
> never, ever going to happen to you!"
>
> Jesus turned on Peter. "Get behind me, Satan!" he
> said. "You're trying to trip me up! You're not looking
> at things like God does! You're looking at things like a
> mere mortal!" (Matt. 16:21–23)

The gospel story of Jesus seen as the launching of the renewed people of God includes, as a central element, the incomprehension, failure, and rebellion of that people, until they are stunned into new faith by the resurrection and energized into new obedience by the Spirit. The themes of kingdom and cross are not simply theological themes that the disciples have to learn, abstract ideas on their way to constituting a creedal "orthodoxy." They are the pattern of their life, both as they follow Jesus around Galilee, despite not understanding what he's up to, and as they then follow him, in the power of the Spirit, to the ends of the earth.

We should not be surprised, then—though many in the church down through the years would be very surprised to hear this—that the early Christians understood their vocation as Jesus's followers to include, as a central and load-bearing element, their own suffering, misunderstanding, and likely death. It isn't just that, as followers of a misunderstood Messiah, they themselves would naturally expect misunderstanding and persecution, though that is certainly part of it. It is, rather—and it will take the later books of the New Testament and indeed much of the Christian writing of the second century to explore this—that the suffering of Jesus's followers is actually, like Jesus's own suffering, not just the inevitable accompaniment to the accomplishing of the divine purpose, but actually itself part of the *means* by which that purpose is to be fulfilled. When Mark's Jesus tells his followers to take up their own cross and follow him, we see a line straight through the New Testament to the theme of suffering and martyrdom that we find in Paul, 1 Peter, and Revelation:

> "If any of you want to come the way I'm going," Jesus said, "you must say no to your own selves, pick up your cross, and follow me. Yes: if you want to save your life, you'll lose it; but if you lose your life because of me and the message you'll save it. After all, what use is it to win the world and lose your life? What can you give in exchange for your life? If you're ashamed of me and my words in this cheating and sinning generation, the son of man will be ashamed of you when he 'comes in the glory of his father with the holy angels.'
>
> "I'm telling you the truth," he said; "some people standing here won't experience death before they see God's kingdom come in power." (Mark 8:34–9:1)

> We sent Timothy . . . so that he could strengthen you and bring comfort to your faith, so that you wouldn't be pulled off course by these sufferings. You yourselves know, don't you, that this is what we are bound to face. For when we were with you, we told you ahead of time that we would undergo suffering; that's how it has turned out, and you know about it. (1 Thess. 3:2–4)

In fact, because of the Messiah I've suffered the loss of everything, and I now calculate it as trash, so that my profit may be the Messiah, and that I may be discovered in him, not having my own covenant status defined by Torah, but the status which comes through the Messiah's faithfulness: the covenant status from God which is given to faith. This means knowing him, knowing the power of his resurrection, and knowing the partnership of his sufferings. It means sharing the form and pattern of his death, so that somehow I may arrive at the final resurrection from the dead. (Phil. 3:8–11)

We have this treasure in earthenware pots, so that the extraordinary quality of the power may belong to God, not to us. We are under all kinds of pressure, but we are not crushed completely; we are at a loss, but not at our wits' end; we are persecuted, but not abandoned; we are cast down, but not destroyed. We always carry the deadness of Jesus about in the body, so that the life of Jesus may be revealed in our body. Although we are still alive, you see, we are always being given over to death because of Jesus, so that the life of Jesus may be revealed in our mortal humanity. So this is how it is: death is at work in us—but life in you! (2 Cor. 4:7–12)

Right now I'm having a celebration—a celebration of my sufferings, which are for your benefit! And I'm steadily completing, in my own flesh, what is presently lacking in the king's afflictions on behalf of his body, which is the church. (Col. 1:24)

Yes, it may well be necessary that, for a while, you may have to suffer trials and tests of all sorts. But this is so that the true value of your faith may be discovered. It is worth more than gold, which is tested by fire even though it can be destroyed. The result will be praise, glory, and honor when Jesus the Messiah is revealed. (1 Pet. 1:6–7)

Beloved, don't be surprised at the fiery ordeal which is coming upon you to test you, as though this were some strange thing that was happening to you. Rather, celebrate! You are sharing the sufferings of the Messiah. Then, when his glory is revealed, you will celebrate with real, exuberant joy. (1 Pet. 4:12–13)

Now at last has come salvation and power: the kingdom of our God and the authority of his Messiah! The accuser of our family has been thrown down, the one who accuses them before God day and night. They conquered him by the blood of the lamb and by the word of their testimony, because they did not love their lives unto death. (Rev. 12:10–11)

Here, the suffering and death of Jesus's people is not simply the dark path they must tread because of the world's continuing hostility toward Jesus and his message. It somehow has the more positive effect of carrying forward the redemptive effect of Jesus's own death, not by adding to it, but by sharing in it. When we speak of the "finished work of the Messiah," as the evangelists intend us to (as far as they were concerned, the story of Jesus was the unique turning point of all history), we are not ruling out, but rather laying the groundwork for, a missiology of kingdom and cross. Jesus has constituted his followers as those who share his work of kingdom inauguration; that is the point of his sending out of the Twelve, and then others again, even during his lifetime and far more so after his death and resurrection. But if they are to bring his kingdom in his way, they will be people who share his suffering.

Reading the gospels as the launching of God's renewed

people, then, is not merely a historical note: "This was where and how our story began." It declares too: "This is the sort of people we are: suffering kingdom-bringers, suffering kingdom-sharers."

This comes to striking expression in Luke's account of the Last Supper. Immediately after Jesus has warned the disciples, as in Mark 10, that, whereas pagan kings lord it over their subjects, he is instituting a different way of power altogether, the way of the servant, he adds this saying:

> "You are the ones who have stuck it out with me
> through the trials I've had to endure. This is my bequest
> to you: the kingdom my father bequeathed to me! What
> does this mean? You will eat and drink at my table, in
> my kingdom, and you will sit on thrones, judging the
> twelve tribes of Israel." (22:28–30)

Then, just in case the disciples might be puffed up by such a promise, Jesus turns to Peter. Addressing him by his old name, Simon, he warns him that he is going to be tested to the limit by "the satan," and he warns them all that tough times are ahead (22:31–38).

All this demands, of course, a strong theology of the Holy Spirit as the one who dwells in Jesus's followers and enables them in turn to be kingdom-bringers. Without that, the vocation would encourage either arrogance or despair. And that theology of the Spirit is, of course, what the New Testament supplies, on page after page.

This, then, is the clue that enables us to understand the whole New Testament vision of the church. It grows directly out of the vision of God's holy ones "receiving the kingdom" in Daniel 7. But it does so insofar as, and only insofar as, the category of the "holy ones" is first shrunk right down to the one man, Jesus himself, and opened up thereafter to his followers. Once this is clear, the way is open for a fresh understanding of the kingdom-and-cross combination, as we find it, for instance, in Revelation:

> Glory to the one who loved us, and freed us from our sins by his blood, and made us a kingdom, priests to his God and father. (1:5–6)

> *You are worthy to take the scroll;*
> *You are worthy to open its seals;*
> *For you were slaughtered and with your own blood*
> *You purchased a people for God,*
> *From every tribe and tongue,*
> *From every people and nation,*
> *And made them a kingdom and priests to our God*
> *And they will reign on the earth. (5:9–10)*

This vision, of a community rescued by the cross and transformed into kingdom-bringers, follows directly from the story the four evangelists are telling. It is, once more, a measure of how far the Western church has drifted from those moorings that it has been possible for Christians in our own day to think of bringing "justice and peace" into the world by the normal, disastrous means of bombs and bullets. Not so. The implicit ecclesiology of all four gospels is a picture of a community sharing the complex vocation of Jesus himself: to be kingdom-bringers, yes, but to do this first because of Jesus's own suffering and second by means of their own. The slaughtered and enthroned lamb of Revelation 5 is not only the shepherd of his people; he is also their template. Sharing his suffering is the way in which they are to extend his kingdom in the world. As I write this I am conscious that today's Western church, and I myself as part of it, have suffered remarkably little by comparison with Christians of other times and, today, other places. I honor those who are leading the way as today's kingdom-bringers and pray for them in their courage and steadfast witness.

Kingdom and Cross in Caesar's World

The fourth speaker, we recall, invites us to listen to the four gospels as the story of God's kingdom confronting that of Caesar. How does the music from this speaker contribute to our understanding of the strange combination of kingdom and cross?

From all that we examined in Chapter 7, it is clear that all four gospels regard the story of Jesus not only as the *confrontation* between God's kingdom and Caesar's kingdom, but as the *victory* of the former over the latter. This theme is continued throughout the New Testament. Toward the end of the previous section we glanced at some passages in the book of Revelation that make this point graphically. The violent death of the Lamb has won the decisive victory over the monsters and their horrid kingdoms and over the old dragon, the satan itself. But there are many other passages too that do not mince their words. It may have looked as if the powers of the world were winning a victory over Jesus (certainly that was how everyone in Jerusalem, both those who followed Jesus and those who hated him, saw things at the time). But in fact the boot was on the other foot. Think of Caesar in his title of "son of God"; think of his (claimed) royal descent, his power, and his claim to worldwide allegiance; and then hear the overtones of Paul's stunning opening for his greatest letter:

> . . . the good news about God's son, who was descended from David's seed in terms of flesh, and who was marked out powerfully as God's son in terms of the spirit of holiness by the resurrection of the dead: Jesus, the king, our Lord!
>
> Through him we have received grace and apostleship to bring about believing obedience among all the nations for the sake of his name. (Rom. 1:3–5)

Or think of Paul speaking of "the wisdom God prepared ahead of time . . . for our glory" (1 Cor. 2:7) and then explaining:

> None of the rulers of this present age knew about this wisdom. If they had, you see, they wouldn't have crucified the Lord of glory. (2:8)

In other words, the powers that put Jesus on the cross didn't realize that by doing so they were in fact serving God's purposes, unveiling the "wisdom" that lies at the heart of the universe. Paul puts it even more positively, seeing the cross as the weapon with which God stripped the armor from the rulers and authorities, as soldiers would do with beaten enemies:

> He stripped the rulers and authorities of their armor, and displayed them contemptuously to public view, celebrating his triumph over them in him. (Col. 2:15).

That is to say, when Jesus died on the cross he was winning the victory over "the rulers and authorities" who have carved up this world in their own violent and destructive way. The establishment of God's kingdom means the dethroning of the world's kingdoms, not in order to replace them with another one of basically the same sort (one that makes its way through superior force of arms), but in order to replace it with one whose power is the power of the servant and whose strength is the strength of love.

It is in this light that we can understand what the evangelists are doing in the so-called trial scenes—the night hearing before Caiaphas and the encounter with Pontius Pilate on the following morning. In both of these it appears, of course, as though it is Jesus who is on trial. But the way the evangelists tell the story—they all share, after all, in something of the nature of "apocalypse," of the Jewish sense that the heavenly reality may need to be "revealed" behind the opaque earthly one—it becomes clear that actually it is Caiaphas and Pilate and the systems they represent and embody that are on trial—and that lose their case. Jesus, having declared that he will be vindicated, goes to his death as to an enthronement, while the Judaean leaders declare that they have no king but Caesar.

Jesus, after all, has come to Jerusalem and found the Temple no longer to be the place where heaven and earth do business, but the place where mammon and violence are reigning unchecked, colluding with Caesar's rule. Jesus himself, the evangelists are saying, is now the place where heaven and earth come together, and the event in which this happens supremely is the crucifixion itself. The cross is to be the victory of the "son of man," the Messiah, over the monsters; the victory of God's kingdom over the world's kingdoms; the victory of God himself over all the powers, human and suprahuman, that have usurped God's rule over the world. Theocracy, genuine Israel-style theocracy, will occur only when the other "lords" have been overthrown.

Behind the actual human beings, whether Caiaphas, Pilate, or even Caesar himself, there stand the dark spiritual forces that they have implicitly invoked. As many scholars have argued, this should not be seen as an either/or (*either* "human authorities" *or* "spiritual powers"). No doubt the "powers" can work independently too; but, like Rome itself in its outlying provinces, the shadowy powers of evil seem to prefer to do their dark deeds through the agency of willing collaborators. Each of the four evangelists highlights this in his own way.

Luke's Jesus declares that he saw the satan fall like lightning from heaven, though this is clearly not the end of the matter; he also says, with a wry solemnity, that the moment of his arrest is the moment when darkness does its worst (10:18; 22:53). Mark's Jesus explains that the rulers of the nations use ordinary power, but that he will use servant power instead (10:35–45). John's Jesus explains to Pilate that his kingdom is of a different sort and so does not use violence (18:36). Matthew's Jesus explains that he is casting out demons by the power of God's Spirit, so that God's kingdom has arrived on their doorstep (12:28); and he then warns that, like an unclean spirit returning with seven worse ones after a temporary exorcism, Israel itself ("this wicked generation") will find that it will end up worse off than it was to start with (12:43–45). All the evangelists see Jesus going to his death in order to win the deeply paradoxical victory over the forces of evil that, throughout Israel's long story, have gathered themselves together to do their worst to the people of God.

This enables us (looking back from the fourth speaker to the first) to understand more fully the reason why it is that Israel's story itself comes to its climax on the cross. The story of Israel, in its own terms within the ancient Hebrew scriptures, was all along the story of the way in which the creator God was going to deal with the problem of evil. Genesis 12 was always designed as the answer to Genesis 3–11. How was this to be done? Not by making Israel a "safe place," a community in which the evil of the world could find no place. Had that been the aim, Abraham would not have been the best person to begin with, as the stories somewhat embarrassingly reveal. Nor was Israel created as a kind of worldly superpower (though it may have looked like that in the time of David and Solomon), a new nation that would beat the world at its own game. Rather—and this is something the early Christians come to with hindsight, only at that stage tracing its earlier stages in the Psalms and prophets—the point is that the story of Israel was to be the story of how God was going to deal with evil. He would draw it onto one place, allowing it to do its worst at that point. And he himself (as we heard through the second speaker) would go to that place, would become Israel-in-person, in order that evil might do its worst to him and so spend its force once and for all.

That message is written right across the New Testament (though the habit of having the first speaker turned way down means that many readers miss it entirely, in the letters and Revelation as much as in the gospels). But it makes enormous sense of the gospels themselves. The way they tell the story of Jesus going to the cross makes this abundantly clear. The greatest religion the world had ever known and the finest system of justice the world had ever known came together to put Jesus on the cross. The misunderstanding, betrayal, and denial of close friends adds another dimension. The mocking of the soldiers and the crowds deepens both the agony and the irony. Finally, the nations rage, as Psalm 2 said they would, rising up against the Lord and against his anointed, and God's response is, "Yet I have set my king, my son, upon my holy hill"—no longer Zion, the ancient Temple mountain, but Golgotha, the ugly little hill a bit to the west.

The cross constitutes Golgotha as the new holy mountain. This is where the nations will now come to pay homage to the world's true Lord. The one enthroned there, with "King of the Jews" above his head, is to have the nations as his inheritance, the ut-termost parts of the earth as his possession. His victory over them will not be the victory of swords and guns and bombs, but the victory of his people and of their derivative suffering and testi-mony. That is how, for the four evangelists, the kingdom and the cross come together at last. That is how the darkest of the "pow-ers" are to be overthrown. For God to become king, the usurping rulers must be ousted.

Throughout his public career, Jesus was engaged in launching that project. But it was on the cross that it came to its triumphant conclusion. That is why, when Peter tried to turn Jesus away from his vocation to suffer, Jesus called him "satan." That is why the mocking voices urging Jesus to come down from the cross echo so disconcertingly the mocking voices in the temptation narra-tives (cf. Matt. 27:39–43; 4:1–10). Without the cross, the satanic rule remains in place. That is why the cross is, for all four gospels (and, as I have argued elsewhere, for Jesus himself) the ultimate messianic task, the last battle. The evangelists do not suppose that the cross is a defeat, with the resurrection as the surprising over-time victory. The point of the resurrection is that it is the immediate result of the fact that the victory has already been won. Sin has been dealt with. The "accuser" has nothing more to say. The creator can now launch his new creation.

All four dimensions—all four speakers, to continue our image—thus contribute to a richly layered narrative that we find, in different ways, in all four canonical gospels (though, noticeably, not in the so-called Gnostic gospels). Getting to this point requires considerable mental effort in today's world and church. We have to reconstruct this story step-by-step, because so many elements of it have been simply forgotten or ignored in so much Christianity, not least, paradoxically, in those parts of the church that like to think of themselves as "biblical." But for the evangelists and their first audiences, the sounds that force us to strain our ears, to readjust our sound systems, would have come through loud and clear with little effort. This dense and dramatic fusion of ancient scripture and in-your-face pagan power, this coming together of the dream of YHWH's return and the surprising launch of a quite new people—all this was their world. They hadn't been expecting it to work out like this. Far from it. But they would have had no difficulty in recognizing that this was the story that was being told. We have to spend a long time carefully adjusting our sound systems. But these were the sounds, loud, clear, and comprehensible, that constituted their world.

Having discovered that adjusting the volume on the speakers enables us to hear, much more clearly, the message of kingdom and cross, what difference will it make? How do our traditional understandings of these two massive and difficult ideas change as a result of our study? To answer this we will need another chapter.

IO

Kingdom and Cross

The Remaking of Meanings

WE NOTED IN PART I of this book the way in which we have been conditioned to read the gospels as though the themes of the kingdom and the cross could be held at arm's length from one another. As we have seen, one very popular understanding of the story the gospels tell is that Jesus's public career began with a time of happy, early fulfillment, when everything seemed to be going well, but that it then turned a dark corner and ran into opposition, unpopularity, and finally arrest, trial, torture, and death. As I have tried to explain, this splitting apart of the story in the four gospels has come about because the story the writers actually tell simply didn't fit the categories that centuries of readers, including some very devout ones, were bringing with them. But we should be in no doubt that, for the gospel writers themselves, there was never a kingdom message without a cross, and Jesus's crucifixion never carried a meaning divorced from the launching of God's kingdom. Our task now, having worked our way back into the gospels by means of adjusting the volume on the four crucial speakers, is to offer a positive statement of what happens when we treat kingdom and cross not as two themes, but essentially as one.

We begin with two scenes that more or less bookend the whole presentation in each of the gospels: Jesus's baptism and the "title" on the cross. In each—and each is decisive as a marker for the writers' meaning—we see exactly the combination of kingdom and cross that has proved so elusive in the history of interpretation.

Baptism and Kingdom

John doesn't mention Jesus's own baptism, but he does describe, through the mouth of John the Baptist, the Spirit descending and remaining on Jesus. Readers hear of this in the context of discovering, in John 1, that Jesus is Israel's Messiah and also the Lamb of God who takes away the world's sin:

> "Look!" said John. "There's God's lamb! He's the one
> who takes away the world's sin! He's the one I was
> speaking about when I said, 'There's a man coming after
> me who ranks ahead of me, because he was before me!'
> I didn't know who it would be, but this was the reason
> I came to baptize with water—so that he could be re-
> vealed to Israel."
>
> So John gave this evidence: "I saw the spirit coming
> down like a dove out of heaven and remaining on him.
> I didn't know who it would be; but the one who sent
> me to baptize with water said to me, 'When you see the
> spirit coming down and resting on someone, that's the
> person who will baptize with the holy spirit.' Well, that's
> what I saw, and I've given you my evidence: he is the son
> of God." (1:29–34)

All this is part of the larger impact of John's first chapter, which ends with the first disciples recognizing Jesus as Messiah (1:41, 45, 49). This, as much as anything, is where we need the first speaker (the Messiah as the climax of Israel's story) not to get drowned out by the second one (Jesus as God incarnate). The two belong together. Jesus has not come simply as a "superman" figure, a "divine hero" parachuted into the world to sort out the mess. He has come—and the gospel story only makes sense if we take this very seriously—as the one who will embody Israel's ultimate vocation in himself.

The title "son of God" expresses both halves of this complex and delicately balanced picture. It was a title, as we have seen, both for Israel and for the anointed king. But it also, in John as in Paul, acquires the associations that John has opened up as a fresh possibility through his prologue. The prologue opens with the "Word" who was God, the one through whom all things were made (1:1, 3), but it closes by telling us that the "Word," becoming flesh, enabled us to gaze upon his glory, "glory like that of the father's only son" (1:14). The son, intimately close to the father as he is, has made him known, has "brought him to light" (1:18). From now on, John is saying, when we think of Jesus in the ancient messianic category of "son of God," we are to understand that this has been fused together with the idea of Jesus as the father's incarnate Word. And we are to understand, a deeper mystery still, that this had been the intention from the beginning. The category of messiahship itself was a category established, as it were, for God's own use.

Though this whole passage has, of course, a characteristically Johannine depth and mystery, we should not think of the synoptics' presentation of Jesus's baptism as any less theologically profound. In them the baptism scene is dramatic and decisive. The heavenly announcement that Jesus is "my son, my beloved one," the one with whom God is delighted, indicates for those with biblically attuned ears that Jesus is marked out as the king of Psalm 2 and the servant of Isaiah 42:

> *I will tell of the decree of* YHWH:
> *He said to me, "You are my son;*
> *today I have begotten you."*
> *Ask of me, and I will make the nations your heritage,*
> *and the ends of the earth your possession. . . .*
> *Now therefore, O kings, be wise;*
> *be warned, O rulers of the earth. (Ps. 2:7–10)*

> *Here is my servant, whom I uphold,*
> *my chosen, in whom my soul delights;*
> *I have put my spirit upon him;*
> *he will bring forth justice to the nations. . . .*
> *He will not grow faint or be crushed*
> *until he has established justice in the earth;*
> *and the coastlands wait for his teaching. (Isa. 42:1–4)*

Jesus was baptized. All at once, as he came up out of the water, suddenly the heavens were opened, and he saw God's spirit coming down like a dove and landing on him.

Then there came a voice out of the heavens.

"This is my son, my beloved one," said the voice. "I am delighted with him." (Matt. 3:16–17)

Teachers and preachers often put these texts together, bringing out two main themes. First, the echo of Psalm 2 says that Jesus is the Messiah; this, frequently, is short-circuited to mean "the incarnate one." Second, the echo of Isaiah 42, and with it of the whole Isaianic "servant" theme, says that Jesus is the "suffering servant." The scriptural echoes of the baptism story thus serve the normal creedal points of incarnation and cross. As I have indicated, there is nothing wrong with this. It is fine as far as it goes.

But the two passages in question will simply not allow us to ignore the kingdom theme, which is so prominent in each. Psalm 2 opens with the nations raging and fighting—raging, indeed, against the true God; and the enthronement of God's "son" is the answer. He's in charge now, and the nations, and especially their rulers, had better be warned. Their power is broken, and he will implement God's victory. There is nothing in the text either of the baptism narrative itself or of the four gospels as a whole to suggest that this kingdom theme has been screened out in favor of an incarnation and atonement theme. All the signs are, rather, that the aim of incarnation and cross is precisely to establish God's kingdom; that, after all, is what Jesus begins to say when, not long after his baptism, he begins his public career (Matt. 4:17, and parallels).

So too with Isaiah 42. Again, the context is important. Isaiah 40, opening with its great promise of comfort for the exiles, continues with the majestic scene of God sitting as sovereign over the world, whose idolatrous inhabitants are like grasshoppers before him (40:22). Chapter 41 continues with a depiction of the nations rushing around in small circles, looking to their idols for help, while Israel cowers in a corner, afraid of what will happen next. But now, with chapter 42, the answer promised in chapter 40 begins to emerge: "Here is my servant." Israel, the family of Abraham, has already been referred to as "my servant" in 41:9, but it has already become clear that Israel as a whole is quite incapable of fulfilling this role. A "servant" is needed who will, so to speak, be Israel for the sake of Israel, who will fulfill the divine vocation to which Israel at its best might aspire, but from which it would always fall short.

And this vocation, exactly like that of the king in Psalm 2, is not simply to be God's agent in saving people from personal sin and its consequences (though that remains at the heart of it). The vocation of the servant is to bring God's justice into the wider world (42:3), to establish it in the world (42:4). The servant is to be "a covenant to the people, a light to the nations" (42:6; 49:6). Israel's God is about to overthrow the wicked nations that have held Israel captive (43:14; 48:14). Thus, when the servant's work is done, "Kings shall see and stand up; princes, and they shall prostrate themselves, because of YHWH, who is faithful, the Holy One of Israel, who has chosen you" (49:7). Or, through a different lens, when they see what the servant's work ultimately involves, "kings shall shut their mouths because of him; for that which had not been told them they shall see, and that which they had not heard they shall contemplate" (52:15, leading immediately to the description of the servant's suffering in chapter 53).

In other words, with the echo of the opening words of the first "servant" poem, the synoptic writers are not inviting their readers merely to contemplate Jesus as the one who dies so that sinners may be forgiven. They are invoking one of the primary scriptural passages in which Israel's God, YHWH, establishes his sovereignty over the whole world, doing so indeed despite the failure of his own people to believe in him. He will rescue them through the servant's work, but merely to do that is "too light a thing." He will provide, through the servant, "a light to the nations, that [his] salvation may reach to the end of the earth" (49:6). At the heart of all this is the ultimate good news: "Your God reigns," *malak elohayik* (52:7). He is king, and has demonstrated this by overthrowing the pagan kingdoms and their idols, unveiling his worldwide justice, and inviting all and sundry to turn to him and enjoy the benefits of his renewed covenant and renewed creation (Isa. 54–55).

The baptism narrative, therefore, in all the gospels, is not simply about Jesus's "divine identity," on the one hand, or a particular program of "atonement," in the sense of a rescue from the world of creation, on the other. Yes, the gospels affirm Jesus's divine identity. Yes, they affirm his death on the cross as the climax of God's age-old plan of salvation. But the purpose of God coming incognito in and as Jesus and the purpose of this Jesus dying on the cross was—so the gospels are telling us—in order to establish God's kingdom, his justice, on earth as in heaven. As in Psalm 2, the point is that in this way the nations are to be called to account. This is how the creator is bringing his creation back into proper shape.

Once we have noticed this theme in the baptism story, we are bound to see it all over the place. We have already noted several of the obvious passages. I think of Mark 10:35–45, where the "servant" work of the "son of man" demonstrates the new kind of power that is to be unleashed in the world, confronting the rulers of the world with God's new way. I think of the Emmaus road story, where the risen Jesus declares that the divine plan always involved the Messiah suffering and then "coming into his glory" (Luke 24:26). We note that "coming into his glory" does *not* mean simply "going to heaven" in the normal sense; "glory" is a way of saying "sovereign majesty," so that the saying exactly combines the two themes we are looking at. The crucifixion was the appropriate and long-prophesied way by which the Messiah would come to be king of all the world, and Luke's second volume, the Acts of the Apostles, describes how that works out.

I think too of John's interpretation of the same theme. As so often in the fourth gospel, it is spread subtly but richly throughout the narrative. When the soldiers dress Jesus up in a purple robe, they do so in order to mock him, but John tells us of it in order to declare that Jesus is indeed the one in purple, the one before whom the nations will bow. Pilate circles around the possibility that Jesus is in some sense "king of the Jews," but without realizing that, according to the Jews' own ancient traditions, their king is to be king of the whole world. John knows that he is telling a story of someone dying the death of a criminal. He is determined that his readers will "hear" the story also as the death of the rightful king. Jesus's kingdom will not come by violence (18:36). It will come through his own death. When he is lifted up from the earth, he will draw all people to himself (12:32).

The "Title" on the Cross

This leads us exactly to the "title" on the cross. The Latin word *ti-tulus* was used to describe the public notice that would be attached to the cross of a condemned criminal, indicating the charge that had led to this extreme verdict. (The practice was well known in European countries until at least the nineteenth century.) Though skeptics have challenged many features of the gospel narratives, this one is generally regarded as very well established, because it fits with normal Roman practice, it is recorded in all four gospels, and it is hardly the sort of thing someone would make up (Jesus's execution was a very public affair, and many people would have seen the notice for themselves). The fullest description is that in John:

> Pilate wrote a notice and had it placed on the cross:
>
> JESUS OF NAZARETH
> THE KING OF THE JEWS
>
> Lots of the Judaeans read this notice, because the place where Jesus was crucified was close to the city. It was written in Hebrew, Latin, and Greek.
> So the chief priests said to Pilate, "Don't write 'The king of the Jews'! Write that he *said,* 'I am the king of the Jews'!"
> "What I've written," replied Pilate, "I've written."
> (19:19–22)

The shaping of John's gospel tells its own story. Jesus has, of course, been disclosed as "Messiah" at various points on the way—when talking with the Samaritan woman, for instance (4:26, 29); and there has been debate and discussion as to whether someone doing and saying the things he is doing and saying can really be the Messiah (7:26–27, 31, 41–42; 10:23; 12:34), with the authorities imposing a ban on the idea (9:22). But, for John, the "title" balances the recognition of Jesus's kingship offered by his first disciples in chapter 1. The title is, of course, heavily ironic. Pilate knows that Jesus doesn't conform to any meaning of the word "king" with which he is familiar. Jesus himself, as we saw, had redefined "kingship" in his conversation with the governor, insisting that his kind of kingship meant bearing witness to the truth (18:37). But now readers are invited to join together the two points, which Pilate was never going to do—the two points that, ironically, much Christian interpretation has also found very hard to combine. Readers are invited to join together not simply a Johannine "incarnational" theology with a Johannine "redemption" theology. Both of those are there, but the middle term between them is once again the evangelist's *kingdom theology.* As Paul saw, the rulers of this age didn't understand what they were doing when they crucified the Lord of glory (1 Cor. 2:8). As the Irish-American New Testament scholar Dominic Crossan commented on Matthew's story of Pilate's wife having bad dreams about Jesus (Matt. 27:19), it was time for the Roman Empire to start having nightmares. Sending Jesus to his death was assisting in the enthronement of the one whose bringing of justice to the nations flowed out of his sovereign, healing love (John 13:1).

The point for our present purpose is that, in all four gospels, readers are strongly urged to see Jesus's death as explicitly "royal," explicitly "messianic"—in other words, explicitly to do with the coming of the "kingdom." Jesus has, all along, been announcing that God's kingdom was coming. His followers might well have expected that this announcement would lead to a march on Jerusalem, where Jesus would do whatever it took to complete what he had begun. And they were right—but not at all in the sense they expected or wanted. That is what the evangelists are saying through this particular moment in the story. This is how the kingdom is to come, the kingdom of God, which Jesus has been announcing and, as Messiah, inaugurating.

This point needs little elaboration in relation to the synoptic gospels, but we may continue to stress it in relation to John, who is not so often seen as a theologian of the "kingdom." In fact, however, as we have already seen, John 18–19 offers an explosion of dense and detailed kingdom theology, so that when we meet the *titulus* in John 19:19, we read it with a special and heightened irony, coming as it does at the conclusion of Pilate's debate with Jesus, on the one hand, and with the Jewish leaders, on the other, about kingdom, truth, power, and Caesar. Jesus, John is saying, is the true king whose kingdom comes in a totally unexpected fashion, folly to the Roman governor and a scandal to the Jewish leaders.

In all four gospels, then, there is no drawing back. This is the coming of the kingdom, the sovereign rule of Israel's God arriving on earth as in heaven, exercised through David's true son and heir. It comes through his death. The fact that the kingdom is redefined by the cross doesn't mean that it isn't still the kingdom. The fact that the cross is the kingdom-bringing event doesn't mean that it isn't still an act of horrible and brutal injustice, on the one hand, and powerful, rescuing divine love, on the other. The two meanings are brought into dramatic and shocking but permanent relation.

If the baptism and the title on the cross are bookends, holding the narrative together in each of the gospels as the narrative of kingdom achieved through cross and cross achieving kingdom, what about the material in between? Is this strong narrative hint borne out by the major structural markers with which the different evangelists have ordered their material?

"You Are the Messiah"

The most obvious central marker in both Mark and Matthew is the complex scene at Caesarea Philippi and immediately afterwards (Mark 8:27–9:1; Matt. 16:13–28). Here is the key passage in the shorter version, that of Mark:

> Jesus and his disciples came to the villages of Caesarea Philippi. On the way he asked his disciples, "Who are people saying that I am?"
>
> "John the Baptist," they said, "or, some say, Elijah. Or, others say, one of the prophets."
>
> "What about you?" asked Jesus. "Who do you say I am?"
>
> Peter spoke up. "You're the Messiah," he said.
>
> He gave them strict orders not to tell anyone about him. (8:27–30)

This functions as the midpoint in Mark, looking back to the voice at the baptism and forward to the paradoxical question of Caiaphas at the trial ("Are you the Messiah, the Son of the Blessed One?" 14:61, which is a statement in Greek; it gets turned into a question by the punctuation and presumably the tone of voice) and then the centurion's statement at the foot of the cross ("This fellow really was God's son," 15:39). Matthew's gospel is more complex in its structure, but this incident is still right in the middle. Luke's equivalent scene (9:18–27) is equally dramatic, but doesn't play the same structural role in Luke's narrative; for him the equivalent is 9:51, where Jesus "settled it in his mind to go to Jerusalem," following what Moses and Elijah had discussed with him during the transfiguration in 9:31.

Here, in any case, we see the evangelists welding together the two elements, messiahship and cross, even while explaining that the disciples, at the time, found such a combination just as puzzling and off-putting as the church has done for much of its history. Jesus asks his followers who they think he is, and they declare that they believe him to be the Messiah. He then tells them that he must suffer, die, and be raised—and that they must suffer as well if they want to follow him. The Messiah is to come into his kingdom through a horrible death; and those who not only follow him, but are called to implement his work must expect that their royal task—for such it is—will be accomplished in the same way, by the same means. There is every sign that the earliest church understood this very well indeed, just as there is every sign (alas) that today's church does not—except, of course, in those parts of the world, like China and the Sudan, where there has been no choice.

As we contemplate the scene at Caesarea Philippi, it is vital that we do not short-circuit the messianic meaning in our quest for creedal affirmations about Jesus's "divinity." Yes, the four gospels do indeed affirm, often in subtle and profound ways (not so often in the rather clunky and obvious ways that some would clearly prefer), that Jesus is the embodiment of Israel's God, come back at last to rescue his people. But the meaning of Peter's confession of Jesus's messiahship is not, "You are the second person of the Trinity," but "You are Israel's Messiah." The phrase "son of God" in this connection is of course once more an echo of the messianic passages in Psalm 2, 2 Samuel 7, and elsewhere. And in those contexts its primary meaning is "Israel's messiah, adopted and anointed by God as his own son."

The much fuller meanings that the phrase "son of God" came to carry quite early in the Christian movement (as early as Paul; see, e.g., Rom. 8:3–4, Gal. 4:4–7) are fresh depths that the early church discovered within this Jewish meaning. They do not indicate that the meaning of "Messiah" had been abandoned and something else ("divinity"?) put in its place. We approach that fuller meaning—and, ultimately, trinitarian theology itself—through the messianic, kingdom-bearing gateway. This is, in fact, the gateway to the meaning both of Jesus's "divinity" and of his "humanity." But how much better to replace those dry, abstract categories with their biblical originals. As Messiah—as the about-to-be-crucified Messiah!—Jesus embodies the vocation of Israel, and with it the vocation of the human race itself. But he also embodies the returning, rescuing, promise-keeping God of Israel himself.

What the four gospels are eager to tell us, then, is that the messianic kingdom that Jesus is bringing will come through his suffering and indeed through the suffering of his followers. But it is Jesus's own suffering in particular, gradually revealed as unique and uniquely effective, that is highlighted as the gospel narratives proceed. The key text of Mark 9:1 and parallels, so often read as an unfulfilled prediction of an imminent "second coming" or even of the "end of the world," was never intended that way by the evangelists or, I believe, their sources or earlier traditions. Coming at the conclusion of Jesus's prediction of suffering for himself and his followers, this is what the text says:

> "I'm telling you the truth," Jesus said; "some people standing here won't experience death before they see God's kingdom come in power."

Faced with this, generations of post-Enlightenment scholars have done their best to fit the quart of the gospels into the pint pot of eighteenth-century political and theological imagination. They maintain that Jesus *must* have meant that either the second coming and/or the end of the world and/or a great political revolution would happen within a generation. Since none of these took place, these critics conclude that Jesus was wrong, or at least that the early church was wrong to put these words in his mouth.

Now, we must of course grant that the version of the saying in Matthew's gospel does look as though it refers to the "second coming," since it speaks of the coming of the "son of man":

> "Some of those standing here will not taste death until they see 'the son of man coming in his kingdom.'"
> (Matt. 16:28)

But this understanding is itself based on an assumption that, however commonplace, is deeply misguided, namely, that "the coming of the son of man" in the New Testament refers to the "coming" *to* earth of one presently in heaven. As we saw in the previous chapter, the text of Daniel 7, which is obviously being invoked at this point, indicates very clearly that the direction of travel is, so to speak, upward, not downward. In Daniel, "one like a son of man," in other words, "a human figure," "comes" *from earth to heaven* to be presented before the "Ancient of Days." It is a move from suffering and humiliation to enthronement and sovereignty.

Matthew 28:16–20 should have taught Matthew's readers how Matthew at least understood this key saying (16:28). He didn't think it referred to a time, still future in his own day, when Jesus would come again. Matthew believed it referred to the events of Jesus's death and resurrection—which, after all, Jesus had been referring to a few verses earlier. Jesus's death and resurrection have constituted him as, already, the one who has "all authority in heaven and on earth" (28:18). It is the church's widespread and long-lasting failure to realize that this was what Matthew and the others were talking about that has left the door open to many generations of misleading readings and consequent puzzles.

The equivalent sayings in Mark and Luke simply highlight the coming of the kingdom itself, with Mark adding "in power":

> "Some people standing here won't experience death
> before they see God's kingdom come in power."
> (Mark 9:1)

> "There are some standing here who won't experience
> death until they see God's kingdom." (Luke 9:27)

These parallel verses, in the intention of all three evangelists, are best read as indicating a kingdom fulfillment that they, the authors of the gospels in question, believe *had already come to pass* in the death and resurrection of Jesus. Luke, as we know, gives more attention in his narrative to the resurrection and ascension than either Matthew or Mark. But I see no reason to suppose that Mark was actually a dark, postmodern sort of writer who wanted his gospel to end with fearful women, because he didn't know or believe anything beyond that point. The best hypothesis is that all four gospel writers believed that with his crucifixion Jesus of Nazareth had indeed been enthroned, however paradoxically, as Israel's Messiah and that, with that event, Israel's God had established his kingdom on earth as in heaven.

They believed this, of course, *because* of Jesus's resurrection— just as it was disbelief in the bodily resurrection that made scholars from Reimarus to Bultmann and beyond assume that there must still be some great coming event to which the evangelists were referring. Such scholars have normally supposed this great coming event to be the Parousia. The word *parousia* is a Greek term meaning "royal presence" or "divine appearing," or perhaps both. It has become the regular technical term used by New Testament scholars to refer to Jesus's "second coming" and its supposed attendant phenomena, which, they maintain, the early church believed to be "imminent." Early Christians thought, say these scholars, that the Parousia would be the final kingdom-bringing moment. That scholarly mistake has fused with the dispensationalism of popular (mostly American) subculture and speculation to give the present state of confusion about the "end-times" that is so prominent a feature of today's American church life.

The four gospels are well aware that this central contention about the kingdom's arrival—that is, the claim that God was already king of the world and had become so in a dramatic new way through the work, the death, and the resurrection of Jesus— was highly paradoxical in their own context, as indeed it has remained so to our day. Then, as now, a claim about God's kingdom being already present was likely to meet with the obvious rejoinder: "Of course God's kingdom hasn't arrived—just look out the window!" The problem was more acute for them, facing hostility and often persecution. However, they were in no danger of having what today we might call an overrealized eschatology, imagining (as some today have suggested, absurdly in my view) that the entire new creation had now arrived and that there was nothing more to hope for.

There is, actually, a secular parody of this that was quite popular in the Western world, at least until the events of September 11, 2001: the belief that history had now developed as far as it was going to do, that Western capitalism and liberal democracy had "won" the Cold War, and that the whole world would now come into line with the brave new "enlightened" world. One does not hear this proposal so often today. But again, we may here be looking at one of the reasons why critics in the modern period were unwilling even to contemplate the possibility that the evangelists might really have believed that God had become king through the work of Jesus. It may not have been objective historical analysis on the critics' part. It could just as easily have been because their whole culture, that of eighteenth- to twentieth-century Europe and America, believed implicitly that some kind of utopia had *now* arrived—through the triumph of "Enlightenment" ideology. The fact of continuing intractable evil in today's world has highlighted the necessity to think again.

But the evangelists did not need to think again, because the claim that they were making was never susceptible to falsification on the grounds of continuing evil, corruption, violence, and death. On the contrary, this merely reminds us that, for all the evangelists in their different ways, the kingdom was precisely *not* to be expected whole and entire, all at once. They highlighted, after all, those parables in which Jesus stressed that the kingdom was coming like a seed growing slowly and secretly or that it would involve strange reversals as well as sudden vindications. The kingdom was not, they insisted, arriving in the way people had imagined. That is Luke's explicit point in 19:11, and it does not appear that he is out on a limb. They constantly remind us that Jesus's kingdom work generated angry opposition from both human and nonhuman (i.e., demonic) sources, that the shadow of the cross hung over the narrative from the start, and that Jesus warned about the need for his followers too to put aside any dreams of an immediate utopia and to be prepared to drink the cup that he was to drink.

That leads us once again to Mark 10, where, in response to the request from James and John that they might sit at his right and his left "in his kingdom" (a request partly echoed, in Luke 23:42, by the dying brigand), Jesus asks a question in return:

> "You don't know what you're asking for!" Jesus replied. "Can you drink the cup I'm going to drink? Can you receive the baptism I'm going to receive?"
>
> "Yes," they said, "we can."
>
> "Well," said Jesus, "you will drink the cup I drink; you will receive the baptism I receive. But sitting at my right hand or my left—that's not up to me. It's been assigned already." (10:38–40)

The significance of this in our present discussion is massive. For Mark, it is clear that the two brigands on Jesus's right and left, as described in 15:27, are the ones to whom "it's been assigned already." But that means, as we might have concluded from other evidence too, that Jesus's crucifixion is the moment when he becomes king, when, as James and John say, he is "there in all [his] glory" (10:37). That is the powerful—if deeply paradoxical!— "coming of the kingdom" as spoken of in Mark 9:1. But the arrival of the kingdom in that way will not mean that James and John, and many others too, can look forward to an easy utopia thereafter. On the contrary, they will still have to drink Jesus's cup and be baptized with his baptism, in other words, to share his suffering and quite possibly his death. (This happened to James quite quickly, as we discover in Acts 12:2.)

It is in this context, as we have already seen, that we find the kingdom and the cross in close juxtaposition. Jesus contrasts the normal practice of pagan rulers with his own vision of power and prestige: "Anyone who wants to be great among you must become your servant" (10:43). This is at the center of his vision of the kingdom. And this is not only illustrated, but instantiated, by Jesus's own vocation: "The son of man didn't come to be waited on. He came to be the servant, to give his life 'as a ransom for many'" (10:45). This saying, so far from being (as has often been suggested) a detached, floating nugget of "atonement theology" within early church tradition that Mark or his source has tacked on to a story about something else (the reversal of normal modes of power), is in fact the theologically *and politically* apposite climax to the whole train of thought. What we call "atonement" and what we call "kingdom redefinition" seem in fact to be part and parcel of the same thing. Ultimately, as we shall presently see in more detail, the cross *is* the sharp edge of kingdom redefinition, just as the kingdom, in its redefined form, *is* the ultimate meaning of the cross.

When we explore the meaning of Jesus's messiahship in all four gospels, then, we find that the central material (of which, naturally, we have only glanced at a small fraction) supports the case we have made from the bookends, the baptism and the "title" on the cross. What about the narratives of the cross themselves? What light do they shed on our question, on the question of the apparent gap in the creeds, the missing link between incarnation and atonement?

Narrating the Cross

It has often been assumed that the four evangelists, in recounting the events that led to Jesus's crucifixion, are doing so with minimal intention to offer theological interpretation of those events. To take a step back once more, when people write about "atonement theology," the tendency has been to go to Paul and Hebrews and to come to the gospels only for those detached phrases that will support (or so it seems) the kind of "theological" construct that has already been culled from Paul. The actual narratives of Jesus's arrest, trial, and crucifixion have, to be sure, been combed for hints of "meaning," and this has been found not least in the use of the Old Testament, of passages like Psalm 22:1. But the thought that the narratives themselves might be theologically freighted has not normally received the attention it should. Indeed, once we realize what the evangelists are doing throughout, we should expect that the stories of the hearings and trials, in all the gospels, may be assumed to serve this purpose, rather than just giving some backstory to Calvary. The trials, in other words, address the theological *and soteriological* "why" of the cross, not only the "how." Learning to read them in this way may be a novel art, but it is one we Western Christians should acquire as soon as possible. John is a good place to start.

I have already written in some detail about John 18–19 and tried to show that, in the great scene of Jesus (and the chief priests) before Pilate, John has said an enormous amount about the significance of Jesus's forthcoming death. John's great scene between Jesus and Pilate is all about the "kingdom," even though it takes place under the shadow of the cross; or, to put it the other way, it is all about the reasons for the cross, and those reasons turn out to be kingdom reasons. The link between kingdom and cross forms the inner logic of the whole narrative, stressing both the inevitability and the necessity (in human terms, it was bound to happen; in the divine plan, it had to happen) of the kingdom of which Jesus speaks being put into effect by his forthcoming death.

Jesus once again takes the initiative in the conversation, introducing the discussion of different types of "kingdoms." "My kingdom isn't the sort that grows in this world," he says (18:36). (We note here that the regular translation, "My kingdom is not of this world," has contributed to, and in its turn also generated, multiple misreadings of all four gospels, appearing to suggest that

Jesus's "kingdom" is straightforwardly "otherworldly." The Greek for "of this world" is *ek tou kosmou toutou;* the *ek,* meaning "out of" or "from," is the crucial word.) There is no question but that Jesus is speaking of a "kingdom" *in and for* this world. The steady buildup, over the previous chapters, of sayings, already noted, about "the ruler of this world" being judged and cast out and about the world being overcome make it clear that in the events now unfolding we are to see the ultimate showdown between the kingdom of God and the kingdoms of the world brought to sharp focus in Jesus and Pilate.

Part of John's meaning of the cross, then, is that it is not only what happens, purely pragmatically, when God's kingdom challenges Caesar's kingdom. It is also *what has to happen* if God's kingdom, which makes its way (as Jesus insists) by nonviolence rather than by violence, is to win the day. This is the "truth" to which Jesus has come to bear witness, the "truth" for which Pilate's worldview has no possible space (18:38). It is at once exemplified, dramatically, by Jesus taking the place of Barabbas the brigand (18:38–40). This is the "truth" to which Jesus bears witness—the truth of a kingdom accomplished by the innocent dying in place of the guilty.

And, in the broader Johannine perspective, we discover that the only word to do justice to this kingdom-and-cross combination is *agape,* "love." The death of Jesus is the expression of God's love, as the famous verse in John 3:16 makes clear. For John, it is also the expression of Jesus's own love: "He had always loved his own people in the world; now he loved them right through to the end" (13:1). And, with that, John introduces the powerful and tender scene in which Jesus washes his disciples' feet. In between these two, we find the "good shepherd" discourse, where the mutual love between Jesus and the father leads directly to Jesus's vocation to "lay down his life for the sheep" (10:15).

Throughout, Jesus remains God's anointed king, crowned as such by the pagans, however ironic the crown of thorns is (John

19:1–3). As such, he is the truly human being. When Pilate says "Here's the man!" (19:5), we are surely to hear echoes of that primal Johannine moment, the Word becoming flesh as the climax of the new Genesis (1:14). But this Genesis, this new creation, is aimed at redemption; and the suffering Messiah, wearing the ironic royal robes, which acquire a second level of irony in John's treatment, does for his people and the world what he had said all along he would do, as the shepherd giving his life for the sheep, as the seed sown in the ground to bear much fruit. The cross stands at the heart of John's kingdom theology, which in this stunning passage is revealed as the heart of John's redemption theology, the vision of the love of God revealed in saving action in the death of his Son, the Lamb, the Messiah.

If the cross is central to John's vision of the kingdom, it is equally true that the kingdom is central to the meaning he gives to the cross. Any attempt to separate out a Johannine redemption theology from the equally Johannine theology of God's kingdom and the new creation is doomed to failure. As the trial scene winds slowly to its conclusion, more ironies emerge: the irony of the charge that Jesus "made himself the son of God" (19:7), which was of course what Caesar had done; the irony of Jesus's acknowledgment of Pilate's God-given authority over him (19:11); the ultimate irony of the chief priests declaring that they had "no king except Caesar" (19:15). Gradually, inch by inch, in a narrative heavy with ironic kingdom theology, we discover the theological "why" of the cross *within* the historical "how." As we should have realized all along, the "lifting up" of Jesus on the cross is his exaltation as the kingdom-bringing "king of the Jews," because the kingdom that is thus put into effect is the victory of God's love. Kingdom and cross fully joined.

How fatally easy it would be for us Westerners to sigh with relief at this point. Ah, we think, God's kingdom is simply the sum total of all the souls who respond in faith to God's love. It isn't a real kingdom in space, time, and matter. It's a spiritual reality, "not of this world." John, though, will not collude with this Platonic shrinkage. We remind ourselves of the earlier passages about the ruler of this world being cast out, condemned, and overthrown. These appear to refer to a being that stands behind the present earthly rulers, but also incarnates itself in them; we are not simply talking about a "spiritual" victory that leaves the present human rulers unaffected.

For another thing, the resurrection scenes in John 20–21 are not about a heavenly existence, detached from this world, but precisely about new creation, the new Genesis arrived at last. The famous *tetelestai* in 19:30 ("It's all done!") matches the *synetelesen* in Genesis 2:2 ("God finished the work that he had done"); on the sixth day, in both accounts, God finished all the work that he had begun and rested on the seventh. The resurrection, as John stresses, happens on the first day of the week (20:1, 19). Mary is sent to tell the others that Jesus is to be enthroned beside the Father (20:17); Peter, to feed and tend the flock (21:15–17). This is how the kingdom, which is *from above,* is coming *into this world.* The work of redemption is complete; now, with Jesus having been "glorified," having completed his work of rescuing his people, the Spirit can be given, and his followers can begin their own work. This is how—remembering how thoroughly it has been redefined!—God's kingdom will come on earth as in heaven. The cross *serves the goal of the kingdom,* just as the kingdom *is accomplished by Jesus's victory on the cross.*

John, then, is certainly not an exception to the generalization that all four gospels bring the kingdom and the cross into the closest possible combination. One could in principle go back to the synoptics and show passage after passage in which the same is true. Think of the kingdom agenda of the Sermon on the Mount (Matt. 5–7), which itself points ahead to the cross: Jesus himself loves his enemies, goes where the Roman soldiers force him to go, and turns the other cheek before being set like a city on a hill, like a light on a pole. To read Matthew's passion narrative in the light of the Sermon on the Mount is to discover just how subtle Matthew has been in constructing his work.

Similarly, Luke insists, again and again, on the necessity of the cross as the fulfillment of the great scriptural narrative, which, as we learned in his chapter 4, was also the kingdom narrative, the jubilee announcement. Jesus's life, after all, was threatened right there, at his opening kingdom announcement in Nazareth (4:16–30). His opening statement of what God was now doing might easily have led to his death, then and there. Any idea of a "Galilean springtime" when everyone thought he was wonderful, before a change of mood set in, is certainly not found in Luke. To announce and inaugurate the kingdom is to go to the cross; the shadow of the cross falls over the kingdom announcement on page after page of the story. Luke insists on his interpretation of why this was:

> "This is what is written," said Jesus. "The Messiah must suffer and rise from the dead on the third day, and in his name repentance, for the forgiveness of sins, must be announced to all the nations, beginning from Jerusalem. You are the witnesses for all this." (24:46–48)

We should not imagine that "forgiveness of sins" here is a purely individualistic thing. In the light of the "Nazareth manifesto" (4:16–21), it seems clearly to extend to the jubilee principle, the release from all debts, the cosmic sigh of relief at God's new exodus achievement, rescuing people from all forms of slavery. Jesus's followers were thereby commissioned and then empowered by the Spirit to announce to the world that there was a different way to be human. Acts, with its many tales of confrontation, persecution, and martyrdom, takes forward exactly this agenda. This is what it looks like, Luke is saying, when Jesus is enthroned as Lord of the world, and his followers go out to put his royal rule into effect, ending up in Rome announcing God's kingdom and Jesus as Lord "with all boldness, and with no one stopping them" (28:31).

In Luke, as in John, the broader picture is filled in with the little telltale touches that show that the larger cosmic kingdom achievement is to be applied vividly to every single person. Over against those who have claimed, absurdly of course, that Luke had no real atonement theology (mainly on the grounds that he does not reproduce Mark 10:45!), we discover Luke saying again and again that Jesus was being accused of crimes of which he was innocent but people all around him were guilty:

> They began to accuse him. "We found this fellow," they said, "deceiving our nation! He was forbidding people to give tribute to Caesar, and saying that he is the Messiah—a king!" (23:2)

> [Pilate] released the man they asked for, the one who'd been thrown into prison because of rebellion and murder, and gave Jesus over to their demands. (23:25)

> "Daughters of Jerusalem," said Jesus, "don't cry for me. Cry for yourselves instead! Cry for your children! Listen: the time is coming when you will say, 'A blessing on the barren! A blessing on wombs that never bore children, and breasts that never nursed them!' At that time people will start to say to the mountains, 'Fall on us,' and to the hills, 'Cover us'! Yes: if this is what they do with the green tree, what will happen to the dry one?" (23:28–31)

Jesus, in other words, is the "green" tree, the tree that is not ready for burning. He is innocent. But all around him, growing up in the streets and lanes of Jerusalem, are the young firebrands who will be only too ready for the fire when the time comes.

The innocence of Jesus continues to be a major motif throughout Luke's account of the crucifixion:

One of the bad characters who was hanging there began to insult him. "Aren't you the Messiah?" he said. "Rescue yourself—and us, too!"

But the other one told him off. "Don't you fear God?" he said. "You're sharing the same fate that he is! In our case it's fair enough; we're getting exactly what we asked for. But this fellow hasn't done anything out of order." (23:39–41)

The centurion saw what happened, and praised God.
"This fellow," he said, "really was in the right." (23:47)

The four canonical gospels thus demand to be read with their two main themes, kingdom and cross, fully and thoroughly integrated in a way that the great majority of the Western church has simply not noticed. And there is more.

Temple, Kingdom, and Cross

One particular symbol stood high above all others in first-century Palestinian Judaism. Indeed, it stood proudly upon a hill, where it could not be hidden. The Temple in Jerusalem was not simply a "religious" building in our modern sense or even in the sense of "religion" that some ancient writers would have recognized. As is now widely acknowledged, our modern distinctions between "religion" and all sort of other things—"politics," "aesthetics," "culture," "economics," and much besides—would have made little sense in the ancient world in general. It would have made no sense in Judaism in particular. Not only was the Temple the center of the whole national life. It was, Jews believed (as many ancient peoples believed about their temples) the place where heaven and earth themselves interconnected and overlapped. It was therefore the place to which one might go for healing, forgiveness, and the renewal of fellowship with Israel's God. It was also—and a glance through the Old Testament will show what this means—the place in which God established his power base. "Heaven," after all, was seen as the throne room, the place from which "earth" would be ruled. But if "heaven" came to be linked with a particular point on "earth," then that point was where power was concentrated. Divine power. Theocracy. The kingdom of God. Long before anyone thought of linking kingdom and cross, the far more obvious link was kingdom and Temple.

And the gospels tell the story of Jesus as the story of a one-man walking temple. Early on in the story we find the hints. "Who then is this?" people ask as Jesus does remarkable things, speaks and acts with authority, behaving as if he is the one who's now in charge. Jesus is portrayed by the gospels as a one-man apocalypse, the place where heaven and earth meet, the place where and the means by which people come and find themselves renewed and restored as the people of the one God, the place where power is redefined, turned upside down or perhaps the right way up. Jesus calls twelve close associates, as though to make exactly that point about the people of God in a more formal and indeed powerful way, even though the twelve themselves remain muddled, dangerously so, as to what he is actually doing. All these are the signs, granted the world of thought in which he lived (so very unlike ours!), that he was indeed launching a new kind of theocracy, and that he really did believe he was the new kind of king.

But just at the moment where we in today's world might be getting worried about this new theocracy, we find the ultimate redefinition. To recapitulate for a moment. Mark, as we saw, gives his story a simple structure, moving in two great loops from the voice at the baptism to Peter's confession and the voice at the transfiguration, and then to the high priest's question (which in the original is in the form of a statement) and the centurion's statement of faith:

> "You are my son! You are the one I love! You make me very glad." (1:11)

> "You're the Messiah." (8:29)

> "This is my son, the one I love. Listen to him!" (9:7)

> "Are you the Messiah, the son of the Blessed One?" (14:61)

> "This fellow really was God's son." (15:39)

This, clearly, is what Mark intends us to learn. But all the way through, this sonship, which as we saw picks up the global royal commission of Psalm 2, is steadily redefined by the vocation to suffer. Mark never envisages a period where Jesus was simply doing kingdom work without the shadow of the cross falling over the page. Hence the great irony (which Paul sums up in the words *Christos estauromenos,* "the crucified Messiah," 1 Cor. 1:23) that characterizes Mark throughout. Caiaphas asks a question, but the words he uses, depending on the tone of voice, are just as much a statement: "You are the Messiah, the son of the Blessed One!" And the centurion confesses Jesus as God's son at the very moment when, as he dies, he seems anything but. Goodness knows what Mark thought the centurion meant. The irony is acute. Jesus will come to this global sovereignty, it seems, only through suffering; and by "through" suffering Mark seems to mean not just that he must pass through it to his goal, as a necessary dark tunnel before coming out into the light, but also that the suffering will somehow be effective in accomplishing his task and establishing his sovereignty.

And it is Caiaphas—the high priest, in charge of the Temple itself—who utters the fullest and the most fully ironic "confession of faith": "Messiah, Son of the Blessed One!" It cannot be that both Jesus and Caiaphas are correct. Either Caiaphas is right, and Jesus is a dangerous blasphemer. Or Jesus is right, and Caiaphas is central to the problem that had gripped the Jewish leadership of the time: they did not recognize the moment of divine visitation (Luke 19:44). The evangelists are in no doubt: Jesus is the reality, the place where Israel's God now dwells, the human being in and through whom the one who called Abraham and uttered his voice from Sinai had now returned to judge and to save. Jesus is the reality, and the present Temple and its official spokesmen must give way before him. It is no accident, from the evangelists' point of view, that when Jesus finally breathes his last, the veil of the Temple is torn in two from top to bottom (Mark 15:38).

In fact, all four evangelists make it abundantly clear that we are to understand both Jesus's kingdom and his death in relation to the Temple—or rather, in relation to the fulfillment of the Temple's role in Jesus himself (this is a major theme throughout John) and his upstaging of it in his last great symbolic actions. It is now becoming more widely recognized, I think, that the synoptic evangelists present the Last Supper as a "new Temple" moment. Jesus, having pronounced God's judgment on the old Temple in his dramatic action and then his discourse on the Mount of Olives, now gathers his friends around him to celebrate a "Passover meal with a difference," a meal that not only looked back, like all Passover meals, to the exodus itself, but forward to the new exodus that Jesus was about to accomplish. Like all Passover meals, it was not just a signpost, but a means, through the sharing of food and wine, of partaking in that event about to be accomplished. When Jesus wanted to explain to his followers the meaning of his death, he didn't give them a theory; he gave them a meal. The synoptics draw this out in one way, John in another (with the foot washing, chap. 13).

But if what we said before about the political significance of the Temple has any significance here, this means that Jesus's Temple redefinition was also part of what the evangelists saw as his establishment of a kingdom vastly superior to those of both Herod and Caesar. For a new theocracy to be inaugurated, a new Temple is necessary, so that the living God may there receive the worship of the world and from there administer his wise rule over creation. This is the point above all, perhaps, that today's attempts at political theology will find opaque. For a genuinely Jewish vision of theocracy, you need God in the midst of it. But what the gospels offer us—especially John, but actually all of them—is a God who is in the midst *in and as Jesus the Messiah,* and a God who is then committed to remaining in the midst, through Jesus, in the person of the Spirit. Jesus himself is the new Temple at the heart of the new creation, against that day when the whole earth shall be filled with the glory of God as the waters cover the sea. And so this Temple, like the wilderness tabernacle, is a temple on the move, as Jesus's people go out, in the energy of the Spirit, to be the dwelling of God in each place, to anticipate that eventual promise by their common and cross-shaped life and work.

All this, I submit, generates a vision of the cross and its achievement so large and all-embracing that we really ought to stand back and simply gaze at it. All the "theories" of "atonement" can be found comfortably within it, but it goes far, far beyond them all, into the wild, untamed reaches of history and theology, of politics and imagination. We have, alas, belittled the cross, imagining it merely as a mechanism for getting us off the hook of our own petty naughtiness or as an example of some general benevolent truth. It is much, much more. It is the moment when the story of Israel reaches its climax; the moment when, at last, the watchmen on Jerusalem's walls see their God coming in his kingdom; the moment when the people of God are renewed so as to be, at last, the royal priesthood who will take over the world not with the love of power but with the power of love; the moment when the kingdom of God overcomes the kingdoms of the world. It is the moment when a great old door, locked and barred since our first disobedience, swings open suddenly to reveal not just the garden, opened once more to our delight, but the coming city, the garden city that God had always planned and is now inviting us to go through the door and build with him. The dark power that stood in the way of this kingdom vision has been defeated, overthrown, rendered null and void. Its legions will still make a lot of noise and cause a lot of grief, but the ultimate victory is now assured. This is the vision the evangelists offer us as they bring together the kingdom and the cross.

Kingdom and Cross
in Mutual Interpretation

What then can we say, in summary, about the evangelists' portrayal of kingdom and cross, and what we ourselves can learn about each from that explosive, and usually ignored, combination?

I offer three reflections about what this combination does to our vision of the kingdom. First, the evangelists insist that the kingdom truly was inaugurated by Jesus in his active public career, during the time between his baptism and the cross. That entire narrative is the story of "how God became king in and through Jesus." But note what follows. We in the West, perhaps ever since Chalcedon or even Nicaea, have read as the main text what the gospels treated as presupposition. In all four gospels, Jesus is the embodiment ("incarnation") of Israel's God. But this is not the gospels' main theme. Not even, I think, John's. The main theme is that, in and through Jesus the Messiah, Israel's God reclaims his sovereign rule over Israel and the world.

In musical terms, we have mistaken key for tune. The key in which the gospels are set is that of incarnational Christology. But the melody is that of the kingdom and of "Christology" in the much stricter sense of "Jesus as Messiah." Those whose catechism was based on the great creeds would never guess what their canonical scriptures were trying to tell them. In the messianic life and death of Jesus, Israel's God really did become king of the world. Again and again I read devout works in which this point, utterly central to the New Testament witness to Jesus, is passed over in silence. Only this morning, as I was redrafting this paragraph, did I read another one of this same type.

Second, this kingdom is radically defined in relation to Jesus's entire agenda of suffering, leading to the cross. This draws the sting of any hint of (what we call) triumphalism. As in the book of Revelation, the victory and sovereignty belong to the slaughtered Lamb—and the slaughtering was not simply a one-time unhappy moment that can now be replaced by the Lamb's followers taking up arms to bring in his kingdom by the methods of Herod and Pilate. Those who would implement Jesus's kingdom are just as prone to forget this as Peter and the others were, trying to dissuade Jesus from his insistence on the suffering and dying vocation with which he interpreted his messiahship, eager to push him toward the vision of a kingdom much more like the kingdoms of the world.

The paradox remains, and those who engage most directly in the work of the kingdom know, again and again, that the principalities and powers they are confronting are cruel, mean, and dirty. Martyrdom of one sort or another, suffering of one sort or another, is what kingdom-bringers must expect. Here, incidentally, is the Christian answer to the postmodern challenge. Our "big story" is not a power story. It isn't designed to gain money, sex, or power for ourselves, though those temptations will always lie close at hand. It is a love story—God's love story, operating through Jesus and then, by the Spirit, through Jesus's followers. This is the building of the church against which the powers of hell, and for that matter deconstruction, cannot prevail.

Third, the kingdom that Jesus inaugurated, that is implemented through his cross, is emphatically *for* this world. The four gospels together demand a complete reappraisal of the various avoidance tactics Western Christianity has employed rather than face this challenge head-on. It simply won't do to line up the options, as has normally been done, into either a form of "Christendom," by which people normally mean the capitulation of the gospel to the world's way of power, or a form of sectarian withdrawal. Life is more complex, more interesting, and more challenging than that. The gospels are there, waiting to inform a new generation for holistic mission, to embody, explain, and advocate new ways of ordering communities, nations, and the world. The church belongs at the very heart of the world, to be the place of prayer and holiness at the point where the world is in pain—not to be a somewhat "religious" version of the world, on the one hand, or a detached, heavenly minded enclave, on the other. It is a measure of our contemporary muddles that we find it very difficult to articulate, let alone to live out, a vision of church, kingdom, and world that is neither of these.

What happens if we ask the question the other way around? What, in other words, do we learn about the cross when we discover that the gospels present it as the means by which God (in Jesus) becomes king of the world? Again, I see three immediate answers to this challenging question.

First, the way we have normally listed options in atonement theology simply won't do. Our questions have been wrongly put, because they haven't been about the kingdom. They haven't been about God's sovereign, saving rule coming on earth as in heaven. Instead, our questions have been about a "salvation" that rescues people *from* the world, instead of *for* the world. "Going to heaven" has been the object (ever since the Middle Ages at least, in the Western church); "sin" is what stops us from getting there; so the cross must deal with sin, so that we can leave this world and go to the much better one in the sky, or in "eternity," or wherever. But this is simply untrue to the story the gospels are telling—which, again, explains why we've all misread these wonderful texts. Whatever the cross achieves must be articulated, if we are to take the four gospels seriously, within the context of the kingdom-bringing victory. This is the ultimate redefinition-in-action of the messianic task, the kingdom-bringing messianic vocation. In all four gospels, not only in John, the cross is the victory that overcomes the world. I am wary of describing this simply as a "Christus Victor" interpretation, because historically that has been associated with other kinds of development and has often been set over against other atonement theologies. But the idea of messianic victory as a fresh interpretation of an ancient Jewish theme is precisely what the four gospels have in mind.

Second, however, when we see the cross in the light of the kingdom, we discover a fresh and helpful framework for understanding the vexed questions that surround substitutionary atonement. I have argued elsewhere, at considerable length, that Jesus understood his own death in terms of several strands of biblical witness, supremely Isaiah 40–55 and within that the great passage on vicarious substitution, the Fourth Servant Song (52:13–53:12). As for the gospels themselves, there should be no doubt that they follow this line. Jesus, for them, is dying a penal death in place of the guilty, of guilty Israel, of guilty humankind. Through his death, the evangelists are telling their readers there will come the jubilee event, the great redemption, freedom from debts of every kind, which he had earlier announced and which is the central characteristic of the kingdom.

All this makes the sense it makes not by playing "substitution" off against "representation," as has so often been done, but through Jesus's role precisely as Israel's representative Messiah, through which he is exactly fitted to be the substitute for Israel and thence for the world. To de-Judaize or dehistoricize this doctrine is to run the risk of the caricatures that have, sadly, been all too common in some evangelical preaching (God demanding blood, eager to punish someone, somewhere, and quite ready to take out his fury on an innocent bystander who happens to be his own son). To ignore the gospels' massive narrative scheme and go hurrying on to Paul for a more abstract formulation is to marginalize the center of scripture and to misinterpret Paul as well. Think, for instance, of Philippians 2:6–11, which on this reading functions more or less as a summary of the gospels. Perhaps that is why twentieth-century scholarship has tried to split that passage off from the perceived Paul of Protestant imagination. Anything, rather than take seriously the utterly biblical concept of kingdom and cross.

Third, if the cross is to be interpreted as the coming of the kingdom on earth as in heaven, centering on some kind of messianic victory, with some kind of substitution at its heart, making sense through some kind of representation, then the four gospels leave us with the primary application of the cross not in abstract preaching about "how to have your sins forgiven" or "how to go to heaven," but in an agenda in which the forgiven people are put to work, addressing the evils of the world in the light of the victory of Calvary. Those who are put right with God through the cross are to be putting-right people for the world. Justification is God's advance putting right of men and women, against the day when he will put all things right, and thereby constituting the justified people as the key agents in that latter project. From this there flows both a new missiology, including an integrated political theology, and the new ecclesiology that will be needed to support it, a community whose very heart will be forgiveness.

There is much more to be said about this, but not here. I suspect, sadly, that this is the point at which my overall argument will encounter some fairly solid resistance, for the same reasons that the kingdom-and-cross split happened in the first place, but now with the added incentive of the implicit Enlightenment divide. Our culture, including much of our Christian culture, doesn't want to know about this kingdom and prefers a cross that takes us safely away into another sphere. The burden of my song is that to think like that is to be radically unfaithful to scripture, to the very heart of scripture, to the four inspired books through which we encounter the Messiah, Jesus, the same yesterday, today, and forever.

Kingdom, Cross, Resurrection, and Ascension

A word, in conclusion, about the immediate sequel. I have written extensively about the resurrection elsewhere (*The Resurrection of the Son of God, Surprised by Hope*) and a fair amount about the ascension too (in addition to the above, see *Acts for Everyone*).* This is not the place to plunge back into that kind of detail. But it would clearly be wrong to leave this account of the gospel narratives without explaining the effect of the resurrection and ascension on the meaning of cross and kingdom that we have been exploring. (The ascension is only explicitly described in Luke, of course, but it is hinted at in Mark and John, and Matthew draws out its meaning in another way.) With regard to the problem this book set out to address—the big gap in the middle of the creed—we have looked in some detail at the way in which "kingdom" can stand in between "incarnation" and "cross." But what happens to the rest of the story?

First, it is obvious that without the resurrection of Jesus the evangelists would never have had a story to tell. Thousands of young Jews were crucified by the Romans. Very few of them are even mentioned in our historical sources, except as a grisly footnote. Even those who think the evangelists were in fact very clever inventors of large-scale fictions designed to revive a Jesus

---

The Resurrection of the Son of God (Minneapolis: Fortress, 2003); *Surprised by Hope: Rethinking Heaven, the Resurrection, and the Mission of the Church* (San Francisco: Harper One, 2008); *Acts for Everyone* (Louisville: Westminster John Knox, 2008).

movement that might not otherwise have survived the death (and continuing deadness, so to speak) of its founder are bound to admit that even within these cleverly designed myths the resurrection plays the vital role in opening the question up again, so that what looked like defeat, like yet another failure of a kingdom dream, was in fact a victory. The resurrection, in short, is presented by the evangelists not as a "happy ending" after an increasingly sad and gloomy tale, but as the event that demonstrated that Jesus's execution really had dealt the deathblow to the dark forces that had stood in the way of God's new world, God's "kingdom" of powerful creative and restorative love, arriving "on earth as in heaven."

That is why the bodily resurrection matters in a way that it never quite does, even to the devout who insist that they believe it, if all one is interested in is a kingdom "not of this world." The resurrection is, from Mark's point of view, the moment when God's kingdom "comes in power." From John's point of view, it is the launching of the new creation, the new Genesis. From Matthew's point of view, it brings Jesus into the position for which he was always destined, that of the world's rightful Lord, sending out his followers (as a new Roman emperor might send out his emissaries, but with methods that match the message) to call the world to follow him and learn his way of being human. From Luke's point of view, the resurrection is the moment when Israel's Messiah "comes into his glory," so that "repentance for the forgiveness of sins" can now be announced to all the world as the way of life, indeed, as they say in Acts, as The Way. Once we put kingdom and cross together in the manner we have, it is not difficult to see how the resurrection fits closely with that great combined reality. It is the resurrection that declares that the cross was a victory, not a defeat. It therefore announces that God has indeed become king on earth as in heaven.

To understand the ascension requires that we recall what was said about Israel's Temple theology. The Temple was the intersection between heaven and earth; but now the place of intersection is Jesus himself, who is equally at home in either or both of the twin halves of God's good creation. Luke's ascension story (John's hint of one, in Jesus's reply to Mary Magdalene in 20:17, shows that he could have told one, had he chosen to do so) is commonly misunderstood, but its proper emphases ought to be clear. Heaven and earth are now joined in the person—in the risen body!—of Jesus himself. But if the Temple was always the sign and the means of the true theocracy, then the Temple-in-person, that is, Jesus himself, is now that sign. The one who sits in heaven is the one who rules on earth. He therefore sends out his followers, equipped by his own Spirit (if the ascension locates a part of "earth" in "heaven," Pentecost sends the breath of heaven to earth), to celebrate his sovereignty over the world and make it a reality through the founding of communities rescued by his love, renewed by his power, and loyal to his name. Jesus's followers, equipped with his Spirit, are to become in themselves, individually and together, little walking temples, rescued themselves from sin through Jesus death, and with the living presence of God going with them and in them.

No wonder the great controversies in Acts 7, 17, and 19 and then the sequence of trials in chapters 20–26 all concern temples. Temple and theocracy are joined at the hip in their new form in the Jesus movement every bit as much as in ancient paganism, on the one hand, or ancient Judaism, on the other. Now, however, because of the cross, theocracy itself has been radically redefined. As Paul would see and celebrate, Jesus has come to his rightful place, claiming the allegiance of every creature in heaven, on earth, and under the earth. But he has come to that place and maintains it by, and only by, his humility and self-giving love.

When, therefore, at the start of Acts, the disciples ask Jesus whether this is the time for him to "restore the kingdom to Israel"

(1:6), his answer is not (as people often suppose) a "no." It is a "yes." As so often, however, it is a "yes but":

> "It's not your business to know about times and dates," replied Jesus. "The father has placed all that under his own direct authority. What will happen, though, is that you will receive power when the holy spirit comes upon you. Then you will be my witnesses in Jerusalem, in all Judaea and Samaria, and to the very ends of the earth." (1:7–8)

And that "witness," as Luke has made abundantly clear, is not a matter of "telling people about your new religious experience" or of informing them that there is now a new prospect of a much better otherworldly destiny than anything the bleak pagan world had to offer. The "witness" of Jesus's followers is the message that there is now "another king, Jesus" (Acts 17:7). It is the witness according to which the temples that presently exist, whether in Jerusalem, Athens, Ephesus, or anywhere else, are now to be seen as at best redundant (Acts 7) and at worst a blasphemous category mistake (Acts 17; 19). Jesus is the true Temple, now ruling the world as the one who was crucified; his followers, as Paul would explain more thoroughly, constitute the fuller version of the same thing, so that the dwelling of the living God is now spread increasingly across and around the world, again evidenced not by coercive or violent power, but by the rule of love.

So where does all this leave us today? How can we address the question of the major misunderstandings that have dogged the footsteps of Christian faith for so long? And, since the kingdom is (as Paul says in 1 Cor. 4:20) not about talk, but about power, how might this begin to translate into the lives of real Christian communities? To put it another way, if this is really and truly the story the four evangelists are telling, is there any way we can retrieve it for ourselves? How might we become true gospel readers, gospel pray-ers, gospel livers in our own day? If it is true, in some sense that we no doubt still find perplexing, that God really did become king in and through Jesus of Nazareth and supremely through the victory of his crucifixion and the launching of his new world in the resurrection, how might we be brought into this story? What might it look like?

PART FOUR

Creed, Canon, and Gospel

II

How to Celebrate
God's Story

IMAGINE A MAN who owns an old car. It still goes; he can drive to work. But it doesn't run as smoothly as it did, it's making odd noises, and he worries that one day it may fall apart altogether. So he takes it to the garage down the road. After a couple of days he goes to speak to the mechanic.

"Well," says the mechanic behind the desk, "this is quite interesting. It's been a long time since I've seen one of these. There are some genuine 1950s parts in there. Pity someone added those extra washers, though—that wasn't what the designer intended."

"But," replies the owner, "is it going to be all right? Will I still be able to drive it?"

"And another thing," continues the mechanic, undaunted. "The tires are the wrong sort for those wheels. They are already quite worn and could get worse. And the cylinders—well, they're a mess. We've been having quite a debate in the garage about whether they will really do the job."

"But where is the car?" asks the owner, getting agitated. "Have you got it going? Can I still drive it?"

The mechanic shrugs his shoulders. "Come and see," he says.

They go through to the garage in the back. There is the car, dismantled into a thousand parts, each one carefully labeled and laid out beautifully, artistically even, all over the workroom floor. The owner stares in dismay.

"My car!" he shouts. "What have you done to my car?"

"Hey, take it easy, man," replies the head mechanic. "Just look at this. What a great machine. People must have enjoyed this old thing all those years ago. These parts—we've all been admiring them. Sure, we've cleaned up some of them, and we'll probably replace some of the others. Enjoy the view! You should be proud."

And the owner, lost for words, shakes his head sorrowfully and walks away.

The Whole and the Parts

The car is the New Testament. The owner is the "ordinary Christian," whether in the pulpit or the pew. The mechanics are a certain breed of New Testament scholar. And the sad little story represents the perception of many "ordinary Christians" about the effect of scholarship on their wonderful old text. Some scholars have said it's unreliable. Some have said people have added bits that shouldn't be there. Some have said you won't be able to drive it much longer. But many others have just taken it apart, analyzed it word by word, drawn cunning parallels with other ancient literature, demonstrated its rhetorical skill—and left it in bits all over the floor. To be admired, no doubt. But not to be driven.

I and many others have done our best to study the New Testament with a different aim. Without skimping on historical and verbal analysis, we have done our best to put the whole thing back together again, even though the owners may have to get used to driving slightly differently in the future. But I can understand why many "ordinary Christians," and many systematic theologians too, have become fed up with a "biblical scholarship" that seems to leave the text all over the floor. However "true" such scholarship may be on one level, it is deeply untrue on another. The text was, after all, written to be part of the lifeblood of a community.

It is because of that perception of "scholarship" that many theologians in our own day have tried to make a virtue of ignoring "historical" scholarship and reading the New Testament in other ways. They have waited long enough, they say, and all the biblical scholars have given them is historical fragments. So they will put all that to one side and read the canon of scripture as a whole. What's more—this is a fairly new move, but it's gaining ground in some circles—they will read the New Testament in the light of the church's ancient creeds. "Nicene Christianity"—that's the criterion. Nicaea, after all, clearly taught the incarnation of Jesus (challenged by many biblical scholars), his atoning death (questioned by many), his resurrection (denied by many), and so on. It represents a historic landmark; this is how our forebears understood the faith! Give us the canon, give us the creeds, and we will drive the old car down the road in fine style rather than handing it over to those mechanics who only want to take it apart.

In this brave new posthistorical or even antihistorical world, canon and creed are supposed to be made for one another. One eloquent writer puts it like this, opposing the view that the creeds are simply the record of ancient squabbles now resolved: "Creed is more than putting out theological brushfires. It is letting Scripture come to its natural, two-testament expression. Just as the Old Testament leaves its father and mother and cleaves to the new, so the Scriptures cleave to the creed, and the creed to them, and they become one flesh."*

---

*Christopher R. Seitz, "Our Help Is in the Name of the Lord," in C. R. Seitz, ed., *Nicene Christianity: The Future for a New Ecumenism* (Grand Rapids, MI: Brazos, 2001), p. 20.

I understand the sentiment, and in many ways I applaud it. The creeds were remarkable, a unique postbiblical innovation to meet a fresh need. They have functioned as the badge and symbol of the Christian family (not for nothing is the creed referred to in Latin as a *symbolum*) for a millennium and a half. They are more than merely a list of things we happen to believe. Saying we believe these things marks us out as standing in continuity with those who went before us as well as with those around the world who today, in other places very different from our own, share this common faith and life.

And yet. As we observed in the first part of this book, it simply won't do to say that the Bible and the creeds can come together in that ultimate, intimate way. The creeds simply do *not* "let Scripture come to its natural, two-testament expression." Indeed, for many who have said the creeds down the years, the Old Testament has remained a largely closed book. There are many who would be horrified to have their status as catholic, creedal Christians questioned, but in whose life, worship, teaching, prayer, and Christian thinking the scriptures of Israel play no visible part. The creeds do virtually nothing to challenge this form of truncated, quasi-Marcionite Christianity. (When I say "virtually nothing," I allow the two exceptions: that calling God the "maker of heaven and earth" at once invokes Genesis 1, for those who have ears to hear; and saying, in the Nicene Creed, that the Holy Spirit "spoke by the prophets" acknowledges—assuming with most that the reference is to the "prophets" of the Old Testament, not the New—that the gift of Pentecost was simply the universalizing of the special inspiration of the ancient biblical writers.)

But that is only the start of it. As we saw, directly following from the creeds' nonmention of the whole story of Israel is the complete absence of anything to do with God's kingdom. This is fine so long as the creeds are regarded as the key markers in areas where there had been serious controversy. But as soon as they are made *the* syllabus, the master list of vital topics, there is a major gap.

Again, it would, I think, be uncontroversial to propose that the great majority of people in today's church who consider themselves to be firmly "creedal" Christians, affirming the Trinity, the incarnation, the atonement, the resurrection, the Holy Spirit, and the second coming, have never imagined for one moment that the gospels are telling the story of *how God became king* or that the rescuing sovereignty of God is *already* a reality in the world through the public career, death, and resurrection of Jesus. There is a kingdom-shaped gap at the heart of their implicit story. And the problem with leaving that gap unfilled is that *everything else in the story changes its meaning,* ever so slightly but significantly. Like somebody who has lost a central piece of the jigsaw puzzle, but is determined to finish the puzzle anyway, other pieces have to be pulled a little out of shape if they are to be made to fit. By themselves, the creeds are fine—excellent, solid, evocative, upbuilding. But if their enthusiasts claim that they teach exactly the same thing as the canon, they have deceived themselves, and the truth is not in them.

Here we touch on another huge topic toward which the present book hopes to make a small contribution, even though we cannot say very much about it here. Among the many old controversies between Catholics and Protestants was the question of authority—scripture or tradition? My understanding of the classic Catholic theology of, say, Thomas Aquinas is that for him and others like him "tradition" consisted simply of "what the church has said as it has read scripture." The distinction between "scripture," as the bedrock or ultimate source and standard, and all church "tradition" was maintained. Indeed, that distinction is still firmly enshrined in the church's liturgy: the church, to this day, reads the Old and New Testaments in public worship, but not the works of Irenaeus, Augustine, Thomas Aquinas, or any of the other great and revered theologians of old.

But today there are many voices suggesting that the distinction between scripture and tradition is overdrawn. Scripture, they say, is simply the early part of "tradition"; we can see scripture itself growing, developing, and producing that ongoing stream of Christian thought and writing we call "tradition," but is not thereby to be distinguished sharply from "scripture" itself. This means, such writers suggest, that the church today should simply look back down the centuries and understand the scriptures in the way they have been understood during the larger and longer story of church history. Tradition, in other words, will tell us, securely and faithfully, what the earliest parts of that tradition—that is, "scripture"—really meant.

It is by no means a merely knee-jerk Protestant reaction to say that this too will not do. (Quite apart from anything else, it raises all kinds of unanswerable questions: Whose tradition? Which writers? Who says?) It is no discredit to the great, holy, and wise writers of the patristic age, not to mention the later periods, to say that, though they had many wonderful things to contribute and were no doubt equipped by the Holy Spirit to say those things, this does not mean that they, any more than we today, glimpsed the full sweep of the biblical story or grasped the precise nuance of every apostolic phrase. They saw things we did not, and we must learn from them. But they, like we, stand under scripture itself, appealing to it, being judged by it. And, as we will no doubt be found wanting by that standard, so will they.

Let me show what I mean by offering two readings of the Apostles' Creed. The first is the implicit reading of much modern Christianity. It maintains its hold on the great doctrines that are there in the creed, but, as we have seen already, it distorts the narrative as a whole and those great truths with it. The second is the implicit reading to which I believe the canon of scripture, particularly the four gospels, compels us.

It might be tempting at this point to write a new, expanded "creed." I am deeply resistant to that idea. I have seen various attempts to do so over the years and, frankly, they quickly become banal. Contemporary agendas shoved in between ancient and venerable phrases simply don't cut the mustard. Part of the point of the creeds, in any case, is precisely that we receive them humbly from our elders and betters in the faith, men and women whose shoes we are not worthy to untie.

Rather, I propose that with each clause, or set of clauses, we hold in our minds the ideas that the canon of scripture, particularly the gospels, provides. C. S. Lewis speaks somewhere of learning to pray the great prayers like the Lord's Prayer by allowing the mind to "festoon" other ideas around each clause, so that the clause becomes the center of a little cluster of ideas that flesh it out and enable us to include particular topics, people, and situations within the prayer. This is perfectly possible with the creeds as well. In fact, I suspect that all of us who say the creeds regularly (and who are determined not to do so parrot-fashion) may well have some such set of associations in our minds connected with the quite brief clauses themselves.

My purpose in offering these proposals, then, is not at all that I wish to smuggle in new ideas that would distort the great creeds. Rather, I wish to show that it is possible to read them in the light of the canon of scripture, rather than the other way around, thereby allowing the hugely important points they make to be made in a more fully biblical manner. The points I wish to make stand out well in the Apostles' Creed, and I will follow it through, noting occasionally some interesting points where the Nicene Creed adds extra clauses. I use the "traditional" language for the creed, partly to avoid getting caught up in questions of different modern renderings.

One Way of Reading the Creed

The first way of reading the creed might go like this. (This is not a caricature. I know many churches, impeccable in their "orthodoxy," where this is more or less exactly what you might be taught.)

The Apostles' Creed opens with a brief but powerful statement about the first person of the Trinity:

> I believe in God the Father Almighty, maker of heaven
> and earth.

Many Christians today, saying this first article, recognize that it was designed to rule out any suggestion that the world of space, time, and matter was the work of a lesser divinity. The world we live in is God's world, not a nasty dark place from which we should want or try to escape. Not all, however, will see it like that. Many traditional Christians may think instead of the debates about "creation and evolution" and may hear in this statement an affirmation of the former rather than the latter, which was not, of course, the original intention. The anti-evolutionary belief can quite easily accompany a belief that the early Christians strenuously resisted, that "this world is not my home, I'm just a-passing through." Indeed, the picture of God "intervening" *from outside,* as it were, to "create," can all too easily accompany the picture of Jesus as a kind of superman or spaceman, coming to earth to snatch saved souls from their dark prison. And that is classic Gnosticism, not Christianity.

The fact that we jump straight from this clause to the second one, "And in Jesus Christ . . . ," makes it easy for many Christians to maintain their silent and unrecognized Marcionism—that is, their view that the Old Testament is a kind of parenthesis in the story, replete perhaps with signposts and promises, but in the last analysis not essential to the whole theme. What many think, then, as they jump from God to Jesus, might go something like this: "Yes, God made the world, but we are sinners, and so God sent Jesus to save us from our sins." Creation, sin, Jesus. That is the implicit narrative of millions of Christians today—and it guarantees that they will never, ever understand either the Old Testament or the New.

And in Jesus Christ his only son, our Lord . . .

One word and one clause might give such people pause at this point. The word is the title "Christ," and the clause is the mention of Jesus as "son of God." But, sadly, most people, saying the creed, do not at this point think, "Jesus, the Jewish Messiah." They think of "Christ" as, effectively, Jesus's second name or perhaps a word that implies his "divinity." And they think of "son of God" not in the light of Psalm 2 and 2 Samuel 7, but simply as a way of referring to Jesus as the second person of the Trinity. I fear that most will understand "our Lord" quite vaguely, meaning "the one we worship and invoke," rather than anything more wide-ranging or substantial.

Who was conceived by the Holy Ghost, born of the virgin Mary, suffered under Pontius Pilate, was crucified, dead and buried.

Here we have the central pair of statements, as we saw near the start of this book. The virgin birth and the crucifixion, with nothing but a comma in between. Sadly, here most modern Christians who say the creed from the heart barely even notice the comma, let alone think about the wealth of biblical emphasis that is thereby dwindled down to nothing. Jesus, for such people, is the miracle man, the supernatural being who came miraculously into the world to save us from our sins. For them, it really would be true that Jesus could have been born of a virgin and died on a cross and done and said nothing whatever in between. The miracle of the birth and the death for sinners—that's the heart of it, think "orthodox" Christians. (The Apostles' Creed does not mention the purpose of the death, as does the Nicene Creed—"who for us men, and for our salvation"—

but most modern creedal Christians will think of it at this point, and be rightly grateful.)

But will they understand the incarnation as God becoming human *in order to become king*? Will they understand the cross as *the means by which God completed his incarnate kingdom work*? Pretty certainly not. As I have repeatedly said, it is possible to check all the "orthodox" boxes and still miss the point. Indeed, I sometimes fear that people have been all the more eager to affirm the official doctrines in this truncated sense as a way of carefully avoiding the implications of God's actually being king on earth as in heaven. Far safer to have a superman Jesus who zooms down into the world to snatch us away from it.

He descended into hell.

I doubt if most modern Christians give too much thought to this. Those who have known hell in their own lives may sense with gratitude that Jesus came into the worst place imaginable, the place where we sometimes are, to rescue us.

The third day he rose again from the dead; he ascended
into heaven, and sitteth on the right hand of God the
Father Almighty.

Traditionally minded Christians will celebrate this gladly. Here's the great miracle, the supernatural intervention! The tomb was empty, and Jesus, having risen, was taken up into heaven. I suspect that most won't bother too much about Jesus's precise location now, "sitting at God's right hand"; we sense that the idea of God having two hands and Jesus being at one of them is at most a metaphor. For many, though, the ascension itself basically means that Jesus has gone away, leaving us to get on with the task (in the power of the Spirit, of course). It won't, of itself, conjure up any idea of his present sovereignty over the world.

> From thence he shall come to judge the quick and the
> dead.

Fine, think creedal Christians. Final judgment may be a fearful prospect, but we know that we, having been justified by faith, need fear "no condemnation," as Paul says (Rom. 8:1). We may have in our minds at this point an image of the great wall of the Sistine Chapel, with the living (that's the meaning of "quick" here) and the dead summoned to face Jesus and hear their ultimate fate.

> I believe in the Holy Ghost, the holy catholic church, the
> communion of saints, the forgiveness of sins, the resur-
> rection of the body, and the life everlasting.

Most devout Christians, when they think about it, are aware of the gentle prompting of the Spirit. This doesn't necessarily happen all or even most of the time, but it is a reality. Most are happy to trust that even when they are not explicitly conscious of that work, the Spirit is getting on with the job behind the scenes. But most, however "orthodox," are happy to leave it at that, to think of the Spirit as basically given to make us like Jesus, to help us to be holy, to teach us to pray. All that is true, of course. But the truth of which the creed speaks at this point is so much more.

Likewise, most well-taught Christians know that "catholic" here doesn't mean "Roman Catholic." (When I worked at Westminster Abbey, with a few hundred or more tourists coming to services every day and hearing the creed, one of the most frequent questions I was asked afterwards was, "Is this a Catholic church?" "Yes," I used to say, "but not in the sense I think you mean.") The word "catholic" here has its proper sense of "universal," "worldwide." Many, however, have not been taught even that much about the "communion of saints" (though for some it means that we are still able to be in touch, in some sense or other, with those we have loved and see no more). Forgiveness is something most creedal Christians quietly and gratefully celebrate, without being quite clear why it occurs here in the creed at all.

When it comes to "resurrection" and "the life everlasting," we still have a major problem. Most Christians, certainly in the Western churches, still assume that the whole purpose of the Christian faith is so that we might "go to heaven when we die." God wants to share fellowship with people, and those who have faith will be those people. For some, "resurrection" functions simply as a fancy metaphor for "eternal life," seen in terms of a spiritual bliss outside the world of space, time, and matter. For others, this ultimate goal still dominates the horizon, not least because countless prayers and hymns reinforce it. The word "resurrection," especially the resurrection "of the body," remains a puzzle. As I heard one elderly man say, "I'll be going to heaven when I die, and I certainly don't want to take this old body with me."

It is possible, it seems, to affirm everything the creed says—especially Jesus's "divine" status and his bodily resurrection—but to know nothing of what the gospel writers were trying to say. Something is seriously wrong here.

A Different Way of Reading the Creed

So what's the alternative? What ideas might we "festoon" around this magnificent document, doing justice to the fact that those who framed it undoubtedly intended it to illuminate and to be illuminated by the scriptural witness, rather than closing it down? One could at this point write an entire systematic theology, and this is obviously not the place for that. Let me simply suggest a few pointers in what seems to me the biblical, canonical direction.

> I believe in God the Father Almighty, maker of heaven and earth.

Here the wise worshipper will celebrate the God of Abraham, Isaac, and Jacob, knowing that this confession of him as "father" resonates back to the Jewish scriptures and that the delight in him as maker of all, heaven and earth, puts us on a level not only with the author of Genesis 1, but also with such majestic writings as Psalm 19 ("The heavens are telling the glory of God," v. 1) and Isaiah 40 ("Lift up your eyes on high and see: Who created these?" v. 26). This is, in particular, the Israelite and Jewish confession of faith, which carried with it an implicit social, cultural, and political edge: the gods of the nations are mere idols, but *our God made the heavens* (Ps. 96:5; Ps. 96 is one of the great psalms of creation and its renewal).

Again and again the plight of Israel, threatened and oppressed by the nations, causes the psalmists to invoke God precisely as creator, as the one who, having made the whole world, is responsible for bringing it back to order when chaos threatens:

> *O God, why do you cast us off forever?*
>   *Why does your anger smoke against the sheep of your*
>   *pasture? . . .*
> *How long, O God, is the foe to scoff?*
>   *Is the enemy to revile your name forever? . . .*
> *Yet God my King is from of old,*
>   *working salvation in the earth.*
> *You divided the sea by your might;*
>   *you broke the heads of the dragons in the waters. . . .*
> *Yours is the day, yours also the night;*
>   *you established the luminaries and the sun.*
> *You have fixed all the bounds of the earth;*
>   *you made summer and winter.*
> *Remember this, YHWH, how the enemy scoffs,*
>   *and an impious people reviles your name.*
>   *(Ps. 74:1, 10, 12–13, 16–18)*

That is a classic statement in which the pagan nations rage against Israel, but Israel appeals to God precisely as creator and, we note from verse 12, as king.

Think back too to "father." The primal statement of God's intention to liberate Israel from Egypt came in the form of the fatherly call: "Israel is my firstborn son. . . . Let my son go, that he may worship me" (Exod. 4:22–23). The opening statement of the creed, despite what many today might think, is full of appropriate echoes of Israel's most central traditions.

Even the Shema, the traditional monotheistic prayer, was seen in this way. To us it appears a bare, almost dry confession of "monotheism" ("Hear, O Israel: YHWH is our God, YHWH alone"). But when the rabbis prayed that prayer they spoke of it as "taking upon themselves the yoke of the kingdom." To confess God as the one and only creator of all that is is already to invoke the God of Abraham, Isaac, and Jacob and to claim his sovereignty over the whole world. And to confess him as "maker of heaven and earth" is already to invoke the Temple theme (the Temple was the place where heaven and earth came together), which is also the promise of the ultimate end. According to Paul, it is God's plan eventually to sum up all things in heaven and on earth in the Messiah (Eph. 1:10). The whole creation is to become a Temple for the one true God.

This then sets us up far more promisingly to "festoon" the right things around the opening of the second clause:

And in Jesus Christ his only son, our Lord . . .

The Christian who is wise as well as "orthodox" will know the two things we mentioned earlier. First, that "Christ" means "Israel's Messiah" and that with that title the whole history of Israel is brought into one place—as Paul says, "when the fullness of time arrived" (Gal. 4:4). The history, then, of the people who invoke the one creator God as king of the whole world—that history has become a person, and that person is called Jesus. Second, when we call Jesus God's "son," we not only hail him as the second person of the Trinity, but we celebrate him as the one spoken of in Psalm 2, the one enthroned over the nations of the world. To call Jesus "son" is to celebrate him as the agent of the kingdom of God. And to hail him as "Lord" was never, in the canon, a merely honorary word. It was one of the regular imperial titles. It declared that Jesus is Lord of the whole world. The word "our" doesn't restrict the scope of Jesus's sovereignty; it merely indicates that "we," the people saying this creed, are those who acknowledge gladly and openly what the rest of the world doesn't yet know. That worldwide sovereignty of Jesus has been the burden of our song for much of this book.

> Who was conceived by the Holy Ghost, born of the
> virgin Mary, suffered under Pontius Pilate, was crucified,
> dead and buried.

Now we are in a position to "festoon" around these great affirmations of incarnation and cross something more like what the canon of scripture is trying to tell us. The "incarnation" of the second person of the Trinity, in the strange and mysterious birth reported in Matthew and Luke, is, as we saw earlier, a highly political moment when Herod (in Matthew) and Caesar (in Luke) are both caught napping. Both even collude unwittingly with the event, Herod by sending the wise men to Bethlehem, Augustus Caesar by sending Joseph and Mary there. The virginal conception of Jesus thus speaks of the living God coming precisely to establish his sovereignty, dependent on no human agency; the attempt to make Mary's "Fiat" ("Let it be") into a kind of equal and opposite contribution to that of God misses the point entirely and makes another that leads us a long way off track. Wise readers of the creed already know at this point, then, that the one who is thus born to Mary is the one who has come to establish the kingdom of the one true God. To make "virgin birth" mean "miraculous divinity" and thereby to screen out "inaugurating God's kingdom" is to falsify it—however "orthodox" it may sound. What it means is the launching of God's kingdom purposes by the one who is, precisely, the sovereign of all.

This means that we must now read the statement of Jesus's suffering, death, and burial as the climax of *this* project, rather than some other. "For us men, and for our salvation," says the Nicene Creed at this point. Yes, indeed, but that "salvation" is not a rescue *from* the earth, from God's creation, but in and *for* the earth, and for us as creatures of earth. The mention of Pilate in the creed (a remarkable enough point at the best of times, scarcely to be explained by some early Christians thinking, in their misguided enthusiasm, that Pilate was actually a hero, perhaps even a saint, for facilitating Jesus's saving death!) is no mere historical marker, though it is important in that respect as well. The mention of Pilate and of Jesus's suffering at his command speaks loudly and clearly into the world of early Christianity, after those three initial centuries of persecution, of Jesus as the one who won the great initial victory over the dark powers of which Caesar's rule (and Pilate's subrule) were the immediate instrument. "Suffered under Pontius Pilate." Yes, we think, because that is how the great scene in John 18–19 comes to its close, with Jesus speaking of kingdom, truth, and power and going to the cross to make them all happen!

He descended into hell.

And to his death and burial we then join "descended into hell"; those who know the single biblical reference to this (1 Pet. 3:19) know that it is not simply (though it may be this too) a statement of Jesus's sharing in our worst nightmares. It is principally a statement of Jesus announcing to the "spirits in prison" that through his death God has won the ultimate victory. Peter goes on to speak of the immediate sequel, in which Jesus is at the right hand of God, with angels, authorities, and powers subject to him. That makes the point exactly.

The third day he rose again from the dead; he ascended
into heaven, and sitteth on the right hand of God the
Father Almighty.

Now at last Jesus's resurrection can mean what it meant to the
gospel writers. It isn't (as some, remarkably, still imagine) simply
an "intervention" by God to rescue Jesus as a kind of special favor
while leaving everyone else still in the grave. If Jesus is the one
who is carrying the destiny of Israel, and if Israel is the people
who are carrying the ultimate purposes of God to bring his justice and new creation to birth, then the resurrection of Jesus is
the launching of the new world in which that justice and new
creation have arrived at last, on earth as in heaven. "Some people
standing here," said Jesus, "won't experience death before they
see God's kingdom come in power." Yes, and now they have.
And the ascension is then, as Luke certainly intends and John and
Matthew hint, not Jesus "going away" in the sense of being out
of sight and out of mind. Heaven, in biblical thought, is after all
the "control room" for earth. For Jesus to be now "at God's right
hand" is for him to be given full authority over heaven and earth,
as Matthew's Jesus says explicitly. Every line of this section of the
creed thus speaks powerfully about the kingdom of God.

From thence he shall come to judge the quick and
the dead.

To the objection that the kingdom seems not to have gotten
very far just yet—an objection that actually ignores the massive
positive changes in the world and in our own society brought
about by faithful and usually unknown Christians—this clause
gives the answer: "From thence"! This is a direct allusion to Philippians 3:20–21, in which Jesus comes "from heaven," from his
place of utter sovereignty, to complete the work of establishing
that sovereignty on earth. The scene here is not so much that
of Michelangelo's *Last Judgment,* though it may include elements

of that as well. It is more a question of Jesus's last confrontation with the representatives of Caesar and all that he stands for, not to mention the dark powers that stand behind him. As Paul says, Jesus comes as "the savior, the Lord, the king" (Phil. 3:20)—all of them titles for Caesar. The "last judgment" will be the moment when the powers of the world are overthrown by the power of God, the power that was displayed fully in the crucifixion of the Lamb.

This is the moment when the Nicene Creed adds "and his kingdom will have no end." By itself and read in the usual (misleading) manner, this can easily give the impression that the "kingdom" is something that *only* happens at the very end of the process. But, if we have followed the creed in the way I have now suggested, this simply tops off the whole process. The kingdom (which Jesus launched in his public career and established through his death and resurrection) will never end. It will not be subject to the ravages of time or fresh rebellions. Nor will the son of God be eventually swallowed up without trace into the oneness of the father, as some might have suggested, at least in the early period. (This is not the same thing that Paul is talking about in 1 Cor. 15:27; there the "son" will be properly subordinated, but will remain separate within the mystery of the Trinity.)

> I believe in the Holy Ghost, the holy catholic church, the communion of saints, the forgiveness of sins . . .

For anyone who has grasped the picture of the kingdom so far, each of these elements has a *missionary* orientation. The Holy Spirit is given not simply so that God's redeemed people may be blessed with his presence and love, though that does indeed follow, but so that we may be witnesses to Jesus and his resurrection, so that we may be for the world what Jesus was for Israel (John 20:19–24). The Spirit is the one who enables the church to extend the work of the kingdom, and the transformation that takes place personally and corporately within and among those who are thus energized for the work is the necessary by-product of that vocation. To read the creed from a "kingdom" point of view is thus to look outward and to invoke the Spirit, not to provide private "blessings" (they may or may not come; they are not the point), but to glorify Jesus in the wider world.

That too is the reason why there is a "holy catholic church." It isn't there because God simply wanted to found an institution in which his people could sit down and feel safe. It is a worldwide community that (as has been rightly said) exists by mission as fire exists by burning. And that, in turn, is why the "communion of saints" matters; read the book of Revelation and see. Those who have gone before us include, especially, those who have lived, suffered, and died to bear witness to Jesus as the world's true Lord over against the other "lords" that try to claim our allegiance. To be "in communion" with them is far more than simply hoping that our departed loved ones will actually still, in some sense, be in touch with us, that there will be some kind of mystical contact beyond the grave. It is to share in fellowship and solidarity with all those who have been the "kingdom people" of their day and to gain strength and courage from them for our own witness. It was highly significant, in view of the vocation he already sensed, that Dietrich Bonhoeffer chose to write his doctoral dissertation, "Communion Sanctorum," on this clause.

Within this context, the "forgiveness of sins" gains an entirely new dimension. It includes, of course, just what it says to most of us: we are all overdrawn at the moral bank, and need to know again and again that God wipes out the debt and fills the account with his own freely given treasure. But when we step back from our own personal anxieties and awareness of guilt, we recognize that the world as a whole needs, longs for, aches and yearns and cries out for *forgiveness*—for that collective, global sigh of relief that means that nobody need seek vengeance ever again; that nobody will bear a grudge ever again; that the million wrongs with which the world has been so horribly defaced will be put right at last; that in God's ultimate new world there will be no moral shadow, no lingering resentment, no character warped by another's wrong. "Forgiveness of sins" is not a purely negative term, getting rid of the moral stain and guilt that we all incur, though it is that too. It is the positive presence of God and the Lamb, the Lamb whose shed blood has wiped the record clean.

. . . the resurrection of the body, and the life everlasting.

And so, finally, we come to the "resurrection of the body, and the life everlasting." Here we must "festoon" around the well-known words the great New Testament hope: "the life of the age to come," the "coming age" in which the whole creation will be transformed to share the liberty of the glory of the children of God. And, within that new creation, the coming together of heaven and earth of which Paul spoke (Eph. 1:10), God's people are promised new bodies. I have written about this elsewhere, but it is perhaps worth reiterating it. If you belong to Jesus the Messiah, if his Spirit dwells in you, if you are a worshipper of the one true God, maker of heaven and earth—then however you may feel at the moment, whether you are sick or healthy, handsome or jaded, you are simply a shadow of your future self. God intends to transform the "you" you are at the moment into a being—a full, glorious, physical being—who will be much more truly "you" than you've ever been before. Sin, by distorting and downgrading our specific God-given capacities and vocations, makes us more and more alike in our degradation. Jesus makes us more and more alive in our uniqueness, and the resurrection will complete that in a great act of new creation. Thomas à Kempis put it like this in his great hymn "Light's Abode, Celestial Salem" (translated here by J. M. Neale):

> O how glorious and resplendent,
> Fragile body, shalt thou be;
> When endued with so much beauty,

> *Full of health, and strong, and free;*
> *Full of vigor, full of pleasure*
> *That shall last eternally.*

And Jesus will do this, declares Paul (Phil. 3:20–21), *by the power that enables him to submit everything to himself.* Our resurrection, in other words, like the whole new creation, will come about because Jesus is king and Lord. Once you get the kingdom back in its place, everything else—Trinity, incarnation, atonement, resurrection itself—all gain in meaning. They stop trying to do jobs they were not supposed to do and can play the parts they were originally given.

Conclusion: How to Read the Gospels

My case throughout this book, then, is that we have all misunderstood the gospels. We have either followed the apparent implication of the great creeds and allowed ourselves to tell a pseudo-Christian story from which the story of Israel, on the one hand, and the story of God's kingdom, on the other, have been quietly removed. Or we have formulated a concept of the kingdom that did in fact grasp God's passion to put the world to rights, but we were then unable to integrate that with the incarnation and death of God's own son. And to correct this misunderstanding it is not enough, not nearly enough, to affirm airily that we believe in the "canon" (many say that who, alas, continue to assume that the canon merely supports the "orthodoxy" they already know), still less that we are supporting something called "Nicene Christianity" and determining to read the Bible in that light. That may get you a little way down the road, though if all you do is affirm traditional orthodoxy in the face of the proper historical questions that must still arise, you may find the journey increasingly uncomfortable.

But there is a long way to go, and, to be frank, the only way to travel the distance is to go back to the gospels themselves and to the integrated message they contain of the kingdom and the cross, or rather the incarnation, kingdom, cross, resurrection, and ascension—with all of those understood in carefully worked out relation to all of the others. And yes, that may mean that the car needs to be taken to the mechanic, and the mechanic may have to take it apart and clean or even replace its various parts. This time, however, the point will be to put it back together again and to drive away in proper style.

I understand the frustration of those who are now saying we should, as it were, start with the creeds, so that we shall at least read the Bible in a "believing" way. But if we start with the creeds, granted the way our Western Christianity is now more or less bound to read them, we will never understand the gospels, and hence the whole canon itself. If, however, we start with the gospels, which form the heart and balance point of the whole Christian canon, and if we understand them to be telling the story of how God, the creator God, Israel's God, became in and through Jesus the king of all the world, then we can return to the creeds and say them in a very different spirit. Put tradition first, and scripture will be muzzled and faded. Put scripture first, and tradition will come to new life. Better still, as Jesus himself said, put God's kingdom first—put first the revelation that, as the gospels have been eager to tell us, this is the story of how God became king!—and all these things will be added to you.

The question of how we might then read the gospels, publicly and privately, is a challenging one. I have enjoyed exploring, over many years now, different ways of undertaking this central task. Most congregations, I think, have never heard a gospel read, or "performed," all the way through. There are plenty of people in our churches who have the dramatic talent to undertake that. Many clergy have never thought of allowing large sections of scripture to frame their liturgy, rather than the other way around;

that was done as an experiment in one of the Durham churches in Lent 2010, and it worked wonderfully well. Equally—and this is really astonishing when you stop to think about it—most practicing Christians, including most clergy, have never sat down privately and read right through one or more of the gospels in a single sitting. These books are not long. They are hardly *War and Peace*—but they are every bit as much page-turners as some of the great novels. We need to shed some inhibitions and experiment with ways of allowing the gospels to speak their message afresh. Preachers and teachers too need to face the challenge of communicating the excitement and drama of an entire book, so that hearers are led both into fresh worship then and there and into an eagerness to read it, and live it, for themselves.

Equally, we need to try new ways of *praying* the gospels. Many have used, with great profit, the Ignatian method of entering into a story, becoming a character within it. Think of yourself as a bystander or onlooker as you watch Jesus asleep in the boat with the disciples panicking all around him, or as an extra guest at the supper table, suddenly wondering, "Lord, it's not me, is it?" Stay there long enough to hear what he has to say to you in particular. That method is well known, and rightly so. But there are ways of doing this corporately too. Again, be innovative. Read the gospels for all they're worth; and they're worth a lot more than we have usually supposed. Consider, for instance, reading through Matthew and allowing the Lord's Prayer, which Matthew puts at the center of the Sermon on the Mount, to become the prayer you pray after each chapter or section to sum up and draw together all that you've been reading. Or try doing the same with John's gospel, using Jesus's great High-Priestly Prayer in chapter 17. The point is that if it's true that in Jesus God was genuinely "becoming king," that is something that cannot remain a matter of mere "information," something we learn about with our heads. It's something we must pray, something that, through prayer, must become a new reality in our lives and our communities.

This whole book has been about new reality, the new reality of Jesus and his launching of God's kingdom. The new reality of a story so explosive (unlike the muddled, murky, "self-help" world of the noncanonical gospels!) that the church in many generations has found it too much to take and so has watered it down, cut it up into little pieces, turned it into small-scale lessons rather than allowing its full impact to be felt. Part of the tragedy of the modern church, I have been arguing, is that the "orthodox" have preferred creed to kingdom, and the "unorthodox" have tried to get a kingdom without a creed. It's time to put back together what should never have been separated. In Jesus, the living God has become king of the whole world. These books not only tell the story of how that happened. They are the central means by which those who read and pray them can help to make that kingdom a reality in tomorrow's world. We have misunderstood the gospels for too long. It's time, in the power and joy of the Spirit, to get back on track.

FURTHER READING

There are, of course, thousands of books about the four canonical gospels. What follows is an alphabetical selection, not quite at random, of those I have found stimulating over the past couple of decades. It is worth remembering that one is often most stimulated by works with which one disagrees. Within my own earlier writings, the background to the present book is mostly found in *The New Testament and the People of God* (London: SPCK; Minneapolis: Fortress, 1992), especially Part IV. If I had to choose one of the following books to take to a desert island, it would almost certainly be Ben Meyer's *The Aims of Jesus,* a neglected work with more wisdom and learning per page than many other scholars could provide per chapter.

Adams, Edward. *Parallel Lives of Jesus: Four Gospels, One Story.* London: SPCK, 2011.

Bailey, Kenneth E. *Jesus Through Middle Eastern Eyes: Cultural Studies in the Gospels.* Downers Grove, IL: InterVarsity, 2008.

Bauckham, Richard J. *The Gospels for All Christians: Rethinking the Gospel Audiences.* Grand Rapids, MI: Eerdmans, 1998.

Bock, Darrell L. *The Missing Gospels: Unearthing the Truth Behind Alternative Christianities.* Nashville, TN: Nelson, 2006.

Burridge, Richard A. *What Are the Gospels? A Comparison with Graeco-Roman Biography.* 2nd ed. Grand Rapids, MI: Eerdmans, 2004.

Dunn, James D. G. *Jesus Remembered.* Vol. 1, *Christianity in the Making.* Grand Rapids, MI: Eerdmans, 2003.

———. *Jesus, Paul and the Gospels.* Grand Rapids, MI: Eerdmans, 2011.

Griffith-Jones, Robin. *The Four Witnesses: The Rebel, the Rabbi, the Chonicler, and the Mystic*. San Francisco: HarperSanFrancisco, 2000.

Keener, Craig S. *The Historical Jesus of the Gospels*. Grand Rapids, MI: Eerdmans, 2009.

Koester, Helmut. *From Jesus to the Gospels: Interpreting the New Testament in Its Context*. Minneapolis: Fortress, 2007.

Lemcio, Eugene E. *The Past of Jesus in the Gospels*. Cambridge: Cambridge Univ. Press, 1991.

McKnight, Scot. *The King Jesus Gospel: The Original Good News Revisited*. Grand Rapids, MI: Zondervan, 2011.

Meyer, Ben F. *The Aims of Jesus*. 2nd ed. San Jose, CA: Pickwick, 2002.

Stanton, Graham N. *Gospel Truth? New Light on Jesus and the Gospels*. London: HarperCollins, 1995.

―――. *Jesus and Gospel*. Cambridge: Cambridge University Press, 2004.

Stuhlmacher, Peter, ed. *The Gospel and the Gospels*. Grand Rapids, MI: Eerdmans, 1991.

Swartley, Willard M. *Israel's Scripture Traditions and the Synoptic Gospels: Story Shaping Story*. Peabody, MA: Hendrickson, 1994.

Theissen, Gerd. *The Gospels in Context: Social and Political History in the Synoptic Tradition*. Minneapolis: Fortress, 1991.

SCRIPTURE INDEX

Scripture references are in bold.

Also by N. T. Wright

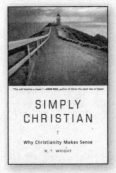

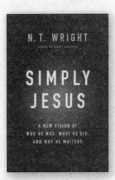